The
Trial
of the
Edmund
Fitzgerald

Also by Michael Schumacher
Published by the University of Minnesota Press

Mighty Fitz
The Sinking of the Edmund Fitzgerald

November's Fury
The Deadly Great Lakes Hurricane of 1913

Torn in Two
The Sinking of the Daniel J. Morrell *and*
One Man's Survival on the Open Sea

The Trial of the Edmund Fitzgerald

EYEWITNESS ACCOUNTS FROM THE U.S. COAST GUARD HEARINGS

Edited by Michael Schumacher

University of Minnesota Press
Minneapolis
London

Published by the University of Minnesota Press
111 Third Avenue South, Suite 290
Minneapolis, MN 55401-2520
http://www.upress.umn.edu

Printed in the United States of America on acid-free paper

The University of Minnesota is an equal-opportunity educator and employer.

24 23 22 21 20 19   10 9 8 7 6 5 4 3 2 1

Library of Congress Cataloging-in-Publication Data
Schumacher, Michael, compiler.
The trial of the Edmund Fitzgerald : eyewitness accounts from the
U.S. Coast Guard hearings / edited by Michael Schumacher.
Minneapolis : University of Minnesota Press, 2019. | Includes bibliographical
references. | LCCN 2018061116 (print) | ISBN 978-1-5179-0644 3 (pb)
Subjects: LCSH: Edmund Fitzgerald (Ship)—Trials, litigation, etc. |
Courts-martial and courts of inquiry—Ohio—Cleveland. | United States.
Coast Guard Marine Board of Investigation. | Shipwrecks—Superior, Lake—
Sources. | Marine accidents—Investigation—United States—Sources. |
Shipwrecks—Law and legislation—United States—Sources.
Classification: LCC KF228.E372 S38 2019 (print) | DDC 343.7309/64—dc23
LC record available at https://lccn.loc.gov/2018061116

To the 29

Contents

Preface

The story of the *Edmund Fitzgerald* is unquestionably the most popular, compelling shipwreck story in Great Lakes history. It is the largest vessel to sink in the Great Lakes, and it is the most recent. Gordon Lightfoot's song "The Wreck of the *Edmund Fitzgerald*," of course, has much to do with the public's interest in the shipwreck, but, arguably, the aura of mystery has captured the most serious attention. No one will be able to say for certain what brought the *Fitzgerald* down without warning or so much as a distress call. One minute she was battling through a rugged November storm on Lake Superior; the next she simply disappeared from radar. All that is known is that she lies in two pieces on the floor of the lake, in Canadian water. In 2005 when Canada declared the *Fitzgerald* an official grave site (all twenty-nine of its crew perished in the wreck, with no bodies recovered), the book on exploring the wreck was closed. She is in more than five hundred feet of water and will no longer be explored.

When the *Fitzgerald* left Superior, Wisconsin, loaded with 26,000 tons of taconite, bound for a port just outside Detroit, Captain Ernest McSorley, a seasoned Great Lakes mariner, knew he would be facing a storm, but he had no reason to suspect that he would be up against anything his boat couldn't handle. The *Fitz* was relatively new, in good repair, and had faced November storms in her past. McSorley ran into the storm earlier than expected, but the massive ore carrier handled it well, without incident, until midafternoon on November 10, 1975, when *something* happened to the *Fitzgerald* near Michipicoten and Caribou Islands on the eastern part of Lake Superior. The waters near the islands were especially fierce, and McSorley reported a fence rail down

◀ *Launching the* Edmund Fitzgerald *at the Great Lakes Engineering Works in Ecorse, Michigan, June 7, 1958.*
Courtesy of Great Lakes Maritime Institute.

ix

and water boarding the *Fitzgerald* shortly after he navigated his vessel through the area. He had also lost the boat's radar. He reported all this to Captain Bernie Cooper, whose ore carrier, the *Arthur M. Anderson,* was sailing fifteen to twenty miles behind the *Fitzgerald*. Cooper volunteered to act as the *Fitzgerald*'s radar, and from that point on, the two vessels were in frequent contact.

Shortly after 7:00 p.m., Morgan Clark, the *Anderson*'s first mate, asked McSorley how he was handling the storm and his boat's problems with taking on water. "We are holding our own," McSorley responded. These were the last words heard from anyone aboard the *Edmund Fitzgerald*. Cooper and Clark watched their radar as the *Fitz*, heading toward the safety of Whitefish Bay, disappeared in a snow squall. It never reappeared. Stunned, Cooper radioed Charles Millradt, the nearest Coast Guard commander, and expressed worry that the *Fitz* might have taken a nosedive. Millradt dispatched any vessels in the area, including the *Anderson,* to the site where the *Fitzgerald* was believed to have sunk, but there were no signs of the boat or any of its crew. She had simply disappeared.

Whatever happened must have happened very quickly, because no one on the *Fitzgerald* sent out an SOS, and the radio was within arm's reach of anyone in the pilothouse. Thus began the mystery. The wreckage was located quickly, and the fact that it was in two enormous pieces that had come to rest near to each other only fueled speculation. Had it broken on the surface, similar to the recent losses of the *Carl D. Bradley* (1958) and *Daniel J. Morrell* (1966), two large freighters lost in similar storms? Had the *Fitzgerald* taken on water through its hatches (or even lost a hatch cover or two) and lost buoyancy? Or had it taken a nosedive, as Cooper feared? It had been pitching badly in the roiling seas, and it was entirely believable that the *Fitzgerald* had her bow pushed beneath the surface and, unable to recover, had been driven by her own power to the depths of Lake Superior.

The Coast Guard wasted no time in seeking answers. A four-man Marine Board of Investigation was formed, and almost immediately after the loss of the *Fitzgerald* the board interviewed crew members from the *Anderson* (including Cooper and Clark), former crewmen on the *Fitz* (including its most recent captain), search and rescue personnel (including Millradt), ship designers and inspectors—just about anyone who might shed light on what might have happened on that fateful night, and more than forty "witnesses" in all. In a final report that remains very controversial to this day, the Board of Investigation concluded that the *Edmund Fitzgerald* sank as the result of water boarding through its hatches. To his dying day, Cooper contested these findings; the *Fitz*, he strongly felt, had hit bottom near the islands, torn its hull plates (not enough to immediately sink it, but enough to allow enough water in to eventually sink it), and, sailing very low in the water, had been overwhelmed by one or more enormous waves that pushed her beneath the surface.

———

The idea for this book came to me one December afternoon while I was engaged in my annual end-of-the-year ritual of sorting and filing research papers. I ran across a large box labeled FITZ. Inside were thousands of pages—photocopies of the transcripts of the complete Coast Guard Board of Investigation hearings into the loss of the *Edmund Fitzgerald*. Seeing the pages, carefully sorted by witness, brought back memories that I shall not forget: one of my initial phone calls to the Coast Guard headquarters in Washington, D.C., and another of my visit to those offices, where I examined the huge deposit of *Fitzgerald* holdings on file. The transcripts had come from that visit.

I remember the phone call because it was unintentionally funny, at least to me. I was connected to a Coast Guard historian, who was friendly, almost disarmingly polite, and very helpful. I told him that I was working on a book (*Mighty Fitz*) and mentioned that I hoped to see the Coast Guard holdings. He responded that that should be no problem, but just to be on the safe side, he gave me the name of another individual to contact for further confirmation. At this point I asked about the Coast Guard's photocopying policies. I was accustomed to being charged outrageous per-sheet prices by university and historical society libraries. I envisioned a hefty price tag on the transcripts.

"There's no charge for photocopies," I was told.

I paused for a moment before revealing my intentions.

"I don't think you understand," I said. "I'd like to photocopy the entire hearing transcripts."

It was his turn to pause. "Well, sir," he said, "maybe if you brought your own paper."

When I arrived in Washington, D.C., I was armed with a couple of cases of paper. I spent two days at a photocopying machine, making my own copies of the transcripts. Each witness was in an individually bound folder. I, too, kept the witnesses individually separated, and I knew better than to bother to seal the boxes. Security at Reagan Airport looked through the boxes, okayed their contents, and I duct-taped everything before checking them in. It was an experience.

I read every page, highlighted passages, and made notes in the transcript margins, knowing full well that I would have room for only the tiniest fraction of the material in *Mighty Fitz*.

All this came back to me when I opened the FITZ box that December afternoon. I pulled out one of the witness transcripts (Bernie Cooper, as it fortunately turned out to be), and I began reading. I was once again brought back to the immediacy of the testimony, offered so soon after the loss of the *Fitzgerald*. I thought, "This is really good material. It's a shame that it sits in storage, with only a handful of people ever seeing it." This really struck home as I continued reading the lengthy testimony, recorded over two sessions. Not only was Bernie Cooper captain of the boat following the *Fitz* during the storm, but he was also one of the last people to talk to those in the *Fitzgerald*'s pilothouse.

Gradually the idea for this book developed. I strongly felt that a book based on the Marine Board hearings would be unlike any book yet published on the *Fitzgerald*. I could present material I had not included in *Mighty Fitz*. For instance, in that book there were no photographs. There were three paintings (one of the *Fitz* in her glory days, one of her caught in the storm, and one of her wreckage), but I avoided photographs because I wanted the story to carry the book. I caught some flak for this decision, but I'm still glad I did it that way.

I had excluded the documents (Marine Board of Investigation report, the Lake Carriers' Association letter stating its findings, and the National Transportation Safety Board report) for the same reason. I referred to these documents, of course, when I was researching *Mighty Fitz*, but I did not want to include them in the book. Finally, there was the testimony itself: obviously, there was no way I could even consider using large extracts from the hearings and still hope to hold the book to any reasonable length.

I saw this new book in a different light. It tells the story of the *Edmund Fitzgerald*'s fateful final journey through the immediacy of the words of those who were out on Lake Superior in the storm, those who frantically coordinated the search efforts for the missing vessel and her crew, and, ultimately, those who eventually discovered the wreckage. From there, the book moves into a detailed account of the Marine Board hearings and the need for answers. These hearings, along with the accounts of the *Fitzgerald*'s demise, will lead the reader into understanding the documents that make up the third part of the book. This could be both a companion volume to *Mighty Fitz* and a stand-alone book.

The testimony gave this book its form. The descriptions of the *Fitzgerald*'s troubles, the storm on the lake, the vessel's sudden disappearance, and the ensuing search were detailed and dramatic, lending themselves to an oral history narrative. On the other hand, the Coast Guard's questioning of what might have led to the disaster, of the inspection history, loading practices, lifesaving equipment, and the overall seaworthiness of the *Fitzgerald* formed a different type of narrative. The exchanges between the board and the witnesses tended to be snappy and more official in tone, suggesting a courtroom transcript narrative. This, I felt, was ideal—a natural lead-in to the final documents.

On a handful of occasions, I silently corrected a witness's grammar, but aside from that their words remain unedited. In the oral history section, I combined answers into a single statement—but only sparingly and only if the board asked and repeated the same question, in the same context. In many other cases, I used only the nuggets from longer answers—testimony that supported the topic at hand. After all, the transcripts are thousands of pages.

When I was researching *Mighty Fitz,* I interviewed several people unavailable to the board—most notably Captain Jimmy Hobaugh, skipper of the Coast Guard cutter *Woodrush,* which participated in the search and rescue efforts and assisted in locating the *Fitz* and the subsequent CURV mission that explored the wreck, and Captain Don Erickson, who commanded the *William Clay Ford* in the search and rescue operations. I also spoke to two of the board members. Their observations were exceptional. Some of this interview material made its way into *Mighty Fitz,* and I weighed the option of including some of their words as parenthetical asides in this book. I rejected the possibility because I wanted this book to be exclusively about the Coast Guard hearings. Readers, I decided, ought to be privy only to what the Marine Board members heard. The documents at the end of the book represent a controversy that is debated to this day, and I felt that, in all fairness, readers should know only what the board knew when it published its conclusions.

These conclusions were not easily reached, and the testimony proves, beyond all else, the difficulty in explaining how a huge ore carrier, recently inspected and deemed seaworthy, could be "holding [its] own" in a storm and then, without warning, suddenly disappear beneath the waves. There is disagreement about what happened, but the witnesses are unanimous in their belief that whatever it was, it was extremely quick in occurring.

I have my own ideas about what happened to the *Fitzgerald,* and I am certain that nearly everyone who has heard an account of the sinking has a theory about what led to the boat's demise. It's a timeless, unsolvable mystery. The testimony herein should answer some questions, though it's likely to present others. Such is the nature of this tragic and extraordinary story.

Routes of the Edmund Fitzgerald *and* ▶
Arthur M. Anderson, *November 9–10, 1975.*
Courtesy of NOAA Historical Map and Chart Collection.

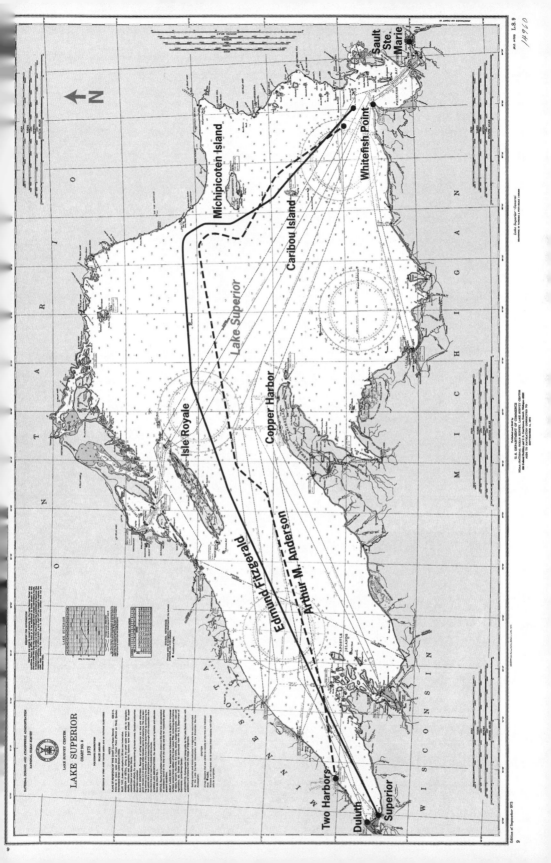

DOES ANYONE
KNOW WHERE
THE LOVE
OF GOD GOES

I. The Loss

WHEN THE
WAVES TURN
THE MINUTES
TO HOURS?

—GORDON LIGHTFOOT,
"THE WRECK OF THE
EDMUND FITZGERALD"

Loading
the Boat

At the time of her first trip on September 22, 1958, the *Edmund Fitzgerald,* named for the president and CEO of Northwestern Mutual Life Insurance Company, had a reputation that exceeded her expectations. The 729-foot *Fitzgerald* was the largest vessel on the lakes, the most expensive bulk carrier ever built, and strong enough to haul unprecedented cargo from port to port. She was well appointed, the envy of every sailor not part of her crew. This was no ordinary freighter. People would line the shoreline, cameras at the ready, to watch her glide by. Larger vessels would be built; others would be lengthened. But in her lifetime, the *Edmund Fitzgerald,* nicknamed the *Mighty Fitz* or *Toledo Express,* was truly the Queen of the Lakes.

The 1975 shipping season was nearing its conclusion when the *Fitz* arrived at the Burlington Northern docks in Superior, Wisconsin, on Sunday, November 9. In the aftermath of the *Fitzgerald*'s sinking, the Coast Guard Board of Investigation devoted substantial time to reconstructing the final loading of the *Fitzgerald,* but to those working on the docks that day, there was nothing out of the ordinary about the loading, as 26,000 tons of taconite (an average load) dropped into the boat's massive hold.

Captain Ernest McSorley, the sixty-two-year-old skipper, and First Mate Jack McCarthy, who supervised the loading, led one of the finer crews on the Great Lakes. This run would find the *Fitzgerald* delivering her cargo to a steel processing plant near Detroit. November could be rough sailing on the Great Lakes, and stormy weather was predicted for a period of the trip, but at the time of the loading, the weather was overcast but unseasonably warm.

◀ *The* Edmund Fitzgerald *during the Milwaukee Seaway celebrations, 1959.*
Courtesy of Great Lakes Marine Collection of the Milwaukee Public Library / Wisconsin Marine Historical Society.

CLARENCE DENNIS *boat loader, Burlington Northern docks*

It was a nice day. It could have been a little cloudy, but it was not a stormy day. I didn't mind being out there at all. There were no troubles. The mate was jolly. With pellets, you never have any trouble with the boats at all. It goes so good compared to raw ore.

BERNIE COOPER *Master,* Arthur M. Anderson

Taconite is a processed iron ore. It is about 25 percent iron when they take it out of the ground. The iron is extracted, and through a process developed by the corporation, it forms a pellet almost like a marble, and it runs about 65 percent iron.

JAMES VILLAR *Manager, Research and Development, Cleveland Cliffs Iron Company*

The procedure is to re-mine the crude iron ore by open pit methods. The material is drilled, blasted, and crushed. Then it is ground to a fairly fine-sized consistency, depending on the particular iron ore property. Then the iron is oxidized and liberated from the silica material and waste material. The iron ore concentrate is essentially a fine powder. It is dewatered to about 10 percent moisture, rolled into balls or formed into balls, spherical objects. It is then placed upon a heat machine, and there are various processes where the water is driven off. The material is permitted to form some strength on a grate. This can all be done on a grate with a heat treatment process taking place, and it is then either discharged into a kiln, which is one method, integrated into temperatures in the neighborhood—oh, it will range about twenty-two to twenty-four hundred degrees Fahrenheit. It is cooled and placed either on a stockpile or in railroad cars for transportation to a facility or a stockpile near a port. The weight of an individual ball I am not certain of. The bulk density of the material is generally in the range of 130 pounds per cubic foot. That's dry, incidentally.

DONALD AMYS *General Foreman, Burlington Northern docks*

[The cargo] is brought down in pellet cars, and it is put on a belt and brought up onto the dock. Unless our belt is down for repairs, the cars are shuffled to the docks, and pellets are put into pockets. A pocket holds on the average of about 300 tons. These are the holds or the pockets in the dock, and they are all numbered. . . . A chute is lowered into the boat, and doors are tripped. It just runs into the holds of the boat.

DELMORE WEBSTER *former Fitzgerald crew member*

As first mate, I was responsible for laying out the cargo and had complete supervision of the loading, and as the unloading took place I was watch stander as second mate. They have a loading manual about. I looked it over when I went aboard to relieve in January. They also had other records from previous loads and previous cargoes to use as a guideline.

The Edmund Fitzgerald *takes on iron ore at the docks of the Duluth, Missabe and Iron Range Railway in Duluth, Minnesota, circa 1970.*
Photograph by Basgen Photography. Courtesy of Great Lakes Shipwreck Museum.

PETER PULCER *former Master,* Edmund Fitzgerald

The mates had a loading pattern. They kept track of all the tonnage in every hatch, what they put in through the ship. They had a loading book, a record for every load for every different draft and all that, like the summer draft. They made out a pattern of every load. They would make out a pattern just how they were going to load the ship. According to our experience on the ship, we load it carefully so that we would not stress the ship.

You put a run through, say, of four or five hundred tons in each hatch, and then you go back and put another run through and then the third run, and you are trimming your ship. You load more in the ends. You put it in the hatch where she will go down aft and not come up forward. You can't go ahead and put the same amount in the middle. It would break it in two. You have to load the end a little heavier than the center of the ship.

THOMAS GARCIA *former* Fitzgerald *crew member*

If you fill every hatch all at once, your boat will sink. If you get all that weight at one time, you will break the back of the ship.

DONALD AMYS

There are 374 pockets on the dock in total. Half are on the east side, and half are on the west side. I estimate how many pockets he is going to take, taking on an average of 300 tons per pocket, and our boat loader puts it into the boat according to the mate, which is according to how he wants it in the boat and when and how much he wants. . . . When I was out observing this load, he was loading in a normal procedure as other vessels do.

The *Fitzgerald* doesn't come to the ore docks too often. He loaded four times in our dock in 1975. She did not load at our dock in '74. On a boat that size, we figure anywhere from five to six hours [to load]. [On November 9, 1975], it started at 7:30 and loaded at 1:15.

When the loading was complete, crew members went about the task of placing the long, heavy hatch covers on the hatch coamings and tightening them down with clamps—"knee busters," as Thomas Garcia called them—in an effort to make the vessel as watertight as possible. This was especially important if the weather forecasts indicated stormy weather ahead.

CHARLES LINDBERG *former* Fitzgerald *crew member*

[The hatch covers] are laying flush on the deck, and in some places there is one stacked on top of the other. You have a motorized hatch crane that is run by the watchman or the AB maintenance man, and the two

Each of the Fitzgerald's *twenty-one watertight cargo hatches was secured with Kestner clamps, seen here during the vessel's construction in 1958. The operation of the hatches would prove crucial to the Coast Guard's investigation.* Courtesy of Great Lakes Maritime Institute.

deckhands are with him. They will put the hooks in, and it is picked up by a winch and picked up to the height it will to clear the coamings and set down onto the hatches.

ROBERT O'BRIEN *Master,* Benfri

I was quite strict about that [securing the hatches]. I used to walk down the deck when we left port or shortly after. If I went back for a meal and it was daylight, then I used to take a piece of chalk with me, and I would walk down one side, and when I came back from the galley, if the weather was all right, I would come back on the other side, and I would notice if they didn't have her battened down right, they would have to go out and do it over. I know that the crew didn't like it, and I told them, "I don't give a damn whether you like it or not. It could be your life as well as mine," and then it got to the point where they knew that they better do it right in the first place. We very seldom had a problem. Well, once in a while the men would miss getting the battens in properly when it was night. It was hard for them to see. So you could allow for that, but then they would correct it in the daylight.

Weather Predictions

WILLIAM KENNEDY *National Weather Service, Cleveland*

I am responsible mostly for data acquisition. We have forty Great Lakes freighters . . . completely equipped with National Weather Service anemometers, barometers, and thermometers. We take observations every six hours, and there are special observations when the winds exceed the forecasted winds. In other words, if there are no warnings out and a vessel gets into a storm, which is up into the storm or gale warning, they take a special weather observation and let us know if the winds are higher than the forecast.

We have forty Coast Guard stations surrounding the Great Lakes, but on Lake Superior we have ten Coast Guard stations, two Canadian stations and two automatic [unloading] stations. The local weather office is responsible for the Coast Guard station in their area. The Coast Guard takes the observations every two hours. They are put on a form. At the end of the month, these forms are sent to the Weather Forecast Service and checked for quality control. Then these forms are mailed to the National Climatic Center in Asheville, North Carolina, for filing.

We have a Coast Guard station at the Soo. Then we have the automatic weather station at Whitefish Point. Then the next station over is Grand Marais Coast Guard, and then it runs over to Marquette Coast Guard Station. Actually, the Grand Marais would be the closest station, Whitefish being automated.

We make up what we call the lake weather bulletin, which are measurements comprised of the forty Coast Guard Stations and the ship reports, and the barometric pressure readings from stations around the

Great Lakes. This is made up every six hours at the Cleveland office and broadcast to the ships every six hours at 2:30 a.m. and p.m., and at 8:30 a.m. and p.m. . . .

Canada has a port meteorological officer who does the same work I do in Canada, and we get the Canadian ship reports and reports such as from Caribou Island on Lake Superior. They come into our office, and it is incorporated in this Lake Weather Broadcast. We start out with each lake. We give [it to] the land stations around each lake, and then it is followed by the ship reports on that lake.

RAYMOND WALDMAN *National Weather Service, Chicago*

The fact that we are able to use satellite pictures helps a great deal in determining the movement of such things as low pressure centers and fronts, and we get a satellite picture once every half hour. The satellite pictures tell us what the density of the cloud coverage is, and we delineate that or we try to identify the storm centers and the positions or locations of cold fronts and warm fronts and other weather features, but [satellite pictures are] used for all forecasts including marine forecasts.

I believe we certainly could use more vessel observations than we have, and we could use observations of temperature, pressure, wind speed and direction, from fixed locations in the Great Lakes. We now depend on vessel observations, and the vessels, of course, are always moving. We have very few places from which we get weather information from a fixed point on a continuous basis, so we have an urgent need for that kind of information.

WILLIAM KENNEDY

When a ship makes an observation, he reports the day of the month, the latitude and the longitude, the time, the total cloud amount, his true wind and degrees and knots, his visibility, his present weather, his past weather, his air temperature, and his Celsius, his water temperature in Celsius, ice secretion, which is information given when the temperature is below freezing, his wave, the average period of the wave in seconds and the average height of the wave in half meters on his observation, and

Storms are frequent on Lake Superior in the late fall, and the National Weather Service uses satellite imagery to track ice cover and shifting winds. This image from November 2014 depicts rapid evaporation as a cold front moves over the lake. Courtesy of NOAA Great Lakes CoastWatch.

also any other information if he has time to put in remarks. He has this little block called "Remarks" where he can put in things such as "Heavy snow, visibility half mile," or maybe "Peak Gusts," if he can observe a peak gust. That is put in the Remarks of the observations he takes.

The weather observations go back with a little history back to the November 11th storm in 1940 when several ships and many lives were lost. The ship masters asked for more weather information for the Great Lakes, and we had a meeting over at Milwaukee at the Shipmasters' Convention with Mr. Andrus, who used to be in charge of the Cleveland Forecast Office. It is very hard sometimes to make a forecast in an area unless you know what the weather is, and at the time we agreed to furnish forty ships with anemometers, thermometers, and barometers in return if they took the observations for us, and we could make a better forecast for them, because we would know what was going on out on the Great Lakes.

So, through the years, it is their observations on the ships, and they put their very best into these observations that they take for us, and of course we give the forecasts back to them or the warnings, whatever. Many times this has happened where on the lake in a certain area of the lake, winds may be up in a gale category and we don't have the gale warnings up. We get that report, and we immediately put a gale warning on for the other ships, and this is the service that they give to us. They have done it over the years, and we furnish the forecasts back to them.

Q. Was the Fitzgerald *one of these reporting ships plying the Great Lakes?*
Yes, one of the better ones.

RAYMOND WALDMAN

I would say that we have intense storms on the Great Lakes on an average of about four or five times a year. November is a particularly critical month for storms. It is what we call a transitional month, where we are well into the fall and we begin to have intrusions of cold air from the north, and we have the kind of collision of air masses that is conducive to the development of intense low-pressure systems which produce strong winds. . . . A well-developed storm is often easier to forecast than one that develops extremely rapidly, so generally, I would say, yes, that often in November we do have well-developed storms that are easier for the forecaster to cope with.

There are years that we do not get this kind of storm, definitely. We might get through several seasons without getting this intense a storm. So it is not something that I would say that happened every year since the time that we have been keeping records.

The storm that affected Lake Superior on November 9 and 10 was a very intense storm. Winds began to increase on Lake Superior at 1:00 p.m., Eastern Standard Time, Sunday, the 9th, and except for a brief period Monday morning, on November 10 continued very strong through Monday evening. Rain and some thunderstorms and squalls occurred on Lake Superior between 1:00 a.m., Eastern Standard Time, to about 9:00 a.m., Eastern Standard Time, on Monday, November 10,

1975. There was also some snow along the northern shore of Lake Superior during the afternoon of Monday, November 10.

The strongest winds that we had reported to us—that is, from either a Coast Guard station or from a vessel that cooperates with our observational system—was from the west-northwest, and this is an average of the winds taken over a period of time. The period of time would have been 3:00 p.m., Eastern Standard Time, Monday, November 10, to 7:00 p.m., Monday, November 10. The average wind was from the west-northwest at 40 knots to 56 knots, with gusts to 66 knots. We also had an observation from the *Arthur Anderson* at 7:00 p.m., Eastern Standard Time, Monday, November 10, 1975, winds from the west-northwest at 50 knots with waves of 16 feet.

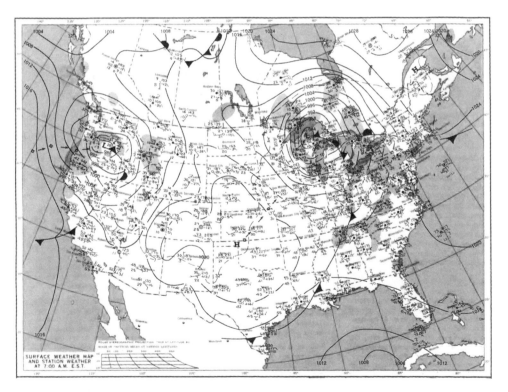

The national weather map from November 10, 1975, shows a powerful low-pressure zone forming around Lake Superior. Courtesy of NOAA Central Library Data Imaging Project.

The forecasters at the National Weather Service Forecast Office in Chicago raised the gale warnings on Lake Superior as of 4:39, Eastern Standard Time, Sunday, November the 9th, 1975. The gale warning was increased to storm warning as of 2:00 a.m., Eastern Standard Time, Monday, November the 10th, and storm warnings were kept up on Lake Superior from 2:00 a.m., Eastern Standard Time, Monday, November the 10th, until 1:00 a.m. early Tuesday morning November 11, 1975. The storm warnings were maintained for approximately a seventeen-hour period before the time of the tragedy, and they were kept up until 1:00 a.m. early Tuesday morning, November 11th.

They were disseminated over the NOAA Weather Radio System, and we have three such systems on Lake Superior, one at Duluth, one at Marquette, and one at Sault Ste. Marie.

Q. The **Fitzgerald** *left Superior Piers at 1452, so I would be interested in your findings and in telling me what the forecast was at that time.*
At that time, the forecast that we issued at 10:34 a.m., Eastern Standard Time, read as follows: South-southeast winds, 8 to 16 knots this afternoon, becoming southeast to east and increasing to 20 to 33 knots tonight and becoming east to northeast 28 to 38 knots Monday; cloudy, occasional rain tonight and Monday, waves 1 to 3 feet increasing to 3 to 6 feet tonight and 4 to 8 feet Monday. So we were indicating a general increase of winds and an increase in the waves. It was replaced by another forecast issued at 4:39 p.m., Eastern Standard Time, Sunday, November 9. In that forecast we indicated that gale warnings should be hoisted at 7:00 p.m., Eastern Standard Time. We were indicating that waves would be continuing to increase and would be 5 to 9 feet on Monday.

The *Arthur M. Anderson*

The *Edmund Fitzgerald* was two and a half hours into her run when another massive bulk carrier, the *Arthur M. Anderson*, left the docks at Two Harbors, Minnesota. Measuring 647 feet when launched in 1952, the *Anderson* had been lengthened to 767 feet after the 1974 season, giving her more room for cargo.

Captain Jesse "Bernie" Cooper, a thirty-eight-year veteran of Great Lakes shipping, had commanded the *Anderson* for the past three seasons. Cooper prided himself in his extensive knowledge of weather on the lakes. Unlike Captain McSorley, who preferred to set a course and adhere to it as closely as possible, Cooper made constant adjustments throughout a trip in stormy weather, the changes dictated by developing weather forecasts or by his own observations and predictions.

BERNIE COOPER

Any time there are gale warnings or whatever, any time there is an indication that there is a storm that is going to be in the Great Lakes area that will possibly involve us, I always plot my own weather along and in conjunction with what we get from the Weather Bureau and also what I pick up from TV stations, because there are two or three real good meteorologists along the Lakes, especially when they agree with me [*laughter*]. . . . To give you an indication on my part, why I had plotted the storm and why I figured that the winds. . . . I have been through three typhoons and I have been through a lot of storms here on the Great Lakes, and every time you pass through the eye of a storm, the wind changes very fast. It's like a direct opposite than what you had been going [through] previously. If you are on the outer edge of a storm, it's less drastic. The wind does not change around like you're going through an eye. I was in the eye, and I plotted this on this 1430 map.

We left Two Harbors on November 9th at 1630. Shortly after we left, they put up a northeast gale warning. At that time the gale warnings were fringe. When I say fringe gale, I mean 34 to 38 knots, which is not unusual at this time of the year. We proceeded on a course to Devil's Island. From Devil's Island we proceeded down toward the middle of Lake Superior. The wind at this time, which was at Devil's Island, was east by north, 31 knots, cloudy weather, and it was practically right on our stem, a fresh breeze.

The gale warnings still were all up, but at 0100 in the morning when

The Arthur M. Anderson, seen here in January 1972, had been lengthened more than 120 feet at the Fraser Shipyards in Superior, Wisconsin, just months before the storm.
Courtesy of National Archives.

I was in the wheelhouse, I got a report from Duluth Coast Guard. They put up storm warnings.

At that time, I notified the *Fitzgerald* that I had heard this and called them, initiated a call, and asked him if he had received this notice. So at this time he was alerted like I was, and we talked over what we were going to do as far as going up on this course.

Now, the *Fitzgerald* had been right close by us all this time, pulling ahead of us a little. She was a little bit faster a ship than we were.

A double sea was rolling. It wasn't big seas at the time, but we got in close enough to the eastern edge of Canada there to knock off the northeast sea, and we both proceeded on down to Michipicoten Island, the west end. And in the meantime I had been charting—in fact I have got the two plots that I had on the weather. I thought we should save those and not erase them, right?

I talked with the *Fitzgerald* on several occasions there. He asked me what I was going to do, what we were going to do, and we kind of generally decided that it wasn't that bad, that we would keep on moseying down.

Well, when he got down just below Michipicoten, I was about 7 miles behind him, and the wind went around to the northwest, northwest by west, and was blowing a gagger. Up on Lake Superior, it usually takes one to two hours for a sea to build up. I don't know what the captain of the *Fitzgerald* thought, but in my own thinking, I figured we would be down a couple of hours above Whitefish before the seas would get big enough to bother us, but that sea built in an hour, and it was blowing. I don't know what I have got it in the logbooks. I can't remember exactly, but it was blowing a pretty steady 55 knots and gusting up to 70 at times.

Well, I steered for Michipicoten. There is a 6-fathom bank in close to Caribou, and I wanted to avoid that and the 15-fathom bank down in there called the Chummy Bank, south of Michipicoten Island, because when you get over those banks, the seas become tremendously huge because of the water being shoal, and the waves, you know, they just break crazy.

The Seas

BERNIE COOPER

I would consider it a severe local storm because it was intense, but it was not a vast wide two-day storm. To me, it looked more like a hurricane storm, which I am familiar with, plotting down in Florida. As I remember correctly, it followed along pretty much with what I anticipated, except I don't think they had as much wind predicted as what I plotted or what my plot showed.

CEDRIC WOODARD *Master,* Avafors

It was very severe. There were big seas and everything and strong winds. I don't know how you measure seas, and I never did, but it was one of the biggest and wildest seas I have been in. I mean, fast. The tops were blowing off them, and there was white water. Then the blue water would come, and then there was white water. The sea was straight up and down and a lot of them were coming at you. . . . I have no idea how they measure them, but it was a big sea. To say how far, I wouldn't.

It was the worst noise I have heard on a bridge, I would say. It was loud. It was up in the superstructure. It was really howling.

LEDOLF BAER *Waves, NOAA*

I am director of the Oceanographic Services Office. I have something on the order of twenty years' experience in wave forecasting, wave behind forecasting, and wave observations and other research in that area.

What studies show is if you are on a small boat, you tend to overestimate the waves. If you are on a big boat, you tend to underestimate the waves. Waves themselves are fairly complicated, and in the last years we almost always speak about a wave spectrum in the scientific discussion of waves, because this allows us to recognize that the waves vary from one wave to the next. When I say spectrum, I am really saying a superimposition of a lot of different wave lengths, and when those are superimposed, you get a complex sea much as what you actually observe, with one exception: that has to do with the non-linear properties of the wave, which makes the crests steeper and the troughs flatter.

There are several formal definitions of shifting wave height. One of them is that it is the average of the highest one-third of the waves. That's a difficult definition to apply because you don't know what is a wave. If you have something 1 millimeter high, is that a wave or not? A most modern definition of that is that it is four times the square root of the variance of the record. Now that's a statistical definition. The square root of the variance is essentially the RMS [Root Mean Square]. We are talking about the same as the area under the spectrum.

How does that tie in with what we are talking about here? Well, there are a bunch of studies, and I can't remember the exact dates, but they were in the era of the late '40s. They showed that what people think they see from a ship, what they talk about wave height, is the significant height. That's when these basic comparisons were made.

There is a great deal of variance between eyeball estimates, but the average of the upper one-third has been found to be a reasonable estimate of what people do see when they look out over the waves. In other words, you don't see the little ones. You just see the large ones.

WILLIAM KENNEDY

Q. How is the wave height data obtained?
It is difficult for a mate, because of his responsibilities in the pilothouse, but he normally looks out and takes several waves, because one wave right after the other would be different, so he looks out and takes the average.

Q. Does he have any instruments to measure that?
No. It is one of the most difficult observations to make on the Great Lakes.

RAYMOND WALDMAN

The source of that [wave height] information is based on a calculation that the weather forecaster makes considering the strength of the average wind and the wind direction and the period of time that the wind blows from a given direction at a certain strength, and what we are trying to indicate. Our wave forecast indicates the expected wave heights at the downwind end or side of the lake, this being the area where the wave heights are expected to build up to their greatest heights.

By the wave height, we are trying to forecast the mean wave height over a period of time, and we certainly recognize that there could be waves that are higher. We are not trying to forecast the highest wave conditions. We are trying to achieve a mean over a period of time, a range of the wave heights over a period of time. One of the things that we would strongly depend on would be the fetch, the length of the fetch, and the average wind speed. That would be one guide. In addition, we would use actual observations that would be available.

Wave height always mattered in a storm. Cooper and McSorley traded observations and strategies for handling the weather, most notably after their respective freighters made the turn to go south on Lake Superior, and they eventually passed through the eye of the storm. They now had following seas growing in height as the wind velocity increased. The waves weren't consistently enormous, as Cooper eventually testified, and he was surprised by how well the *Anderson* handled the waves. When asked if the *Anderson* had rolled in the storm, Cooper responded by quoting his cook: "It wouldn't roll an egg off the table." The *Fitzgerald,* Cooper surmised from his exchanges with her wheelhouse personnel, was responding similarly to the storm.

BERNIE COOPER

Looking aft and watching the stack on the horizon, her stern would rise maybe seven or eight degrees up on the horizon before it would come back. I was watching it, and I estimated the seas at 200 feet apart, crest to crest. To me, this indicated that I was riding on three waves at all times. Now, I am not riding on one here and here and nothing on the front end. You look at my average speed, and I never checked, but you will find that I questioned the engineer if the governor took over, because we were throwing our wheel. None of this happened. She rode beautiful. We were taking water over our deck, but she was riding absolutely phenomenal. I couldn't believe it myself.

The seas were coming up from aft, and in effect we would hit a trough between a sea. The deck would be clear. Like if a 25-foot sea would come over, you have 5-foot-high water that would come over your ship, and it would roll across your deck with a following sea. It would just roll right on across. It was almost like dropping it on. It was not a breaking sea like

ABOVE AND FOLLOWING PAGE
Snapshots taken by a crew member on board the William H. Truesdale *in the late 1930s show how following seas can begin to swamp the decks of a massive ore boat.* Kenneth Thro Collection, Lake Superior Maritime Collections, University of Wisconsin–Superior.

if you were running into it head-on. It was like a thumping wave coming down and splashing across, but there was no driving across. . . . She didn't even wiggle at all. She had a little bit of movement to her, which is a normal spring. I mean if they don't bend, you are going to break them.

In 1975, two of the Great Lakes' most recent shipwreck disasters involved two of the longest ships on the lakes at the time. *The Carl D. Bradley* and the *Daniel J. Morrell* both suffered structural failure when excessive bending, coupled with frigid water, broke them into pieces. Both of these freighters had been constructed before 1948, when new, more flexible materials began to be used to give vessels more flexibility in cold water. But even that did not end captains' worries. The biggest, strongest bulk carriers would "work" in heavy seas, often with a springing effect that threatened to hog a vessel. Or, in some cases, a wave could lift a stern out of the water, its propeller spinning with no resistance, causing a massive shudder when the stern returned to the water. In such cases, good communications between the pilothouse and the engine room became essential. If necessary, an engineer would check down the engine to hold down the spinning effect. Cooper admitted that he never checked down throughout his entire trip down Lake Superior.

BERNIE COOPER

When a ship is springing, it is the movement of the end as compared to a stationary object in the middle of the ship. The ship will bend or spring, whichever you want to call it. If a ship is completely rigid in a seaway, you will break in two. There has to be give to the ship, like our lakers that are built to carry a lot of cargo on a shallow draft. So you can actually discern springing in a seaway. Your stern will dip down as sea runs out from under it and it will dip a little bit and come back up, and the same way as the wave progresses forward on the bow. The bow will go down, and you can actually see the movement of the two ends and compare it to a stationary spot amidships.

ANDREW RAJNER *former* Fitzgerald *crew member*

Q. On the ships that you ever sailed on the lakes, where you had this effect [springing], have you ever been concerned or were you ever worried about this?

I sure was. . . . Everybody would be. It is a funny feeling to walk down the ship and have that ship springing. Even if you go down the tunnel, it is a long way down to the other end. . . . You have something moving underneath you, and you really are not sure of what you are standing on, but after a while, you get used to it. You just forget about it.

[McSorley] never said anything about it. The only thing he would say, if she gets to springing too much, to just check her down. He would say, "Don't hesitate to check her down." That's all he told me.

RICHARD ORGEL *former* Fitzgerald *crew member*

On one occasion, he [McSorley] told me that the action of the vessel, the hull, in the seaway sometimes scared him. We were in the heavy water, if I remember. It was north-northwesterly weather. We were coming out of Whitefish going up toward the north shore for shelter. It was of gale force winds, what I would call a moderate sea, perhaps 10 or 12 foot, pretty near stem on. We altered course, altered speed from time to time, trying to ease the working of the vessel. . . . She bends and springs considerably. When you are standing forward and looking aft, it would remind you of a diving board just after somebody jumped off the board, the diving board of a swimming pool. She did this whippingly. It seems to be when you are standing forward, it looks like it is starting around midship, so then going to the stern, and then when you are standing aft and looking forward, it sometimes would appear like the forward end is doing it, and just where all this is taking place, I just don't know. It's along the length of her somewhere.

It seemed to be much more noticeable, at least this was my experience, when you are standing forward and looking aft. It seems that when the sea piled up under her stern and then falls away, she just doesn't drop down into the trough. The stern doesn't drop into the trough like you would expect it. It whips is the best word, or springs is the best way I could describe.

The difference between the bending and springing is, I would say, that the springing is the rapid bending; it does it fast. It isn't—there is a difference between a vessel bending when the sea is rolling underneath it and this action that I am trying to describe to you is this is a fast thing. I mean, it would probably occur in a matter of two or three seconds, and then it will do it again in two or three seconds, I would say. It shudders. [McSorley] said that this sometimes scared him. This springing was quite noticeable at that time. It wasn't jest. I was working back out on the deck, and I asked him if it was possible that this action could actually cause the hatch clamps to come off. He said no, he had never seen that happen, and I remarked to him that there was sometimes a lot of action back there, and he was walking away. He was leaving the chart room, and we were standing back in the pilothouse. He was going toward his room, and as he walked away, he said, "Oh, this thing, this sometimes scares me."

The captain told me that before this, before he had left the wheel-house, when he first came up, he was there perhaps forty-five minutes, and he told me that if she started working too much, that I should alter course or call him. He said he would be laying on top of his bed. He wasn't going to dress or anything, and if I had any problems or I thought it was working too much, I should call him.

Dangerous Shoals

The early portion of the *Fitzgerald*'s (and *Anderson*'s) trip across and down Lake Superior had been uneventful. The weather continued to deteriorate. The taconite cargo helped stabilize the *Fitzgerald*, and Captain Ernest McSorley, closely monitoring the weather, never gave an indication that the run was out of the ordinary.

That changed when the *Fitzgerald* and, later, the *Anderson* navigated near the shallower water near Caribou and Michipicoten Islands.

BERNIE COOPER

We came across the whole north end of Lake Superior with northeast winds—I mean you can look at the logbook, 30 to 40 knots. No big seas that would bother us. We came across at full speed. The ship wasn't working or pounding or anything else. But that damn low [pressure system] intensified when it hit the water, and that water was warm, and, of course, that makes the storm center much more intense, and, brother, when we got down to Michipicoten, she was blowing a gale. And I, of course, from previous experience on Lake Superior, this being a deep lake, [knew that] it takes a couple of hours for the sea to build, and I figured I had it made. It's only 30 miles from there down to Whitefish, and I am sure that the captain of the *Fitzgerald* felt the same way. But it got nasty, and nasty very quickly.

The shoals in the area presented hazards to vessels being bounced around in heavy seas. Pitching boats could touch bottom in such seas. Captain McSorley maintained his regular pattern of passing through the area, while

Captain Cooper took a more cautious approach. In their testimony before the Board of Investigation, several experienced masters spoke of the hazards of sailing though the area during stormy weather.

BERNIE COOPER

If you have big seas, usually the seas are a little larger over your shallower waters, which is normal. . . . As a general rule, if you can avoid a shoal area with a big wind and sea, you avoid it.

ROBERT O'BRIEN

We always try to give it [Caribou Island] a wide berth—5 or 6 miles. I have always felt that you should not try to come too close to places like that.

I remember the old man saying to the mate that he wanted to make sure we had plenty of room off Caribou because he said if we get a pretty good rolling there, and, as it was, we did, we rolled like hell until we got by it. That's why I feel you should try to keep as far away as you possibly can.

ROY ANDERSON *Second Mate,* Arthur M. Anderson

[Bernie Cooper] said we will have to be far enough off Caribou so we are well clear of that [Six-Fathom Shoal] and take even more precautions. That's 6 fathoms when the water is calm, and with those heavy seas, it is going to be less. Since we had good water the other side of us, that's the only way to go. He wanted to be in the vicinity of 6 miles off.

ALBERT JACOVETTI *Master,* Nanfri

You certainly try to avoid the shoal waters. Any time you have a sea running out there and you are passing over a shoal water, you are going to get a beating. Like the south seas banks off Caribou Island, you try to avoid those during the time of the sea or storm, because they do react upon a ship, I mean to cause a ship to roll and pitch. . . . It is more turbulent. I would not say it is higher, but it is more turbulent. I think if you run across a shoal or run across shoal water, you would know that right away. The reaction of the ship usually shakes and vibrates more. If the ship is pitching or bobbing, it is going to take you closer to the bottom, and I imagine you would have more reaction.

BERNIE COOPER

We were concerned that he [the *Edmund Fitzgerald*] was in too close, that he was going to hit that shoal off of Caribou. He was about 3 miles off the land beacon. That's a very fringe on that shoal area that extends out northeast from Caribou Island. And when he got in that close, he was over that 36-foot spot in there. There is a 6-fathom spot. Pretty good sized, extensive 6-fathom spot. And then out farther is a 25-fathom bank. I hauled out around both of these because when you get over those damn shallow waters, you can get a hell of a sea. You get a much bigger sea right in those particular areas than you do out in the deep water.

Eyeballing her down there, all I can say it's clear she was closer than I would want to be. Here again, I can't be definite, but— and I think when you talk to my mate he will tell you, he will give you the same—it was an impression that we had that she was in too close. . . . We were eyeballing her going in there near Caribou Island.

The beacon at Caribou Island, Ontario, occupies a small rocky outcropping in eastern Lake Superior. Many believe this is where the Edmund Fitzgerald *struck the lake bottom in her struggle to reach Whitefish Bay.*
Courtesy of Library and Archives Canada.

CEDRIC WOODARD

I would say that she could possibly strike, but grounding to me is stopping. I wouldn't say she would stop, but I would say maybe she could go up and down enough to hit a ship loaded with 27 [thousand tons], which would raise and fall enough to strike her, but I have never seen it. I am not saying it is impossible.

BERNIE COOPER

Normally you figure on Lake Superior in weather, you can figure two hours before you are in deep water, before you get a sea that is going to start to bother you, but from the time I hauled her, from the time I was to Michipicoten West End, the sea had built up to probably 10 to 12 feet. By the time I was down in here [south of the island], seas were running on, say, 12 to 16 feet.

ROY ANDERSON

I overheard the captain—the mate, speaking of the message that the *Edmund Fitzgerald* had lost two, or lost some air vents and had damaged some fence rails and was developing a list. I was off watch, but you never leave. As a rule, you don't go right out the door when you are relieved. I would say this is possibly ten or fifteen minutes after I had been relieved. He had this damage. He had lost air vents, or his air vents had been damaged, and there was some fence rails or something, and he was taking on water.

MORGAN CLARK First Mate, Arthur M. Anderson

The *Fitzgerald* called the *Anderson*. As I turned around to answer the phone, the captain was over looking in the centimeter radar. He turned around and picked up the call. So I continued and started to work on the chart until I heard the *Fitzgerald* say he lost some fence rail. It came over the loudspeaker. [The caller] never identified himself as a captain, [but] the way he was talking, he said, "I have lost some vents," or like, "I have—" he said. "I believe that we have lost two air vents." He said, "I have." If it was a mate, I don't think he would say, "I." He would say, "we" or [something] in that respect.

He said he wanted to know if we would stay with him. Captain Cooper said, "Yes, check and we'll stay with you." He said, "Have you got your pumps going?" [McSorley] said, "Yes, we have got our pumps going." There were a few other things said, but as far as the conversation, that was about it. It was just general talk that the *Fitzgerald* said he would check down, and Captain Cooper said, "Yes, that would give us a chance to close up or watch out for you."

Q. What do you mean when he said he would check down? What did that mean to you?

That he was going to cut his revolutions, because under normal conditions, [the *Fitzgerald*] is a little faster. He was going to give us a chance to close up.

One of the fastest ore carriers on the lakes when built in 1958, the Edmund Fitzgerald *was powered by coal that was stoked in massive furnaces. Like many ore boats of this era, she was converted to oil fuel over the winter of 1971–72.*
Courtesy of Great Lakes Maritime Institute.

BERNIE COOPER

It was the captain of the *Fitzgerald* who called me. I understood him to say that his fence rail was laid down, and I'm probably wrong on this, but the mate and the wheelsman said the fence wire was gone. This was probably correct. He also told me that he had lost two vents, and he said that he had had a list and asked me if I would stay with him, which I concurred that I would stay with him. He said he was taking a list. I asked him if he had his pumps on, and he said, "Yes, I have them both on." He said, "I will check down so that you can close the distance between us," so we could get up closer to him.

In all the years I have been sailing, I have never known anybody to lose a fence rail in a seaway, and I have been out in some pretty good-sized seas, actually or probably bigger than these. A fence rail is a series of stanchions with three cables running through them. That is five-eighths wire rope with three strands running in through there. You might break one, but you can't conceivably think of breaking three. They are set in slots in the deck and there is no buoyancy to them. A sea wouldn't get underneath it and lift it. It might bend them, possibly, because the stanchions are about 3 inches wide. The only solution that I can have to a fence rail breaking is—you can't break one by sagging a ship, but you would have to bend the ship, hog it up in the middle, to put such a tension on the fence rail that you would break it.

ROY ANDERSON

I am not familiar with the *Fitzgerald,* but I believe she had the same type [of air vents] that we have. When you are pumping in ballast or pumping out ballast, you have to have some place for the air to escape when you are pumping water into a ballast tank full of air. Those vents are opened up so the air can escape. Otherwise you will break the tanks. You are pushing water pressure against air pressure.

BERNIE COOPER

There is a good possibility of something that was adrift in the sea that would come along and slap one of those [vent covers] and take it off.

This is a possibility. I can't foresee how the sea could knock one of them off, the way they are built, because they are round already and you have a natural cushion on it. It would almost be a physical impossibility for a sea to knock it off.

I was up in the wheelhouse when he called, and he told me that his fence rail was laid down and that he had snapped off two vents and he was taking water through those vents into the tanks. He didn't say starboard or port list, but I would assume it was a starboard list, because the sea was on our starboard side a little bit.

We were taking a lot of water, but you have got to almost have a 12-inch pipe full of water to go in there to cause you to list that quickly.

Of course, I never saw the *Fitzgerald* visibly from the time it started, or a little before it started, to snow, but there must have been snow where he was at before we ran into it. I never saw him again visibly, but I saw him on radar; I had him on radar all the time.

By the time we were 10 or 12 miles north of Caribou, the seas had picked up in that one hour. They were running 12 to 18 feet, and below Caribou they were running 18 to 25. . . . We had a damaged lifeboat. That particular one [wave] had to be close to 30 feet to go in on top of it. We didn't have very, very many 30-footers. That wasn't water coming up on the deck on a constant rate. You had seas that were 10 foot, and three or four that would come along that were 18, and a couple of dandies would roll by about 25, and maybe you would go by and none would come. It was an intermediate type thing, and we got down to here, 30 to 40 miles northwest of Whitefish, the seas were breaking over. We had seas breaking over the deck all the time.

At this time, after steering west, [the *Fitzgerald*] extended his distance out to 17 miles, which I think was about maximum, which he was ahead of us.

He gave no indication that he was worried or that he had a problem or there was something that he couldn't cope with. There was no excitement whatsoever. This was a problem, but it was under control. This is what you would assume from the way he talked, that there was no problem.

ROY ANDERSON

He had this damage. He had lost air vents or his air vents had been damaged, and there were some fence rails or something, and he was taking on water. . . . I was told that he was not in any standing danger. He was not having any problems, and I believe if he was, that he was to call me on that.

BERNIE COOPER

I firmly believe that he had a damaged ship and didn't know how damaged she was. I believe that she was cracked somewhere. She was taking water fast enough because what he told me was that "I have a list and I am taking water," and I said, "Have you got your pumps on?" And he said, "Both of them." So from my experience on a previous occasion, I think what he did, he took that list which seemed to be real fast, as far as I was concerned, and that water level would have reached a level of his draft and it would stay constant, no matter whether he had the pumps on it or not, if there was water coming in from below from an opening in the hull. No matter how much you pump, if water is coming in faster, you are not going to lower the water in the tank because that water will stay at a constant level with the same list, because you can't bring it down. You have the lake right there.

If, at that time [when the *Fitz* was in the vicinity of Caribou Island], Captain McSorley knew that vessel was in danger, I know he would have gone right up on the beach in Caribou, because he was in that position. He would have put it on the beach. I am sure of it.

Cooper's
Close Call

Bernie Cooper was familiar with the *Fitzgerald*'s plight. Only a year earlier, the *Anderson* had been taking on water while in transit, and he had successfully brought the boat in for repairs.

BERNIE COOPER

Q. Were you aboard the Anderson *in October of 1974? I have a reference to an incident where the* Anderson *required dry-docking because of some fractures in the bottom plating. Were you aware of that incident?*
I was master of the vessel then.

Q. I am particularly interested, Captain, of your experiences during this occasion.
She was loaded, downbound on Lake Michigan. At 2:30 in the morning, the second mate rang my bedroom to inform me that one of our King gauges was showing 20 inches of water. We had one King gauge, and that happened to be the one that was malfunctioning part of the time. I said, "Okay, get a sounding rod and go out and sound the tank, and let me know what you have got." He came back, and he said there was 28 inches of water. It had been dry up above. I told him to put on the pumps and to pump it out, and then sound it every hour to see how much water we were actually making in that specific tank per hour. It wound up that it was making about 28 or 30 inches every four hours. In the morning, after breakfast, I sent the second mate down to check, after we sucked the tank out, to check out the bottom of the ship to see where it was leaking.

In 1973 the Arthur M. Anderson *was placed in dry dock at the Fraser Shipyards in Superior, Wisconsin, to undergo repair work to her bow.*

Kenneth Thro Collection, Lake Superior Maritime Collections, University of Wisconsin–Superior.

It was not anything that was a problem that we couldn't maintain with the pumps. He came up, and he reported to me, and I left him in the wheelhouse. I went down myself and took a look. A half inch in front of the watertight and a welded seam where the watertight was welded to the shell of the ship, there was a crack that extended all the way across the E plate, except for the last inch or two where the crack ended in a rivet hole.

In dry dock, they checked it out, and they tried to find out why it cracked. There was no reason, and there was no apparent damage. They planed it off, but it was on absolute flat bottom. There was no satisfactory explanation as to why it did crack, other than the fact that I, as a qualified American Bureau welder, or was a few years ago, know that if you weld and you weld too long and get the metal too hot, you set up a crystallization process which will not break in your weld, but it crystallizes the metal ahead or behind your weld. I was looking at it and looking at the marks. All I assumed was that either there was a built-in flaw in the plate, or it had been welded with too hot of a machine.

Q. Was this on one side of the vessel or both that you recall?
I think on the port side of 5 and the starboard side of 4. It was No. 4 on one side and No. 5 on the other. There was an identical crack on the other side of the ship, which was not leaking, but it was discernible after they got her in dry dock.

Q. I see. The reason I am asking is that I wanted to see what your procedures were when you discovered that the vessel was taking water from some source that was unknown to you. How often do they look at the King gauges?
On my ship, the King gauges and the ballasting of the ship is checked whenever it is changed, and marked in the logbook. Whenever it is loaded and I have it set up for the mate, he comes on watch at 4:00 in the morning and 4:00 in the afternoon, and he will call back and get a reading on the gauges to see if we are making any water in any specific tank. So every twelve hours it is checked. The oilers are supposed to check the King gauges when they come on watch. All you have to do is punch a button, and it gives you the inches of mercury, and it is measured in feet or inches. It is a practice on vessels in the Great Lakes with King gauges.

Q. How does either the mate or the engineering personnel know what the reading should be in a particular ballast tank?
Well we have a set of plans, specific plans drawn up, ballast plans 1, 2, 3, and 4, and they are informed on what ballast plan to pump out or into when we are in ballast. When we are loaded, sometimes when we leave the dock, it will show an inch or two of water in the tank. This is primarily maybe here there is a little water left in there that they didn't completely strip dry, but very seldom do you have more than one or two inches. In fact, maybe in one or two tanks that is all you would have leaving a loading. The more water you take out, the more cargo you carry. In ballasting conditions, it is a different story, because it is set up by a marine consultant as to what specific ballasting plans we can have, so there will not be a stress on the ship.

The Whitefish Point Lighthouse

WILLIAM KENNEDY

The station at Whitefish Point is an automated weather station at the Coast Guard station. The readings are transmitted from Whitefish Point into the Soo Coast Guard Station, using telephone lines. On the day of the 10th at 1600 the station went out of commission, and I understand when I called up the Sault Ste. Marie weather station that the wires went down at 1600, so the reports after that—the 1500 report was the last report from the Whitefish Station.

GARY WIGEN *Coast Guard, Grand Marais, Michigan*

At 1639, I received a call from the *Edmund Fitzgerald,* and I asked them to switch to channel 22. When he called back on channel 22, he asked us if Whitefish Point radio beacon was inoperative. I told him to stand by because we didn't have the equipment here at Grand Marais to see if it was operating properly.

I got to talking to the Soo on the teletype, and they told me that as far as their equipment showed, Whitefish Point radio beacon was not operating. They also said that they were having a power failure and that when the power came back on, they would call me back and give me some more information on the beacon.

I called the *Fitzgerald* back and told them that as far as the Soo knew, that the beacon was not operating at that time. He said, "Okay, thanks. We were just wondering because we haven't been able to get it for a while." He said he would call us back and went back to channel 16.

CHARLES MILLRADT *Commander, Coast Guard, Sault Ste. Marie*

Whitefish Point is an unmanned station that we monitor by radio from Soo Control. To the best of our knowledge, we had a malfunction with the Whitefish Point radio beacon fog signal and light. This is an automatic operated light beacon and fog signal, which is monitored from the Control Building at Base Sault Ste. Marie, and our monitor equipment indicated that there was a failure of the signal intermittently during the evening of the 10th of November. It was possibly partly due to the bad storm that we were having, which caused the failure or might have caused the failure of the monitor equipment, and maybe the light and radio beacon were actually operating, but we are not exactly sure because the light is designed with an emergency generator. If there is any power failure, the emergency generator comes on and the light should operate, but we did get a report that it was inoperative, and I have a statement here from the radio watch stander.

I will read this statement from the radio man which pretty much sums up the situation.

> "November 10, 1975, at approximately 1630 Romeo Group Soo received a call from Grand Marais Station requesting to know if Whitefish radio beacon was operative. I told Grand Marais to stand by until I had a chance I would get to them. Approximately 10 minutes later, I called Grand Marais back and told them that Whitefish Point was inoperative. The watchstander at Grand Marais inquired as to whether or not that was the entire light radio beacon and sound signals, and I replied that it was."

If I could divert for a moment from the statement, I don't have it with me, but we were getting a statement from the Grand Marais Coast Guard Station of the operator on watch there that said what prompted this inquiry was a radio call from the *Fitzgerald* asking if the radio beacon at Whitefish Point was operative because he couldn't pick it up. Upon getting this information from the Soo, the Grand Marais watch stander called back the *Fitzgerald* at about 1630 Romeo or Local Time and advised them that the Whitefish Point radio beacon fog signal and light were inoperative.

Now, I will continue on with the statement.

"We were very busy that evening and when time permitted, I called the Rescue Coordination Center and informed them that the Whitefish Point light beacon and sound signal were inoperative. This was at approximately 1715 Local Time. I was told to initiate an informal safety broadcast due to the fact that our, meaning Group Soo and RCC, were very busy and it would take quite a while to get an official broadcast sent. At approximately 1730, the officer in charge of the aids to navigation team from the Soo arrived and reset Whitefish Point radio beacon sound signal and light. This could be done from the monitor.

"Approximately 10 minutes later, the monitor gear showed all systems were inoperative again. This operation repeated itself several times and at one point all systems were operative for longer than the rest, so I called the Radio Coordination Center and told them that Whitefish was once again operative. During the time I was on the phone to the Rescue Coordination Center, the Whitefish Point monitor equipment showed all inoperative again. While still on the phone, I informed the Rescue Coordination Center of the same and stated, even though we were trying to reset it, I will originate a broadcast due to the fact that I was not staying operative for very long at a time. I then originated a broadcast and sent it when time permitted, signed RM-2 radio second class, PM Branch."

CEDRIC WOODARD

When I was just a little past or abreast of Whitefish, the *Fitzgerald* called for any ship in the vicinity of Whitefish Point, and nobody answered, so we answered them. He wanted to know if the beacon was working or the light was on. I replied then that I couldn't see no light, and we couldn't get the beacon. It may have been on, but I couldn't get it. I could see between the snowstorms the tower or structure of the lighthouse. I told him the light was on, and we could see it good between the snow squalls. Then we talked about the weather a little. I just asked him how

*Built in 1861, the Whitefish Point beacon is the oldest operating light
on Lake Superior. The station's fog signal and radio beacon were automated
in 1971 and controlled from Sault Ste. Marie.* Courtesy of National Archives.

the weather was up there. He said it was one of the worst he had ever
seen. The only thing he told me was that he had a list and his radars were
out. He said he had two and both were out. I asked him, I said, "You got
the radars?" and he said, "Yes, and they are both out."

Q. Did he tell you where he was?
Well, he didn't tell me, but I heard the *Anderson* tell him. I heard the
Anderson tell him about where he was. When the *Anderson* called him, I
heard him twice. The last position he was about 20 miles, he said, above
Whitefish as near as he could tell. He said as near as he could tell, and I
heard say, "I am 10 miles, about 10 miles behind you and gaining about a
mile and a half an hour on you." The *Anderson* said he was 10 miles from
him, and he said that he was gaining a mile and a half an hour on him.

He said he was taking heavy seas over the deck when I asked him how he was going and how the weather was up there. He said he was taking heavy seas over the deck, and he said he did have a bad list. It takes a lot to take the sea over a deck like the *Fitzgerald* because she had a high side. It takes a fairly good sea to go over the deck, to get the blue water, as you call it, to go over the deck.

Through the information I heard him say something. He was not talking to me but [to] someone else. He said, "Don't allow nobody on deck." That's all I heard. There was something said about a vent, but I didn't get it. There was something about, "Don't let nobody out on deck." I don't know whether it was to close a vent or open one or what it was, but he said, "Don't allow nobody on that deck."

ROY ANDERSON

Well, the way those seas were, any man who ventured to go out on deck or the aft, any portion of the open deck, and up around the boat deck area, he wouldn't make it.

MORGAN CLARK

I don't know why anyone would be out on the deck in a life jacket. I know on the *Anderson* we had all of our ports on our doors, all our hallway doors. Everything was secured. We used our tunnels going aft and everything. The crew said, one man said to me, "I will go and get the wheelbarrow," because some stuff went over the side. I told him that he better not have the thought of going out there. I said, "I don't care how many wheelbarrows we lose, but I can't replace a man."

So I don't know of any reason that anybody would be out there.

The
Final
Minutes

BERNIE COOPER

I was looking on the deck, and I think we were damn near under 6 feet of water on our deck. Not the houses or anything else, but [on] the deck.

ROY ANDERSON

The seas? I would estimate them to be about 25 feet . . . on our starboard quarter . . . between the quarter and the stern. The seas were coming right up to the deck, but we had been on a quarter. There was very much water on the deck. The seas were faster than the vessel, and they were hitting the aft side of the forward cabin.

Q. Were you taking any water on the spar deck?
Very much; the sea was coming right up to the deck, yes.

BERNIE COOPER

Almost 1910 the mate had talked to the *Fitzgerald*. When I came in the wheelhouse, Morgan said that I had come in practically just as he hung up and just got done talking to him. He said it was just about two or three minutes before that. After he talked to the *Fitzgerald* at 1910, he was down here on the scope about 9 miles away and barely discernible. The radar—the sea return, the center of the scope was just a white blob, and the *Fitzgerald* was disappearing into the sea return at 10 miles. When I walked into the wheelhouse, I think we picked him up, and he was about 9 miles away. I asked Morgan where the *Fitzgerald* was, and he showed me. He said, "He is here." We had had him on the radar all this time.

We were closing on him at this time, too. That was up to 10 miles, so we picked up 7 miles or 8 miles, you might say, down to the 9 miles when he disappeared into the clutter.

MORGAN CLARK

We were talking [at 1900]. I said, "We haven't got far to go, now. We will soon have it made." He said, "Yes, we will." Just before I hung up, I said, or before I signed off the telephone, I said, "It is a hell of a night for Whitefish radio beacon to not be operating," and he said, "Yes, it sure is." That was the end of the conversation.

About ten minutes [later] I was watching the radar and a target popped up that was about 19 miles ahead. I watched it for a minute or so to make sure that it was a steady. It looked like a ship coming. I called the *Fitzgerald* up, and at this time he still—well, it was still under the 10 miles. I didn't measure it for the exact distance, but ten minutes elapsed there that we had been gaining on him because he was supposed to have been waiting for us to catch up.

I told him there was a target 19 miles dead ahead of the *Anderson*. "You are ahead of us, so the target is 9 miles on ahead." Then he asked me, "Well, am I going to clear?" and I said, "Yes. He is going to pass to the west of you." And he said, "Well, fine."

I just started to sign off the phone, and as an afterthought, I said to him, "Oh, by the way, how are you making out with your problems?" And he said, "We are holding our own." That's the only thing he said. I said, "Okay, fine. I will be talking to you later." That was the sign-off.

CEDRIC WOODARD

I had known him [McSorley] to talk to him for probably fifteen years. . . . He stammered. I didn't recognize his voice at first, and I asked him who I was talking to, and he said, "Captain McSorley." It sounded like he had a cold or he was weary. He had been up a long time. It just wasn't his voice.

MORGAN CLARK

The last conversation that I had—I am talking about 1910 . . . he sounded like he was—as I said, it had been a long drag down the lake. The skipper

It is difficult to imagine the conditions the Fitzgerald *faced during her final minutes. In a chilling photograph taken on January 2, 1976, just months after the sinking, the steamer* Irving S. Olds *barrels through a ferocious sea on upper Lake Huron.*

had been up and down, and it seemed like his voice was a little different from the gentleman who had been talking back and forth.

As I say, as I was getting ready to sign off, as an afterthought, I asked him how he was making out with his problem. That's what he called it. We hadn't talked about it recently. You don't like to discuss over the phone that a guy has a problem. At least at the time he said it wasn't serious. He said he was holding his own.

BERNIE COOPER

About 1910, Morgan talked to the *Fitzgerald*. Morgan was giving him positions, because one of his radars was out and the other was ineffective. We were looking at the radar. I asked Morgan where the *Fitzgerald* was, and he showed me. He said, "He is here." We had him on the radar all this time. We were closing on him at this time, too. We got another target coming up around Whitefish Point. It was still snowing when I walked in the wheelhouse, but after ten or fifteen minutes, it cleared up. You could see for miles. We had also two other targets on radar. I can't remember if the two salties were visible or what.

We picked up two saltwater vessels about 17 or 18 miles away, and then I started looking for the *Fitzgerald* and there were no lights around. I couldn't find him. I thought maybe he had a blackout, which happens once in a great while. You lose your steam or if your engine goes down, your generators don't work. We were looking for him—everybody in the wheelhouse was looking for him. It was a change of watch, too.

ROBERT MAY *Wheelsman*, Arthur M. Anderson

When the salty or some boat showed up on the screen, the mate said that the *Fitzgerald* was approximately half the distance, and we could see the lights on the other boat, but we could not see the lights on the *Fitzgerald*.

MORGAN CLARK

I think I might have still been on the phone, but I could hear the captain come in. He has an inside stairway from his office to the pilothouse, and you could always tell when he opens the door because there is a breeze that comes in through the front window. And he was up on his way to the pilothouse just about the time this conversation at 1910.

About that time I turned around and I was looking, and I could see the lights of the ship that I had been picking up on radar, which at that time was probably up around 17 or 18 miles. So the *Fitzgerald* was still showing on the radar, and I made the remark as the captain was just walking up, and I made the remark to the wheelsman and the watchman up there. I said, "We should be able to see if that is the *Fitzgerald.*" We could see the guy coming, and so the watchman, he was standing over there looking and everything, and the captain, we all started looking and we never seen no navigation lights or no lights of any kind.

When this salty had broken through, it had been snowing, and when we could see the lights of the salty, that is when I made the remark and that is when I had the glasses. And the watchman was looking. I had the glasses, and I thought maybe he had a blackout or we could see a silhouette or something on the horizon, but then I told the captain—well, not told, but we started discussing that we should see his lights and then we started calling him, and I must have made, I don't know, six or seven calls at that time and everything, and I couldn't get ahold of him. And the captain tried to get ahold of him.

BERNIE COOPER

I called the *Fitzgerald* on the FM, and I got no response. The mate tried to call him several times. Then I was wondering whether my phone was putting out. I called the *William Clay Ford,* which was by Whitefish Point, and he told me that my signal was excellent. He said that I was coming out loud and clear. I also asked him by any chance could the *Fitzgerald* [have come] under the point. He told me what ships were there. There was a *Hilda Marge Ann,* and I can't remember the others. There were about four at the time under the point.

About this time, I tried to call the Coast Guard. They were having trouble at the Soo. I think their big antenna was down, and I found out a little later that their high antenna was down.

At that time I was trying to call the saltwater vessels. I can't say which was which, or where, because I was calling like on a constant basis, trying to get an answer from somebody somewhere. But I do know that I didn't get ahold of the Coast Guard the first time. I think I got them and tried to go to channel 12, and nothing came through. I asked the saltwater vessels if they could see the *Fitzgerald* on their radar, because at that range they would have been outside of that big sea return. I was talking to the *Nanfri,* and that was Captain Jacovetti. He told me that he was only making 1 or 2 miles an hour and the sea was big. He could see the lights of one vessel, and there was nothing on his radar, which pretty near convinced me at the time that there was something that happened.

MORGAN CLARK

We should be able to see his range lights, and under normal conditions we have all kinds of lights on our vessel, cabin lights, he had a lot more lights than we had. There was sufficient, probably a hundred bulbs on the cablings and decks, and we should be able to see.

BERNIE COOPER

I felt that he [McSorley] practically hung up the phone and practically dove under. I don't believe the fellow had a chance to get out of the wheelhouse. This is the only thing I could believe, because she couldn't disappear that suddenly. It cleared up about ten after when I came back in the wheelhouse—about 1910 or shortly after, and you don't think that the *Fitzgerald* could go. We started looking for a blackout. If she lost her power, she would have blacked out. I have had that happen to me and it can happen. I didn't know that if she was drifting out there, we might even hit her. So, we were trying to do everything we could with our radar to bring her back on target. We could see the other targets of the salties extremely well. Well, she was so very close to the point where we last talked to her where you were finding some of the echoes, the sonar type echoes, we thought she must be in that general area, so she had to go over right then, but the seas were big at that time.

Three saltwater vessels on Lake Superior that night—the *Avafors,* the *Nanfri,* and the *Benfri*—symbolized the debate over sailing on the Great Lakes versus sailing on the oceans during a storm. Great Lakes captains with experiences on both insisted that storms on the lakes were more difficult to handle: the seas were more violent, with waves coming in more rapid succession than you would find on the oceans. It was not uncommon to get two sizable waves under a freighter at the same time, which led to elevating or sagging a vessel in a potentially dangerous way. This rarely happened on the ocean.

The American crews on all three saltwater vessels opposed the idea of heading out in the storm. Their captains favored waiting for the storm to pass. However, in all three cases, officials from the vessels' overseas owners, present on each of these ships, had the final say, and they ordered the ships and crews to head out, even before the *Fitzgerald*'s plight was known. When the Coast Guard called and asked them to turn around and search for the *Fitz*, none of these officials, now fully aware of the storm's intensity, was interested in doing so.

CEDRIC WOODARD

I tell you, most of the time in these saltwater ships, a weather report means nothing. They tell you, you're on the lakes, and you just go because they say go. They are the boss. I recommended to go to the anchor, and he said, "No, pilot, we go." I also called O'Brien and told him that he shouldn't come out. He had the same orders I did. The captain had said no. I said I didn't think we could make any headway. I don't know if I said unsafe or not. I don't think I said that. I said, "we have no business out here."

ROBERT O'BRIEN

I can't remember all of it [his conversation with Captain Woodard of the *Avafors*], but he said that we were a bunch of damn fools for coming out of here like this, and he said he wanted to stop but the old man wouldn't stop. He said, "We are not going to make any time," so we come out there and just, you know, were making a poor time of it. We figured we were making about 3 [miles per hour], and he had less power than I did.

CEDRIC WOODARD

He [the company official] was talking about conserving fuel all the way up the [St. Marys] river. He wanted heavy fuel and not heavy diesel fuel. He said, "We're burning too much expensive fuel," and I said, "Here we are, going out in the storm, and you are going no place with your fuel. I didn't think it was really unsafe, but I didn't think we could go anyplace with that ship."

The Nanfri, seen here in Toronto's Oshawa Harbor, was one of three saltwater vessels on Lake Superior the night of the storm.

I advised him not to go out, and he said, "This is only a lake." He said, "We'll keep going." The next day, he said, "This is a pretty big lake, ain't it."

ROBERT O'BRIEN

The *Benfri* is one of the largest oceangoing vessels that comes up here. She is 709 feet in overall length with a 75-foot beam. Her molded depth was 9 feet, and she had 15,000 horsepower.

The wind was quite heavy, and when we were steering at 290, it seemed we were heading right into it. It was dark, and I would say [the waves] were in the neighborhood of 20 to 25 feet. I heard someone calling the *Fitzgerald,* but I didn't pay any attention. I don't even know if he answered or not because I just figured it was somebody calling him and wanted to talk to him.

The Search

GARY WIGEN

I heard the *Anderson* calling either the Group Soo or else Group Control. I don't know which one exactly. And he told them that he was concerned about the *Fitzgerald*. He said he was extremely concerned, that he didn't know what had happened but that he had lost the radio and radar with him, that he couldn't get in touch with them.

After we heard that the *Fitzgerald* might have sunk, everybody at the station had been talking about it, and I was telling them that I had just talked to them, just before people started getting worried about it, and I told them that they didn't sound like they were worried at all about anything. Everybody sounded like they were in real good spirits.

ALBERT JACOVETTI

I heard the master of the *Anderson* repeatedly calling the *Fitzgerald,* and I got ahold of Captain Cooper on the *Anderson,* and I told him that his transmission on 16 was very loud and clear, and if the *Fitzgerald* was in the area, there was no reason why he shouldn't hear him. Captain Cooper told me then that he had been in contact with the *Fitzgerald* and the *Fitzgerald* had taken this damage aboard the vessel and asked him to sort of shadow him, and he said that he was within 5 miles of the *Fitzgerald* and then all of a sudden he lost radar contact and telephone contact, and yet, at the same time, on his radar he could see the three of us that were down below that area. I told him that I would attempt to contact the *Fitzgerald* also, which I did on channel 16 of the FM. No result. No result. I couldn't see anything on the radar.

PHILIP BRANCH *Group Soo Radio*

Group Soo is a SAR facility where, as Soo Control, they are almost like a vessel traffic system. They control the St. Marys River and the ships within. There were various outages that evening. I was only capable of using three of my five radios. In addition to that, I lost two of my distress frequency guard receivers.

I myself had attempted to contact the *Fitzgerald*. I also [contacted] WLC Rogers City, [Michigan], which is a commercial station to ask them to try to contact the *Fitzgerald* for me.

CHARLES MILLRADT

Our involvement with the rescue operation started with the initial notification from the steamer *Anderson* of the *Fitzgerald*'s disappearance from his radar screen, our making initial inquiries over the radio to try and contact the *Fitzgerald* to see if we could establish communications with her, and then passing the information received from the *Anderson* and our inability to contact the *Fitzgerald* on to the rescue coordination center here at Ninth District Office in Cleveland, and then thereby from therein taking direction from the Rescue Coordination Center participating in the search effort with the facilities that were available in Group Soo. This involved primarily the Coast Guard Cutter *Naugatuck* and a 40-foot utility boat stationed at Sault Ste. Marie.

Bernie Cooper's frustration with the Coast Guard nearly boiled over. First, he struggled to get anyone to seriously regard his concerns about the *Fitzgerald*. Then, when men in charge at the various Coast Guard stations conceded that something serious had happened to the *Fitzgerald*, as difficult as that was to accept, the Coast Guard were woefully unequipped for a disaster of this nature. The personnel and equipment were more than adequate when asked to rescue a small craft broken down on the lakes in the summertime, but a situation like this was another matter. The *Naugatuck*, a 110-foot harbor tug stationed in Sault Ste. Marie, was under repair, and even if it had been immediately able to join the search, its vessel classification prohibited her from heading out on open water in the kind of wind the storm was producing. Other vessels of similar or greater lengths were stationed too far away to provide meaningful assistance in the search for survivors. The *Woodrush,* for instance, was willing to join the search, but it was 300 miles away, anchored in the Duluth, Minnesota, harbor.

The only solution was to contact the huge freighters already on Lake Superior, fighting their own battles against the storm, or those anchored in the safety of Whitefish Bay, near Whitefish Point.

As the weather intensified, distress calls went out to available vessels, but few were able to respond immediately. The Coast Guard cutter Naugatuck, *seen here on the St. Marys River, was undergoing repairs while stationed at Sault Ste. Marie.*

Kenneth Thro Collection, Lake Superior Maritime Collections, University of Wisconsin–Superior.

CHARLES MILLRADT

According to our log, the call we received from the motor vessel *Anderson* was at approximately 2025 Romeo [EST] on that evening. That is a broadcast of a notice to mariners. Following that entry, it says, "NOG," which is the call sign of the radio station.

"This is the *Arthur M. Anderson*. Over."

"This is NOG. Over."

"This is *Arthur M. Anderson*. I am very concerned with the welfare of the steamer *Edmund Fitzgerald*. He was right in front of us experiencing a little difficulty. He was taking on a small amount of water, and none of the upbound ships have passed him, and I can see no lights as before and don't have him on radar. I just hope he didn't take a nosedive. Over."

"This is NOG. Roger. Thank you for info. We will try and contact him. Over."

"This is *Anderson*. Roger. Thank you, and also you might try WLC Rogers City. Have him ring his buzzer on AM and he might be able to contact him just to be sure that he is there. Over."

"This NOG. Roger. We will try that. Over."

"This is *Arthur Anderson*. Roger."

"This is NOG. We'll get back to you. Out."

And the time of the completion of the transmission, and I assume after he finished logging it, is 0132 Zulu, which would be 2032 Local Time, so my original statement was that we were notified at approximately 2025 Local Time, assuming that's when the transmission started from the *Anderson*.

Following that entry, there is an entry, the next minute from NOG where he tried to call the *Fitzgerald* three times and received no reply. The following minute, he tried again to call three times and received no reply. The very next entry, which is logged at minute 0140 Zulu, which would be 2040 Local Time, was with WLC Rogers City.

"This is NOG. Over. Request you contact steamer *Edmund Fitzgerald* on AM. Over."

"This is WLC. Roger."

And that is the end of the transmission.

Then, two minutes later, Rogers City came back and they said, "NOG, this is WLC. Something wrong with AM antennas. We'll go take a look and get back to you. Over."

"This is NOG. Roger. Out."

And that was it. That was at 0142 Zulu.

As far as I can see here, I don't see any further communications with Rogers City, but Radio Soo tried to contact them several more times.

The radio room watch notified our Group OD [Officer of the Day], and he, I guess, along with the radio operator, they tried several times to call. Chronologically, our log indicates that the OD notified the Rescue Coordination Center in Cleveland. Our log indicates that our OD notified the Ninth District Coordination Center in Cleveland at 2040 Romeo, or Local Time, which would be 0140 Greenwich Mean Time, which was while the conversation was going on with WLC Rogers City. According to the radio log here, we continued to try to call the *Fitzgerald*. There is another transmission here that took place with the *Arthur Anderson* getting some work details of confirming the report. The time of that is at 0203 Greenwich Mean Time or 2103 Local Time.

"NOG, this is *Anderson*. Over."

"This is NOG. Go ahead."

In other words, the *Anderson* originated this call.

"This is *Anderson*. I have the mate here at this time. He was the one up here when all this went on. Over."

"This is NOG. Roger. What was the last known position of the *Fitzgerald*? Over."

"This is *Anderson*. Approximately 15 miles due north of Crisp Point was the last I talked to him."

"NOG. Roger. And what time was that? Over."

"This is *Anderson*. Approximately 1900 Eastern Standard Time. Over."

"This is NOG. Roger. And did you alter your course in any way to look for the *Fitzgerald*? Over."

"This is *Anderson*. Negative. I am taking seas over my decks also and I am taking a beating. Over."

"This is NOG. Roger."

"This is *Anderson*. We were following at an approximate distance of 10 miles. We knew he was experiencing a little difficulty due to the fact he took seas over his deck and lost a couple of vents and was taking on a small amount of water and was listing. We asked him how he was doing, and he said he was holding his own. Over."

"This is NOG. Roger. That's all for right now. We will get back to you. Thank you. Out."

Following that, four minutes later, at 2107 Local Time, there is another call recorded there of the calling of the *Fitzgerald* with negative response.

BERNIE COOPER

I tried to call the Soo again, and I finally got them. I think it was around 1950. I informed them of my concern over the *Fitzgerald,* that I thought

Coast Guard officials coordinated search and rescue operations from Soo Control at Sault Ste. Marie. Their early efforts at communicating with the Arthur M. Anderson *and other vessels were hindered by high winds and weak radio signals.* Courtesy of Great Lakes Shipwreck Museum.

she had floundered, and they reported to me to be on the lookout for a 16-foot boat that was lost in Whitefish Bay, and there was another ten- or twelve-minute lapse. I called them again. I think they were like I was. I don't think they could believe a ship could go down that fast. When I called them the second time, I said, "I know she is gone."

CHARLES MILLRADT

We were working on the case of an overdue 16-foot boat in Whitefish Point near Tahquamenon Island. It was a case of two persons overdue in a 16-foot boat who had gone out before the storm hit and were reported overdue. We were pursing that case at the time when the missing *Fitzgerald* came up. The people were located on Tahquamenon Island the next morning by the sheriff. We were planning to send a boat out, but when we got involved in the *Fitzgerald* case, we sent our 40-footer on the *Fitzgerald* case instead of that, because we had the sheriff's department handling that. We felt they were adequate to handle that at that time.

JAMES RIVARD

Coast Guard, Cleveland, search and rescue
My duties are to act for the District Commander in matters of search and rescue over the entire Great Lakes area. It was my personnel that directed the overall search efforts during the case [of the *Edmund Fitzgerald*].

A call was received, and it was at Group Sault Ste. Marie, who, in turn, called the Rescue Coordination Center at 2040 Romeo Time, or Eastern Standard Time. We all use local time, which is Romeo Time. Word was passed to the Search and Rescue Controller, Lt. J. J. Mumford, that the steamer *Anderson* had lost contact with the *Edmund Fitzgerald*.

CHARLES MUMFORD

RCC Controller, Coast Guard District 9, Cleveland
I was the duty controller that night. At 8:45, local time, I received a call from Group Commander Sault Ste. Marie. He informed that the steamer *Anderson* had the *Fitzgerald* on radar and had lost it, and she was taking on some water through the vents and experienced a little difficulty,

listing a little. He also stated visibility was good to excellent. That was the extent of the phone call. [It was] just to advise us that a ship was in possible distress. The *Anderson* was 10 miles behind the *Fitzgerald*. They had lost her on radar. There were three upbound vessels that should have passed within 1 mile of the *Fitzgerald*, and was negative sightings on radar or visually, and the last report received from the *Fitzgerald* was 1900 to 1915, local.

The action I took was to alert our air station at Traverse City, Michigan, to launch an HU-16 [aircraft], and to have two helos [helicopters] launched as soon as possible and to follow the aircraft up. The next step was 0225 Group Soo advised that the CO of the *Naugatuck* thought it was too bad for her to get underway in these type of sea conditions. I told him to go ahead and get underway and stand by at the mouth of

When it became clear that the Anderson *had lost contact with the* Fitzgerald, *the Coast Guard deployed a HU-16 Albatross from the air station at Traverse City.*

Courtesy of Local History Collection, Traverse Area District Library.

the St. Marys River. I called the Chief of Operations and briefed him on what was happening. He instructed me to start calling the *Woodrush*. I called the Chief of Search and Rescue and instructed him, and he wanted to see if I could get a C-130 to assist. I received a telephone call from the Controller, the Canadian Controller at Trenton. That was at 0240. He advised me that Rescue 325 was available, but it was on another case right now, and he would divert it. He would advise me. Approximately at the same time I called Mr. Kirby, a dispatcher for the Oglebay Norton Company.

CEDRIC WOODARD

I happened to go up and check my radio, thinking, funny, I wasn't hearing nothing, and I found it on channel 11, and then I heard the "Pan, pan, pan," Coast Guard warning anything to look for the *Fitzgerald* or any wreckage, they thought she was gone down. They had lost contact. We just kept a lookout. There was nothing much we could do. We were having all we could do to keep in the sea or keep her going. The skipper wouldn't never let you try to turn around if I did want to, and I don't think I could have.

RICHARD ORGEL

[A PAN-PAN message] is an urgent message by the Coast Guard, an urgent message. It is short of a May Day, but it is an urgent message with regard to safety. The Coast Guard was broadcasting this and it came over our radio.

We were all concerned. We hoped that the vessel would be found and everybody would be all right. Somebody remarked that they hoped it wasn't going to be another *Morrell*.

CHARLES MILLRADT

We tried to talk to the three upbound vessels. I personally talked to the skipper of the *Anderson*. I don't remember exactly what time it was, but I asked the *Anderson* what his present position was. Knowing that we didn't have anything else in the area that would be able to get out there in the near future, I asked the *Anderson* if he could turn his vessel around and go back into the area and look for the *Fitzgerald*. He thought about that one for a few minutes—or a few seconds, anyway—and he said that it would be extremely hazardous. I explained to him that he was the master of the vessel, and it was his decision to make, that I was requesting him to come around if he could, and if he was concerned that it would not unduly hazard his vessel, to come around and go back into the area and to search for the *Fitzgerald* or any survivors. He said he would give it a try.

He was by that time down inside Whitefish Point, and I think he felt he had enough of a lee to come back down and head up into the sea. He thought he would be taking a beating.

BERNIE COOPER

I told him that I would go back and give it a try. So, at that time, at 2155, we were at the Bay of Parisienne, and I hauled the ship around on a reciprocal course and headed back out toward the area where we last saw the *Fitzgerald*. After that, the *William Clay Ford* did come out there behind Whitefish Point, and he was afraid to turn around. So he kept right on going. There were two saltwater vessels, the *Nanfri* and the *Benfri,* I think, and they almost drifted backwards. They tried to stay but they were also afraid to turn. They didn't think they could make them.

CHARLES MILLRADT

We then called any other vessels in the area. We called the three saltwater vessels that were probably upbound and probably just past the last known position of the *Fitzgerald*. Actually, I think the first ones were quite a ways past. The last one might not have been too far from it. I asked them to come back and also search in the area, and they all stated that they didn't feel they could come back without creating a hazard to their vessels. One of them was the *Nanfri*. He said that he would slow down and try to run some disposal courses to the seas, thereby searching in the area where he was, to try to maintain a fairly constant position. None of them, as far as I know, came about to search in the storm.

The William Clay Ford *was shielded from much of the storm in the bay behind Whitefish Point, but in the early hours of November 11 she returned to open water to assist the* Anderson *with the search operation.*

ROBERT O'BRIEN

I think you should go if you would not be jeopardizing your own ship. You should proceed and render whatever assistance you can. I don't think they require you to do it if you will endanger your own ship. . . . I don't know about law or anything, but I would say it would be tradition that you would do whatever you could.

ALBERT JACOVETTI

The wind was right dead ahead. I figured that at that time the wind was in excess of 70 knots. In fact, the wind was taking the top of the waves and blowing them across the water indicating that it had to be a force of at least that much.

CEDRIC WOODARD

The sea was tearing tops off and turning white and stuff like that. I have been in, I think, bigger rollers before, but I never was in one that came up that quick, I don't believe, to go out into it. I have been in seas that came up quick, but we went for shelter.

ROBERT O'BRIEN

I have been in some bad storms with these saltwater ships. I have been in some bad ones on lakers, too. I was always fortunate that I was not in winds that strong, but for the condition of the ships, I would say I was in worse shape on a laker. I blew around on the laker, a couple of times. When you get in the trough of the sea, you really roll.

BERNIE COOPER

I certainly didn't want to go back because I was afraid we were going to get beat all to hell, to be honest with you. I had a decision to make because I had other people involved, but I figured that I was obligated to try. Maybe I wouldn't even be able to do anything after I got out there.

The best way I can describe it is that we had a couple of guys on board who were a little bit of braggarts. They wanted the rough weather, and when I told them that we were going out, they said they were going to get a tape and put it in bee's wax and throw it overboard so they knew where the *Anderson* would go down.

CHARLES MILLRADT

The first on scene were the aircraft, not only the fixed wing aircraft, which was launched at 2206 Local Time, [but] also a helicopter was launched at 2223 Local Time, and a second one at 2249 Local Time. So, in the span of forty-three minutes, three aircraft were launched.

The *Anderson* was back in the area about two o'clock in the morning along with the *Ford,* and I really feel that that was our best line of attack right there, having those two large lakers there who could survive in those kinds of seas and with the aircraft trying to illuminate for them and to search the area around where they were. The aircraft was then in direct communications with the *Anderson.*

JAMES RIVARD

There was an area assigned around the last known positions of the *Fitzgerald* for the HU-16 and the helicopters to search. The HU-16 dropped approximately four flares, one of them not firing. This is nor-

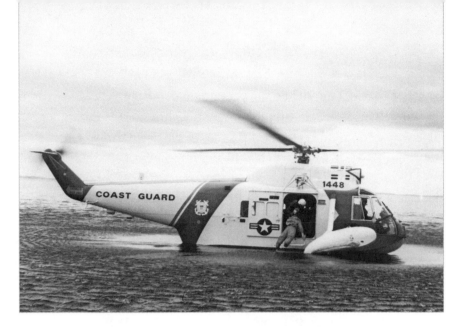

Coast Guard helicopters like this HH-52 Seaguard, seen here during rescue drills, were dispatched to make continuous flights over the eastern side of Lake Superior in the days following the storm.

Courtesy of Local History Collection, Traverse Area District Library.

mal occurrence because a certain percentage of flares will not work. The steamer *Anderson* searching underneath indicated the flares were not very effective.

You have to have a freeboard or something sticking up out of the water at a considerable distance casting a shadow, but the seas were casting so many shadows and such large shadows that it made searching by flares ineffective.

ROBERT O'BRIEN

There are very, very few saltwater ships that have a searchlight. Some do have the Aldis lamp, but there are very, very few of them that have a searchlight.

BERNIE COOPER

Watching the rollers come over the deck, and I was thinking how I could take my boys down without having to hurt them . . . I really have my doubts. We would have been extremely lucky to get somebody. I would have had to check her right down, get upwind and try to hold her while the sea and wind would bring them to the ship. This is the only possible way. If we could get them close, maybe we could throw them a ring buoy, but I couldn't put my crew to the middle because then I would have some broken bones. It would have to be [in] back or on the poop deck up where they would be out of the weather, because the seas were nasty, rolling back to the deck there.

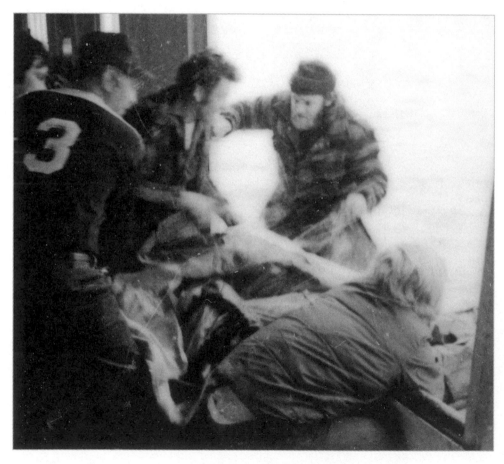

As news of the sinking spread, communities along the southeastern coast of Lake Superior assisted in collecting debris. This local fishing party located and retrieved one of the Fitzgerald's *life rafts.* Courtesy of Great Lakes Shipwreck Museum.

ROBERT O'BRIEN

Even if we did see men, I don't know how in the world we would have been able to pick them up. I would say the only means that would have been available to us would have been—she has cranes on deck, and if we could have got, say, cargo nets and put on the hook and lowered them over the side and just hoped that if there was somebody in the water that they could grab ahold of the net, then maybe you would be okay.

ALBERT JACOVETTI

I don't know how you could have maneuvered your vessel to get anywhere near it, because the minute you stop a light vessel like that, she would have broken right off. I don't think you could have even dropped an anchor there and done any good. . . . You could have tried with what Captain O'Brien said. At least, you could have tried to hang something over there that they could have grabbed onto.

CEDRIC WOODARD

About the only thing we could have done if we could have got above them and put oil in [the water] and calmed it till somebody could have helped, but we couldn't maneuver to help because every time we got off our course, we were in trouble. You couldn't have launched a boat. . . . I don't think you had any chance in a boat. I don't think you could have launched it, or if you could have launched it, nobody could have gotten into it or [done] anything.

CHARLES MILLRADT

On the 11th of November, I had some ships not only pass through the area but I had a number of ships go around in circles and make search patterns in the area. They found or sighted a considerable amount of debris and equipment that we recovered. Pieces of a lifeboat, life-saving devices, and boat oars. . . . The debris that we got from the Canadian shore party from Copper Mine Point was a seven-and-a-half-foot stepladder, one of the inflatable life rafts picked up by a shore party, one broken oar, one boat cover, four—each small, flotation tanks, one rudder

One day after the sinking, the bow of Fitzgerald *lifeboat No. 1
was spotted in the water. What little debris was left of the vessel began
washing ashore soon afterward.* Courtesy of Great Lakes Shipwreck Museum.

from a small boat, three life jackets, one empty boat box, one inflation cylinder for a rubber life raft, one bag of garbage, and one piece of
life ring.

BERNIE COOPER

I don't remember the exact time, but around 4:40 in the morning, before
daylight, we did start to spot some debris, and we were in contact with
the 7236 aircraft, I believe, who was ahead of the search in the area. They
were dropping flares when we spotted the debris, but even then, the sea

was so big, trying to maneuver, that we would drift by and the debris would drift out of our range. It was difficult to even see during the day.

After we picked up the debris, then they started searching more in an easterly direction, back up into Pancake Bay. I found a half lifeboat, and I think it was *Armco* or *Reserve* that came in there [and] found all this debris. I can't remember. Anyway, they were back up in Pancake Bay and Copper Mine Point. The wind direction, being northwest by west, had blown it in the area where the *Fitzgerald* sank back into Pancake Bay and off Copper Mine Point.

DANIEL MANIA *Marine Inspection Office, St. Ignace, Michigan*

The No. 1 boat was the one that was broken just about in half. There is just a 16-foot section left. I saw the No. 2 boat, I believe, on the 13th, but I did not examine it. I saw the boat as it laid there at the base. I did not see the section of No. 1 boat until the 24th.

As an example of the overall and general damaged condition, I will refer to Exhibit 98(a), which is the bow area of the No. 1 boat, where she is holed, the saddle area. This is the position where the boat normally sits in the saddle. Now this would be like the same boat and the same side that the *Anderson* suffered, the same type of damage in the saddle area to the starboard side. This would have occurred, I would assume, before the boat was launched. That's the point I am trying to make. Here is No. 2 photograph in 98(e). The damage here, the structural damage here is also the saddle area damage, so it would be my conclusion that this damage was done while the boats were still aboard the ship. Both boats show holes in the area of their normal cradled positions in the saddles.

Q. Is there anything about the No. 1 boat that is not included either in the photograph or in the report of your examination which you feel is pertinent to this investigation?

Yes. There is one thing that may be some source of confusion on the No. 1 boat. That is page two of my report I discussed the Rottmer releasing gear. What I say is "The Rottmer releasing gear consisting of the hook preventer bars lock, upper and lower guide bearings, universal joints and a complete portion of the shafting to the after universal are present.

The shaft is twisted and distorted. The plate attachment to the stem is in place. The hook is in the unlocked position. The release lever is torn loose from its secured position. The hold down brackets are severed."

One thing that I should have included in here, or I say, "The lock is in the unlocked position," and that is correct, that is the way it appeared. One significant thing though that I did not include here is that the hook lock itself is closed, in the closed position. The photograph shows the hook lock to be in the closed position, and my examination of the boat was the same; the hook lock was in the closed position.

The hook was free. Normally, with the hook lock in this position, the hook would not be able to be moved. It would be locked and secured. In this case, it was not.

Damage to the lifeboats was severe, particularly in the saddle area, where they would have been secured to the spar deck of the Fitzgerald.

Kenneth Thro Collection, Lake Superior Maritime Collections, University of Wisconsin–Superior.

I would say that my opinion would be that there must have been a great stress and probably some sort of dynamic stress, which made the hook jump out from behind the hook lock itself. Otherwise, there is nothing that would make sense.

The first raft which we labeled as Raft A just for identification purposes was in good condition, serviceable and usable. This is the raft which we were able to inflate. This second raft was, as Captain Nurmeste indicates here, was unserviceable. We were unable to inflate the raft. We would have had to patch it in order to inflate it. There were some holes in the raft, and these holes were as the result of being deflated by the Canadian Provincial Police, as I understand the situation. They cut the inflation tubes so that they could handle the raft.

When we finished the inspection, we were folding the rafts back up to return them to the Coast Guard base. [A taconite] pellet was found underneath the second life raft, which Captain Nurmeste refers to as a second life raft and we call it Life Raft B. When we folded it back up to put it on the dolly, Mr. Madigan found that pellet on the floor of the loft, underneath the raft or where the raft had sat.

Q. Is there any indication, Commander Mania, that the rafts may have been occupied by anyone?
No, sir. There is no indication of that at all.

ROY ANDERSON

You couldn't get off on a lifeboat, because you couldn't get back to the lifeboat. If you were back there, the inflatable rafts are all right, but when they are thrown off of the side, your chances of getting to it under those conditions are no good. The only possible thing is sitting in the raft and waiting for the boat to go down and hope for the best. You would inflate it on board the vessel, but then you have got—you must have an area that is snagproof, because if you snag anything, then you get punctured, so the inflatable raft in that respect is the only way I can see. But under those seas, I don't know how you would have been saved.

*The Coast Guard inspected one of the Fitzgerald's life rafts after its recovery
in Whitefish Bay by the steamer* Roger Blough *on November 12, 1975.*

JOHN LARSON *former* Fitzgerald *crew member*

I don't believe you could put a [life]boat in that water, because those seas would have damaged it or something. It would tip her over, but I don't think you could handle a lifeboat even if you get it in the water. I don't think you could have boarded it.

Q. What would you use?
Probably the life raft. After it is blown up, it's got a cover over it and you would be out of the water. You would be protected from the exposure. That time of year, it is very important.

Q. How long do you think you would last in water that was 51 degrees temperature and about 35 degrees air temperature?
I wouldn't last very long. Probably a half an hour or so. That's about all I would last.

ROBERT O'BRIEN

I don't like to be joking about this, but I have said that if the damn ship is going to go down, I would get in my bunk and pull the blankets over my head and say, "Let her go," because there was no way of launching the boats.

BERNIE COOPER

I was the first vessel released from the search. I guess they figured I was a little bit beat. At that time, it was obvious that there were no survivors. They were picking up debris and this sort of thing to try and find out exactly where she went down. The last time I went up on Lake Superior and ran up there, I found an oil slick.

The Oil Slick

Early efforts to locate the *Fitzgerald*'s final resting place focused on trying to find an oil slick on the surface. Planes, helicopters, and boats scanned the area where the *Fitzgerald* was believed to have sunk. Their efforts were quickly rewarded.

CHARLES MILLRADT

The District Commander invoked a joint Canadian-U.S. response team to handle the possibility of a major oil spill in the area, since the vessel was carrying approximately 75,000 gallons of Bunker C and some diesel fuel for their bow thruster and generators, and we had a potential oil spill here. The response team was established and helped to survey the area. The team concluded that there was some oil spilled initially, but the bulk of the oil was probably still in the wreck.

CHARLES CORBETT

Marine Environment Protection, Coast Guard
In the morning hours of Monday, about midnight, I was advised by the Rescue Coordination Center that there had been a sinking in Lake Superior near Whitefish Bay. That is the normal procedure in the event that there is some pollution.

The following morning, we were monitoring the situation, maintaining a low profile due to the Search and Rescue efforts, trying to determine the amount of fuels carried on board the vessel and what the pollution potential might be.

About one o'clock Tuesday, it became apparent that there was in fact some discharge of what seemed to be or what was reported to us as heavier oil. We had learned at this time that the vessel carried about 75,000 gallons of Bunker C and in the vicinity of 75,000 gallons of diesel, and of course there was residual oils normal to vessels. Since the sinking was very near the Canadian border, I recommended to the District Commander that we activate the provisions of the joint Canada pollution contingency plan. The main vehicle by which this plan operates is a joint response team, of which I am normally a member. The team consists of various Canadian and U.S. agencies, oriented towards environmental affairs. Admiral Gracey activated the provisions of the plan, and the team proceeded to Sault Ste. Marie to assist and advise the on-scene coordinator, the captain of the Port of Sault Ste. Marie, Captain Millradt.

We all arrived up there about midnight Tuesday, the evening between Monday and Tuesday, and we met together the following morning.

During the next few days, we assisted and advised the on-scene coordinator, assisting him in directing shore patrols of the beaches, looking for oil, aerial patrols, and there were available aircraft; otherwise providing him any technical guidance when the team could provide.

We determined on late Friday that the pollution potential was negligible, having determined or expressed a unanimous opinion that the majority of the Bunker C which was on board had reached a sufficiently low temperature to reduce or, rather, increase its viscosity so that it was no longer venting. Using an aircraft the next day, we located what we believed to be the oil from the vessel surfacing in that position. We concluded that was the diesel oil used in the bow thruster mechanism, and that oil then, of course, did vent and dissipate. It was never a real pollution threat as far as the environment was concerned.

As I said, on Friday we recommended to the on-scene coordinator that the joint response team disband and the provisions of the joint Canada team be revoked, and we recommended that to the commander of the Ninth Coast Guard District. He concurred, and we disbanded for pollution purposes.

That really is the extent of the pollution activities, and the pollution did not reach the magnitude it might have. I might say also in this

Some of the debris recovered after the sinking was spattered with oil that had leaked from the Fitzgerald. *This provided Coast Guard investigators with clues as to the vessel's final resting place.* Frederick Stonehouse Collection.

expression of opinion that we did conclude that there was a discharge of Bunker C as evidenced by the oil on some of the debris which we saw. But that could easily have been vented close to the time when the accident occurred, since the operating temperature of the Bunker C was sufficiently high at that stage to permit it to vent. As I said, as it cooled, it would cease to vent, reaching a temperature at about 41 degrees Fahrenheit.

I believe that the diesel oil in the bow thruster has vented, and in that event, the Bunker C remains in the ship in a tar-like configuration, very heavy, very viscous, not venting to the environment.

Finding the Wreckage

JAMES RIVARD

The Navy was asked to provide a P3 aircraft to conduct a search of the area for possibly locating where the *Fitzgerald* might rest. They did this search on the 13th, and they located an object. Then on the next Saturday, I think Saturday of the 16th, the P3 went out again with the *Woodrush*, so that they covered the area.

In addition to that, the Coast Guard Air Station Traverse City was directed on, I believe, the 14th, it might have been the 15th, to conduct daily flights over the area, which they did for approximately one week. Now Traverse City is conducting weekly flights over the area. One of the search objects was any oil that might be coming up. They were also on the lookout for personnel and debris.

We have asked the Canadians, during the normal operation, to report any sightings that they might find in the area. Group Sault Ste. Marie's vessels and personnel have been directed, when they were transitioning the area during the normal operation, to report any objects or bodies that they might find. Yesterday we had an H-32 helicopter searching the shoreline from 10 miles west of Crisp Point around Whitefish Bay and then north to the Montreal River. The search conditions were pretty good on the Michigan shoreline, but on the Canadian shoreline, due to ice, the probability of detection was low.

The loss of the *Edmund Fitzgerald* stunned the Great Lakes shipping world. This had been a relatively new vessel, an enormous, powerful ore carrier that should have weathered a storm, vicious as it was, with little trouble. As those out on Lake Superior testified, the storm was a serious challenge, but it was manageable. What, then, had happened? There was no shortage of theories, but with the public clamoring for answers, theories were inadequate. This called for a full-scale investigation.

A search for the *Fitzgerald*'s wreckage began as soon as the weather and sea conditions permitted. The search for survivors ended on November 13, with no victims and only minimal wreckage recovered. The search for the *Fitzgerald* commenced the next day. A navy aircraft, using a magnetic anomaly detection unit to look for large objects on the floor of Lake Superior, circled the last known position of the *Edmund Fitzgerald,* as well as areas where debris had been recovered. It took little time for the plane to detect something large on the lake floor. The Coast Guard dispatched the *Woodrush,* a cutter used in the initial search for *Fitzgerald* survivors, to the area.

Poor weather thwarted these efforts. The *Woodrush*'s crew, equipped with a side-scan sonar, required minimal stability to effectively record images of objects hundreds of feet below the lake's surface. It was a slow, tedious process, and rough seas interfered with the work. Despite the difficulties, the *Woodrush* verified the presence of a large object—two large objects, actually—at the location supplied by the navy aircraft.

But was it the *Fitzgerald*?

LLOYD BRESLAU *Assistant Director for Physical Science and Technology, Coast Guard Research and Development*

I was the team leader of the sonar search group for the R&D [Research and Development] Center, and most of the time I ran the side-scan sonar, a device which utilizes a towed fish with a sound transducer. The fish is towed below the surface and after the vessel, and projects sound to either side of the vessel, and objects on the sea floor will produce a return and a shadow, which will return to the vessel and produce an image on the record. The water was deeper than we are accustomed to dealing with, and we had to purchase a cable the night before and accepted delivery just before the ship left, using a steel cable instead of a rubber cable that we are used to using. We went to a site previously

The Coast Guard cutter Woodrush *assisted in the search for the wreckage but only after being deployed from its mooring 300 miles away in Duluth, Minnesota.*

Kenneth Thro Collection, Lake Superior Maritime Collections, University of Wisconsin–Superior.

given by the aircraft. While we were on station, the aircraft flew out and located the magnetic anomaly and dropped a smoke bomb. We ran over this [immediate area].

I have three sections of [image] records which I will show you, and I will give you the generalities that I have been able to deduce from the records.

There appears to be two ship-like objects on the sea floor. One of these appears to be in the neighborhood of 300 feet. There appears to be something emanating from one of the vessels, perhaps a trickle of oil, something that appears in the water column above the vessel, or perhaps a shroud or something floating secured to the ship, which is floating secured to the ship, which is floating up about 70 or 80 feet.

I notice I have a rough area in the proximity of the two objects, and this rough area could be as a result of natural ocean floor roughness or it could be the result of spilled cargo. There is no way I can say which one.

The [images] are not of adequate quality to give a definite identification. I just have shapes, images. I do believe that there is a strong possibility that this is the remains of the *Fitzgerald*. However, I would like to have clearly stated that this is not by any means a definite identification. Further undersea investigation will be necessary, in my opinion. You can do a side-scan sonar survey over again in a better fashion than we did it. That's the first thing you can do. Second, you can do underwater photography, hanging a camera on a cable and just lowering it. There are cameras which will take hundreds of shots and just shoot randomly, hoping that you will get a few pictures. For positive identification, there is nothing quite as satisfying in my opinion as a photograph. Third, with a bottom grab device such as geologists use, you can go out there and pick up some material in the proximity of the objects. You might find debris and you might find cargo. It is a very easy thing to do. Then, as we go up in complexity, there are underwater television devices, and there are underwater submersibles. Those are all the avenues open to you.

Coast Guard officials weren't content with an educated guess, and with the approaching winter preventing underwater exploration until the following spring, within days of the initial search for wreckage, another firm, Seaward Inc., was dispatched to the suspected wreckage site for a possible confirmation of the earlier findings. Once again, the *Woodrush* was used, and the search took place November 22–25.

BOB KURZLEB *Seaward Inc.*

My occupation is ocean engineering with a firm called Seaward Inc. I am the vice president and in charge of operations. My duties include deep ocean search and recovery, tanker cargo transfer, salvage, and conduct of diving operations.

We were under contract to the United States Navy Supervisor of

Salvage as their commercial contractor for the conduct of search and recovery operations. They were contacted by the U.S. Coast Guard and requested assistance. After an analysis and discussions of the background in the case, we brought a towed side-scanning sonar and operators to Sault Ste. Marie. We utilized the Coast Guard buoy tender, *Woodrush*, and also their navigational line-of-sight system, which was made available to us for precise positioning.

We arrived in Soo and had to stand down because of a fairly heavy storm for a day or two. [We] departed for the scene last Saturday, commenced our search Saturday evening, and searched almost continuously through Monday after at which time we returned to port.

We made approximately eighty sonar runs involving some three hundred fixes, and we came back with a great mass of data which, because of, one, the weather on the scene, which was still marginal, and, two, the immense bulk of wreckage and cargo on the bottom that provided reflections everywhere, we feel we must further analyze to pick out and be more definitive as to more precise details. We haven't had the time as yet.

Q. Did you observe any results of your search as far as the Fitzgerald *is concerned?*

Yes, we feel that we did. Short of seeing the name, yes, sir. The conclusions that we have come to are that the *Fitzgerald* lies on the bottom in two pieces, perhaps three. She is broken clean, cleanly apart between the two major sections. She is essentially lying upright, and when I say "essentially" I mean she could have, at this moment, 5 to 10 degrees list, but no more, I don't think.

The results are firm. That is, the ship is in two pieces essentially upright. We believe there may be another section torn away.

Q. In what depth of water was this trace obtained?

530 feet.

Q. Is it possible, through your analysis techniques, to determine the length of the forward part of the ship which is viewed here?

Yes, sir. Just grossly.

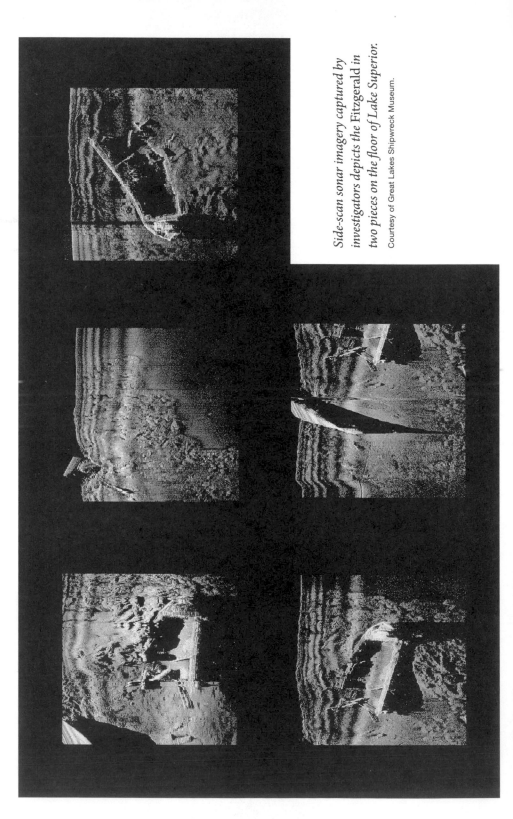

Side-scan sonar imagery captured by investigators depicts the Fitzgerald in two pieces on the floor of Lake Superior.

Courtesy of Great Lakes Shipwreck Museum.

Q. Can you estimate what it is?

Yes, sir. 239 feet. We went to the after section and measured it as near as we could on a first-look basis. The after section, excluding the portion we think that is broken, we came out with an average of measurements between 335 and 350 feet. Then the midship section, that is the other section which we think rolled away, which makes up the difference. Our overall dimensions, when we added them up, came out to be 720 on one analysis, and 739, I think, on the second one. We also counted hatch covers to try and nail it down—hatch coamings, I should say.

Q. You have no doubts, then, in your mind that, based on your experience and based on your judgment, what we have here is the **Fitzgerald**. *Is that correct?*

That is correct, sir.

Q. Do you have an opinion as to whether or not it would be possible to raise either one or two of the three pieces that are down there?

It is possible to raise it if you have enough time and enough money. I think that would depend really on the condition of the ship, which you could only find out from a thorough visual survey.

Q. What is your conclusion, that you are relatively certain or whatever your degree of certainty is upon what that is based as to this being the **Fitzgerald**?

One, it is quite close to the track and the position given by the motor vessel, the *Anderson*; two, the earlier search which was conducted some time before I got here, revealed the visual presence of oil; three, the coamings apparently match the same number that were in the *Fitzgerald*; four, the approximate lengths match the *Fitzgerald*; five, the radar antenna, the disposition of what we believe to be the air whistle, a searchlight and perhaps an RDF antenna.

Q. What further exploration would be in order and feasible to determine with certainty that it is the **Fitzgerald**?

To go down and take a picture of the bow.

LET ME SAY
THIS, SIR:

II. The Investigation

THIS WAS THE
BEST BOAT WE
HAVE IN OUR
FLEET—OR HAD
IN OUR FLEET.

—RICHARD FELDTZ

On November 13, 1975, the Coast Guard suspended its active search for survivors and wreckage. Commercial vessels passing through the area were asked to stay on alert for bodies or objects in the water, but realistic hopes of finding anyone alive had passed within hours of the *Fitzgerald*'s loss. In light of the freighter's sudden disappearance, with no distress calls, it was possible that the entire crew had gone down with the *Fitz.*

There was no shortage of theories of what brought the *Fitzgerald* down. With the discovery of two large objects on the bottom of the lake in the area the *Fitzgerald* was thought to have disappeared, and the belief that these objects were, in fact, the missing vessel, the most popular theory was that the *Fitzgerald* had broken up on the surface, similar to the *Carl D. Bradley* and the *Daniel J. Morrell.* Others, including Bernie Cooper, believed the *Fitzgerald* had taken a nosedive that drove her to the lake bottom under her own power. Still others advanced the theory that she had capsized after being overwhelmed by a gigantic rogue wave.

As it did in all accidents involving loss of life, the Coast Guard assembled a blue-ribbon panel to interview appropriate witnesses and attempt to determine the cause of the sinking. The men selected had never worked together and came from all parts of the country. The four members selected for the Marine Board, all with impressive credentials, quite often disagreed on the focus of questioning, but they worked out their differences in private, away from the scrutiny of attorneys representing Oglebay Norton, Northwestern Mutual, the families of lost sailors, and, in some cases, those representing witnesses. Rear Admiral W. W. Barrow—"the straightest arrow

◄ *A shattered lifeboat and life vests from the* Edmund Fitzgerald *were among the debris lifted from the water after the storm. None of the twenty-nine crewmen were found.*
Courtesy of Great Lakes Shipwreck Museum.

the Coast Guard had ever seen," according to fellow board member C. S. Loosmore—commanded the Eighth Coast Guard District, a reward for a long career in marine safety and inspection. Adam Zabinski, whose occasional impatience and fiery line of questioning made him a formidable presence during the proceedings, had served on every recent Board of Investigation, a background that was vital in hearings that promised to be intricate in nature and probably controversial. James Wilson, like Barrow, could boast of a broad range of experience in safety and inspection. Loosmore, the youngest of the four, offered knowledge in two disciplines that would prove to be beneficial to the board: he was a licensed attorney who had also studied mechanical engineering at MIT and needed only his thesis for his doctorate.

The four gathered for the first time on November 17, one week to the day after the loss of the *Edmund Fitzgerald*. The next morning, Admiral Barrow opened the hearings.

The Coast Guard's four-man inquiry board convened on November 18, 1975. Pictured from left to right are Captain Adam S. Zabinski, Rear Admiral Winford W. Barrow, Captain James A. Wilson, and Commander Charles Loosmore. Copyright 1975 The Associated Press.

W. W. BARROW

Good morning, ladies and gentlemen. It is now 10:10, Tuesday, November 18, 1975. This Marine Board of Investigation will now come to order.

I would like to have each one in the room stand for about sixty seconds in respect for those who lost their lives in this tragic accident.

(brief pause)

Thank you very much.

I am Rear Admiral W. W. Barrow, United States Coast Guard, Commander, Eighth Coast Guard District, and Chairman of this board.

On my right is Captain Adam S. Zabinski, United States Coast Guard, from the Office of Merchant Marine Safety United States Coast Guard Headquarters, Washington, D.C.

The officer on my left is James A. Wilson, United States Coast Guard, Commanding Officer, Marine Safety Office, Detroit.

The officer on his left is Commander C. S. Loosmore, United States Coast Guard, Marine Inspection Office, Seattle, who is also recorder.

Let the record show that the members of this board have been duly sworn and that the court reporters have been sworn. The U.S. Attorney has been notified of the convening of this board.

At this time I have a statement concerning the conduct of this Marine Board of Investigation. This Marine Board of Investigation has been convened by the Commandant, United States Coast Guard, under the authority of Revised Statute 4450 as amended (46 YSC 239), and Part 4 of Title 46 of the Code of Federal Regulations, to investigate the facts and circumstances surrounding the loss on 10 November 1975 of the Ore Carrier *Edmund Fitzgerald* in Lake Superior.

This investigation is intended to determine the cause of the casualty, to the extent possible, and the responsibility, therefore, subject to the final review by the Commandant of the U.S. Coast Guard and by the National Transportation Safety Board.

The investigation and determinations to be made are for the purpose of taking appropriate measures for the promotion of safety of life and property at sea and are not intended to fix criminal and civil liabilities.

The investigation will determine as closely as possible:

1. The cause of the casualty;

2. Whether any failure of material, either physical or design was involved or contributed to the casualty so that recommendation or the prevention of a recurrence of a similar nature may be made;

3. Whether any act of misconduct, inattention to duty, negligence or willful violation of law on the part of any licensed or documented seaman contributed to the casualty so that appropriate action under Revised Statutes 4450, as amended against the license or document;

4. Whether any Coast Guard personnel or other representative or employee of the Government or any other person, caused or contributed to the cause of the casualty.

All parties in interest have the right to be present and be represented by counsel, to cross-examine witnesses and to call witnesses in their own behalf.

Witnesses who are not parties in interest may be assisted by counsel for the purpose of advising them concerning their rights.

However, such counsel are not permitted to examine or cross-examine other witnesses or otherwise participate in the proceedings.

Witnesses will be examined under oath when testifying; a witness is subject to the Federal laws and penalties thereunder for perjury and for making false statements under Title 18 U.S.C., Section 1001.

At this time, I will explain the term "parties in interest."

A person or agency is a party in interest by reason of his position or his part in a casualty. He is not necessarily suspected of wrongdoing. Parties in interest are those who, under the existing facts, or because of their positions, may in any way be responsible for or have contributed to the casualty.

As discussed with counsel at the pre-investigation conference, a person is named a party in interest so that he may have an opportunity to protect himself if facts develop that are adverse in nature to him.

A party in interest may be named during the course of this investigation if it appears that he in any way may have been responsible for or may have contributed to the cause of the casualty.

For the purposes of this Board of Investigation, the following are hereby designated as parties in interest:

The operator of the vessel, Oglebay Norton Company, Cleveland, Ohio. The Master was Ernest McSorley.

The sources of information into which this board will inquire are many and varied. The investigative resources of the Coast Guard have made attempts to locate every available source of information having some bearing on this casualty.

This board will hear all such pertinent evidence.

Should any person have or believe he has information not adduced, but which might be of direct significance, he is urged to communicate such information to the board through the recorder. . . .

The Edmund Fitzgerald

EDGAR M. JACOBSEN *Marine Superintendent, Oglebay Norton*

Q. Captain Jacobsen, one of the things we would like to have you describe for the board is some rather general background on the operation of vessels such as the Fitzgerald and fleets of vessels such as that. Is it fair to say that a vessel such as that operates pretty much on a set round trip from point to point?
Yes. Normally she is in one particular run, but we do divert occasionally to other ports.

Q. What would be the particular run?
Primarily Toledo to Silver Bay [and] back to Toledo.

Q. Could you describe in your own words the conduct of a trip from Toledo to Silver Bay and back, describing such things as the process of taking on cargo and the ballasts, if any, and fuel and water and so worth? Describe the entire operation and the time involved and so forth.
Toledo is an unloading port. We unload pellets in Toledo. During the course of unloading, the ship is ballasted. They use Hulett unloaders to keep it on an even keel.

Prior to finishing the discharge, the remainder of the ballasts are put in to get the stern of the ship down, and then they leave and head for the upper Lakes, passing through the Detroit River, Lake St. Clair, the St. Clair River, Lake Huron, St. Marys River, through the locks at the Soo and across Lake Superior to Silver Bay.

Upon arriving at the loading port, during the loading of the cargo, you discharge your ballasts completely.

In one of the last known photographs of the Edmund Fitzgerald,
the ore carrier takes on cargo at the National Steel Works in Detroit,
October 26, 1975. Photograph by Paul C. Lamarre Jr.

We have been fueling our ships there in Silver Bay toward the upper
end of the Lakes the last few years.

Upon completion when the ship is loaded, it returns and crosses Lake
Superior, which is an easterly course, and you might say that she goes to
the St. Marys River through the locks again and down Lake Huron, the
St. Clair River, Lake St. Clair, Detroit River, and back to Toledo. This
relationship normally takes about five days round trip.

Q. You used a phrase, "Hulett unloader." Can you describe that?
The Hulett unloader gets its name [from] the person who designed it,
George Hulett. It is actually like a large arm with a grab on the end it. It
reaches down in the cargo and picks up, depending on the docks. Some
docks go up to about 17-ton capacity. Toledo, I think, is around 12 or 13.
Depending on what you are unloading and the unloading dock, you may
have three unloaders and you may have four. Some ports have five. The
discharging takes about twelve to thirteen hours.

Q. How much cargo?
For the size of the *Fitzgerald*, 26,000 tons [or] thereabouts.

Q. You said the ship takes on ballast.
Water ballast.

Q. How much quantity could a ship the size of the Fitzgerald *take on?*
I would say roughly 10,000 tons, 10 to 12, depending on weather conditions. You have been furnished with the loading manual for that particu-

*Iron ore is unloaded from a freighter in Cleveland at the Pennsylvania
Railroad docks in 1943. Patented at the turn of the twentieth century,
the specialized Hulett unloader revolutionized shipping on the Great Lakes.*

Photograph by Jack Delano. Courtesy of Library of Congress.

lar ship, which spells out the ballast conditions. [On] these lake ships, the machinery is aft, which puts them down deeper aft normally, to keep the ship on a fairly level plane so these Huletts can unload efficiently.

Q. How long does it take to load one of these vessels?
About five hours.

Q. Who on the vessel is in overall charge of that loading operation?
The first mate. . . . At the time a man becomes a first mate, he already has experience, and when he was a second mate, he had worked with the first mate, and he had experience, a lot of it.

Q. Could you tell us a little bit about what's in that [loading manual] for purposes of describing this loading operation?
It refers to various ballast conditions, normal running, tipping if you have to tip the ship for examination of the propeller. It refers to heavy weather ballasting; it refers to loading and various drafts; it gives the information on what the drafts are on the first or second page.

Q. You said that Oglebay Norton has been having its ships fuel at the upper end of the lake.
The ships that are going up there.

Q. Fair enough. Would that be done before or after the cargo was loaded?
During. Simultaneously.

Q. About how much fuel would a ship the size of the Fitzgerald be expected to take?
For a five-day trip, roughly 30,000 [gallons].

Q. What percentage of the fuel capacity would you expect it to sail from the Duluth-Silver Bay area?
Roughly 75 percent.

Q. When in the season does this operation begin, generally, and [for] how long?
I would say a normal start would be probably April 15, but as you know we have been starting earlier. Last winter some ships went right around the whole season. Not in our fleet, though.

During the 1969 season's winter layup, the Fitzgerald *was put
in dry dock at the Fraser Shipyards in Superior, Wisconsin,
where a diesel-powered bow thruster was installed.*

Kenneth Thro Collection, Lake Superior Maritime Collections, University of Wisconsin–Superior.

**Q. And how long, again, is a normal season? How late would you expect
to operate?**

A normal season I would say would be December 15 to December 30.

**Q. And what do you do between December 15 or December 30 and
April 15?**

Maintenance and repairs. We put it in layup. It goes in port naturally,
and we find a dock to moor it at, and we put extra lines on it, secure it for
the winter, and put anchor chains on it. We drain the systems. This past
winter we did keep some ships warm, because there was a short layup.

Q. Could you describe the sequence, then, of repairs and maintenance such as when you develop work lists, if you do, and what you do during the operating season? What do you postpone until the winter layup and that type of thing?

Prior to September 1, we write to the captains and chief engineers and ask them to make a list of things that they feel should be done, and we have, in our company, a fleet engineer and an assistant fleet engineer, and our hull superintendent visit each ship, go over the ships and look over the ships. They may add to this list or they may not, depending on what the ship needs. When they finish their fall inspection, as we call it, they bring these lists in. They are typed up, and we work out our projections for appropriations. When the ship actually does come in, we start the work.

Q. You make up a work list and accomplish it during the winter. Then what happens? You must have to do something to the ship before you are ready to sail it. Is that right?

We call the engineering crew about three weeks prior to sailing, and they fit out the ship. If there is any machinery that was taken off, like pumps or motors, they are put back on. When they feel that they are all set, they get a date for annual Coast Guard inspection, and whatever date is agreed upon, the Coast Guard hull inspector and boiler inspector come out and inspect the ship. It is done in the springtime, prior to sailing.

Captain
Ernest McSorley

Was Human Error a Contributing Factor?

It was only natural that one would wonder if human error contributed to the loss of the *Edmund Fitzgerald*. Was Ernest McSorley the type of master who took his vessel out in dangerous weather conditions? Did he and his mates chart a good route in navigating the storm? What kind of captain was he?

The answer to this last question was unanimous.

ANDREW RAJNER

He lived in Toledo, and occasionally we would work in the wintertime with each other, shifting boats in the shipyards and back and forth to the winter berths. One winter I wheeled for him, it must have been back around '58 or so, just between Toledo and Detroit. A very good man, competent, sober, about the best captain I ever knew. Cautious in every respect—not to an extreme, but a cautious man.

GERALD LANGE

Captain McSorley was a professional sailor who knew his own capabilities and knew the capabilities of his ship, and he operated accordingly. He was cautious, [but] but not overly cautious. . . . He was more on the quiet side.

EDGAR M. JACOBSEN

Q. You knew Captain McSorley personally?
Yes.

Q. Would you describe him for me, professionally?
I feel that he was the best captain in our fleet. He had the most time in as a master.

Q. You are a licensed master yourself?
Yes.

Q. How would you gauge his professional ability?
He was our top skipper.

Q. Have you observed him underway as far as navigation and ship handling and that type of thing?
Yes.

Q. When was the last time when you would have made note of that?
Well, 1974.

Q. Do you recall what the weather was like?
The weather was good.

Q. There were no problems?
Nothing out of the ordinary.

Q. Do you have any knowledge of the physical condition of the master on the Fitzgerald?
As far as I know, he was in good health.

Q. Or taking medication?
I do not know that, either.

Q. Do you know whether the master intended to retire at the end of the 1975 season, as reported?
The last word I heard, he was going to sail this year and also next year.

Q. If he had been planning to retire at the end of next year—
That would be 1976.

Q. At the end of the 1976 season, but do you know what his reasons would be?
No, not really, other than putting in a good many years sailing. He was what? Sixty-three? I would suppose he felt he better start enjoying life a little bit, more than sailing.

THOMAS GARCIA

To my knowledge that was the best crew that could have been on the *Fitzgerald* with the mates, engineers, and the skipper. The men throughout the Oglebay Norton Co. knew the *Fitzgerald* as the "Mighty Fitzgerald." She was the queen of our fleet. It was unbelievable when we heard that she went down.

Was the
Fitzgerald
Seaworthy?

Like all working freighters on the Great Lakes, the *Edmund Fitzgerald* was required to undergo a series of inspections for sailing approval. Safety was all-important, and the Marine Board spent a great deal of time in making certain that the *Fitzgerald* had received and passed all required inspections. In 1975, the *Fitzgerald* was cleared for service; by all indications, she was fit for all lines of work.

CHARLES STUDSTILL *Hull Inspector*

Q. Did your assignment as a hull inspector include any inspections on the Fitzgerald, *the ship involved in this hearing?*
Yes, sir. I had the dry-dock inspection or examination of the *Fitzgerald*, which was completed on 4–20–74. It was dry-docked at the American Shipyard in Lorain, [Ohio], American Ship Building.

Q. Is this a required examination?
Yes, sir.

Q. How frequently?
Every five years.

Q. What does the examination involve?
In this particular examination, the vessel is placed in the dry dock and is examined throughout extensively, every department, internally and externally, and all the equipment and gear and so forth relative to the safe operation of the vessel.

Q. What is the conclusion? What end results are reached by one of these examinations?

After the examination is completed, the vessel is certified to be, in the opinion of the inspector, as the statement at the last page in the book indicates, "In my opinion, the vessel is fit for service and route specified in the certificate."

Q. Could you tell me what was done during that examination?

Yes, sir, I sure could. . . . The condition [of] the vessel is examined—the hull, the structure externally, all external members and all internal members, bulkhead decks, tank tops, bulkheads, et cetera, throughout the ship. The vessel is carefully examined for all fractures, and if any previous fractures or repairs are necessary, they are accomplished at that time.

The vessel structure is examined to see that it is reinforced in accordance with the applicable instructions for that particular vessel. All the fasteners, rivets, welds, whatever it may be, are examined as thoroughly as possible. The ground tackle or the anchors are examined. If necessary, if there are any available or if they are present, all air ports below the weather deck are examined, but of course, this was not applicable for the *Fitzgerald*.

Q. Why not?

There [weren't] any air ports below the weather deck—or at least when I checked on her.

The spar deck, the side ports, all self-bailing and cockpit-freeing ports, compartments, all interbottoms, were entered and examined thoroughly and throughout; scuppers, draft marks, stern frame, the rudder, propeller, and all the sea chests were opened and examined. The sea valves were looked at by the machinery inspector, and he so indicated here in the book, and he has also signed the Remarks section. That is a quick view of what we do.

Q. Thank you. You mentioned fractures: did you find any fractures?

We found some fractures in the connection between the hull side girder and the hatch in girder or skirt. There were some fractures in the welds. They were of the nature that you usually encounter in this type of inspection. We found some fractures in the keelson, the connection of the keelsons and the floors below the tank tops. I believe we found one fracture—let me refer to the book now. That's all we have here. All these were repaired while part of the vessel was on dry dock.

JAMES GORDON *Hull Inspector, Coast Guard, Toledo*

Q. In connection with your marine inspection duties, were you ever aboard the **Edmund Fitzgerald***?*
Yes, sir. I believe once, the 19th of February, 1975. I boarded the *Fitzgerald* to commence the annual inspection for certification, and my duties were to inspect the hull structure. That day, along with an ABS [American Bureau of Shipping] surveyor, Mr. Will Jeanquart, and, I believe, Mr. Richard Feldtz from Columbia [Transportation Division], we inspected both side tunnels, all cargo holds, fore peak and after peak tanks, and some shell structure through the engine room.

Q. As a result of this inspection, did you find any discrepancies?
No, sir.

Q. You said that you did the hull structure on the **Edmund Fitzgerald***. Just how do you go about doing this? What is the procedure?*
The inspection normally is done in concurrence with the ABS inspection. You meet with the ABS inspector and the company representative and then the procedure from there on, on this particular day, I believe, we entered the after peak tank first, checking the strength members in the after peak. We came up from there, worked up probably the port side, side tunnel, to the fore peak tank and inspected the fore peak tank and related areas there. We worked back to the starboard side, side tunnel, and then up the deck through the hatch openings down into each cargo hold.

Q. What would you be looking for, say, [in] the after peak tank?
Excessive wastage of any of the strength members or mechanical damage to those strength members which impair the seaworthiness of the vessel. You climb in the tank and you have flashlights and you examine the structure that way.

Q. What are you generally looking for in the tunnels?
Since the tunnels were sealed off from the cargo holds, you are looking for mechanical damage which might have occurred through collision or slamming a deck or something.

Q. What does [a visual side shell inspection] consist of?
Before I boarded the vessel, I just visually examined the side of the hull for any mechanical damage that was visible, and once I am aboard, I look over the outboard side and just to make sure, if there is any mechanical damage, I make a note of it and try to see it from down below.

Q. Were there any outstanding requirements as far as hull repairs and so forth that were done during the winter layup season?
No, sir.

HORTON E. GAFFORD *Commanding Officer, Inspector, Toledo Coast Guard*

Q. Did your office or did you issue a certificate of inspection for the Fitzgerald*?*
Yes.

Q. Do you know the date?
April 9, 1975, I believe. Yes, that is correct. 9 April 1975.

Q. Commander Gafford, is there anything in that entry which, if you had read that prior to the issuance of the certificate, the last certificate on the Edmund Fitzgerald, *that would have prevented or delayed the issuance of the certificate of inspection?*
No, sir.

Q. Do both the hull and boiler inspections indicate that the vessel was seaworthy in all respects at the completion of the inspection?
Yes. The block is: "In my opinion, the vessel is fit for service and route specified," both books.

Q. Therefore, there is no information that you have seen now which was made but would not have been called to your attention at the time of the issuance of the certificate?
No, sir.

The cargo hold, ballast tanks, and transport tunnels of the Fitzgerald *begin to take shape in a construction photograph taken at the Great Lakes Engineering Works in November 1957. The tunnels just below the spar deck were used by crew members during bad weather.*
Courtesy of Great Lakes Maritime Institute.

Q. No information in reviewing the books which would have precluded or prevented or delayed the certificate of inspection being issued to the Edmund Fitzgerald*?*
No, sir.

Q. Commander Gafford, we have had testimony from Mr. Paul earlier in the afternoon about spar deck inspections. I asked Mr. Paul if spar deck inspections were required by the regulations; his response to that was that it was not one required by the regulations but a special type of examination done on Great Lakes vessels. Is that correct?
Yes, sir.

Q. Can you give me the background on this spar deck inspection?
Lt. Paul indicated that it came about as a result of the **Morrell** *disaster several years ago.*
This is my understanding also.

Q. What can you tell us about the spar deck inspection?
I don't know of any written history of spar deck inspections. All I know about it is it was word of mouth, and I know that it is an inspection we do up here.

Q. Do you do it on every vessel, every lake vessel?
Every ore carrier.

Q. Every year?
Every year.

Q. Every vessel that comes into your port or for an annual inspection do you do a spar deck inspection?
When a vessel comes into our port on an annual inspection and it hasn't a current spar deck inspection from some other port, we do one.

Q. How do you know she has had a spar deck inspection?
It's on the bridge record card. Or if it isn't, we will tell the port captain: "Do you want to do a spar deck inspection?" He'll say, "Well, I just had it done in Cleveland last month." You get on the horn and call Cleveland, and Cleveland says that's it.

Q. You verify?
Sure.

SIDNEY SPINNER *Fleet Engineer,*
Columbia Transportation Division, Oglebay Norton

Q. Mr. Spinner, would you say that you were on board the **Fitzgerald** *a month before it was lost?*
Six weeks, approximately.

Q. Do you recall the occasion of that visit or what the purpose of that visit was?
Yes. It was to pick up winter work, repair work, which would be done this

winter. . . . I think the largest item on that would be anticipated requirements from the Coast Guard at the annual inspection and the American
Bureau requirements. The rest was just routine maintenance and repair.

We examined the propeller blades and found what we thought was
a 6- or 7-inch crack in the fillet of one blade. It didn't warrant changing,
and nobody would tell us even with die-checking if it was definitely a
crack. This was approximately 6 inches in length, and then we operated
the vessel with the intentions of further survey at a later date, which we
did in October, and it showed the crack was progressing. It was definitely
a crack, and a decision was made to change the blade.

The Fitzgerald's *massive
propeller, seen here during
the vessel's construction
in 1958, was thoroughly
inspected prior to the
1975 shipping season.
A 6- to 7-inch crack was
found, which prompted
one of the propeller blades
to be changed out.* Captain
William A. Hoey III Collection.

The Marine Board of Investigation was particularly interested in the final inspection of the *Edmund Fitzgerald*, which took place eleven days before the vessel's loss. This involved a delicate line of questioning: one might have expected the inspectors to testify that the *Fitzgerald* was seaworthy in the aftermath of their inspection, but had they seen anything that might have affected the freighter's structural integrity in the storm?

WILFORD JEANQUART *surveyor,* Fitzgerald *inspection*

Q. Have you had any occasion to do any surveys of the Fitzgerald *in the last several years?*
Yes.

Q. Could you tell me when the most recent of those inspections would be?
Yes. The 31st of October of this year. That was the commencement of the annual survey of the hull. We made a weather deck or so-called spar deck survey of the vessel.

Q. Can you describe the procedure of the survey that you conducted on the 31st of October, please?
We inspect the deck, all deck erections, the deck area within the hatch coamings, the gunwale connections, the sheer striker which you would look over the side port and starboard, this is all included in our inspection together with a general look at the hatch covers [and] the hatch clamps, what I call erections on a ship.

Q. What did this inspection disclose?
Well, I found some irregularities located in the way of the hatch openings on Hatch No. 13, No. 15, No. 16, and also No. 21 starboard side after-coaming. We discussed and decided that they were merely irregularities and could be dealt with before the completion of the annual survey of the hull. This was ordinary procedure. When the spar decks [inspections] first started, it was an agreement that the Coast Guard, the [American Shipping] Bureau, and the owners should agree as to the resolution of these things.

RICHARD FELDTZ

I am employed by the Oglebay Norton Company in the Columbia Transportation Division, and I am a hull inspector.

Q. What are your duties as hull superintendent? What do they involve?
Hull maintenance and repair of the hull structure, the deck machinery, and the deck department and equipment.

Q. Do your duties as hull superintendent involve visits to the various ships that Columbia runs?
Yes, sir.

Q. Frequently?
Well, sir, in 1974 I was aboard the *Fitzgerald* on sixteen different dates. In 1975 I was aboard the *Fitzgerald* on fifteen different dates. On this one date, it may involve numerous visits, sometimes it is one, two, or three a day, but these are different dates that I am referring to. The last time was on October 31, 1975.

Q. And what was that occasion?
To conduct an annual survey.

Q. Is that something that the company does?
No, that is something that the company does in joint requirements with the Coast Guard and the American Bureau of Shipping.

Q. What was conducted on the list then?
On the list we had conducted a spar deck inspection, which was the commencement of the annual [inspection].

Q. What were the results of that spar deck inspection?
The results of the spar deck inspection on the *Fitzgerald,* I believe there were four minor discrepancies that were disclosed.

Q. And what action was taken by you as a result in your role as hull superintendent, as a result of finding these discrepancies?
Well, after we found discrepancies, we looked at them, and we discussed at the time, to prevent any further discussion, I explained how we would repair them in the future and if that was satisfactory to all those concerned. I was given a statement by the American Bureau of Shipping

at the time that these would be completed before the '76 inspection, and the Coast Guard [inspector], he contacted his office and followed up and gave a requirement that these discrepancies of a minor nature would be completed prior to 1 April 1976.

WILLIAM R. PAUL *Inspector, Coast Guard, Toledo*

The last date that I had been on the *Fitzgerald* for board inspection was on October 31, 1975. This is the annual spar deck inspection.

Q. Could you tell us what that involved?
Basically inspection of the spar deck in the vicinity and in the location of the area of the hatches, and everything associated with it. As a result of this inspection I issued a requirement to the *Fitzgerald* for four items.

Q. What were those four items?
To the best of my recollection, there was a fracture, a fracture in No. 16 port in the hatch and girder, a small one, a gouge, an indentation on each; and on No. 15 and I am not positive of the exact hatch. No. 13 hatch,

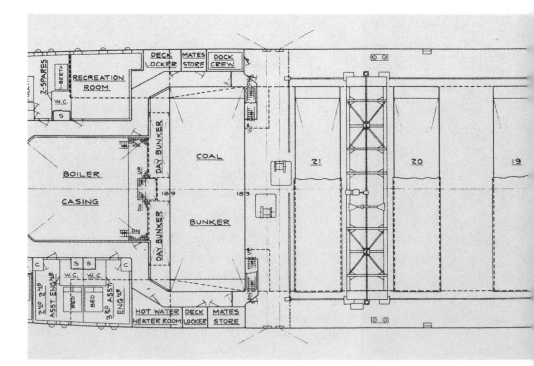

there was a notch in the deck plating. It is a very small notch. No. 15 hatch, there was a small gouge in the deck plating. There again it was adjacent to the hatch itself. No. 1 hatch, there was a fracture, as I said before, in the hatch and girder, and in No. 21 there was a small fracture, the hatch and girder connection after-coaming on the starboard side. That was all.

Q. Would you describe for us what you did from the time you went aboard to the completion of this inspection? How is the spar deck inspection conducted?

I leave the office and attempt to arrive at the vessel at the specified time, and generally the company representative is on board, and I might meet him and have a cup of coffee first, and you meet the ABS inspector, and you go together and you start your inspection.

The aft cargo hatches and ballast vent covers (between hatches 15–16 and 20–21) appear in this detail of the spar deck plan. The Coast Guard and American Bureau of Shipping conducted their annual inspection of the spar deck on October 31, 1975, ten days before the sinking.

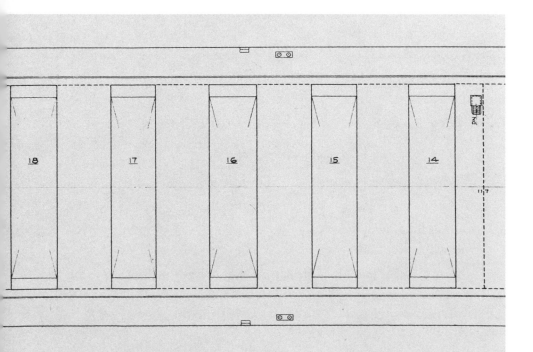

You generally confine your inspection to the hatchings, to the coamings, to the corners, the girders, any weld connections, rivets. You start on one hatch, and you go up one side of the vessel, get through that, and, of course, as you go along you might find some item, and you might discuss it. You record what you find. Then you go to the other side of the vessel, doing the same thing. When this is completed, you have some items which you found, some deficiencies. You discuss how serious it might be or what you should do about it. "Should you require them immediately? Can you wait until the end of the season?" or whatever. That is basically it, sir.

Q. You said you issued a requirement, and what was that requirement issued for?
This was issued on a standard Coast Guard Form CG835.

Q. What was the process of finding these?
In the process of a routine spar deck inspection. We were in the company of American Bureau of Shipping.

Q. And who was that?
Will Jeanquart was in attendance and a new man from Toledo of which I don't recall his last name.

Q. Another ABS man?
Another ABS man. And Mr. Dick Feldtz from Columbia was also in attendance.

Q. What was the physical process of inspecting that you did?
Just by visual observation, these items were spotted. We inspect each individual hatch. There is the process of climbing out and sometimes using a mirror or flashlight and everything we have on hand to aid in the inspection.

Q. What time of day was it?
During the broad daylight. I don't recall exactly the time.

Q. Were these the four listed there, were they the only deficiencies you found in the course of that spar deck inspection?
To the best of my knowledge that's the only deficiencies which we found.

Q. All right. Once you had found these four, what did you do?
After we found these deficiencies, we discussed them. Afterwards I think the consensus was that there was nothing of a serious enough nature to hold the vessel or anything requiring repairs. After this, I personally called my office and advised them of what we had. I talked to Commander Lawrence, the executive officer. He is also the senior inspector [of] materiel. I advised him what we had, and I advised him of what our results were, and he asked me about a couple of things, and I answered him to the best of my ability and that's it.

Q. Did you advise him that you were going to write up an 835?
I don't remember my exact words, but I probably said it would be required. I am sure I said something of this nature in the normal process of inspection.

Q. Now, is there anything else included in that 835 on that particular form?
There is a time element on the bottom of that form. There is a time element involved in this requirement.

Q. What is that, please?
It says, "Above items to be completed prior to the 1976 operating season."

Q. Do you feel that any of these four items, that any of these four items affected the seaworthiness of the vessel, of the Fitzgerald?
No, sir.

Q. Had there been any requirements which, in your opinion, should have been dealt with at that time, you would have required that they be dealt with?
If we had considered anything that was affecting the seaworthiness of the vessel, we would have made sure the vessel did not leave port and required repairs.

Q. As you know, the Fitzgerald was lost within days of this inspection.
Yes, sir.

Q. Is there anything that you observed on board that comes to mind now that could have contributed to the loss of the Fitzgerald?
Nothing to my knowledge, sir.

Stress
and Stability

How Could Loading
Have Affected the *Fitzgerald*'s
Ability to Handle the Storm?

Seaworthiness of a vessel did not necessarily translate into smooth sailing in stormy conditions. Two of the most recent losses on the Great Lakes—the *Carl D. Bradley* and the *Daniel J. Morrell*—involved vessels deemed seaworthy, but both were older freighters, built before 1948, when newer, more flexible steel was used in shipbuilding from that point on; both vessels had been riveted, rather than welded. Stress and stability had been components in their breaking on the surface and sinking.

The *Edmund Fitzgerald* was much newer and sturdier, but that did not mean that it was capable of handling the kind of stress presented by the storm. The Marine Board was especially interested in how the vessel had been loaded. Could this have been a factor in her sinking?

ROBERT MASON *Lieutenant Commander, Coast Guard, Cleveland*

We have a stability criteria for Great Lakes vessels, and we have the regulations which state that if the commandant is satisfied that due to the vessel's proportions and arrangements more than adequate stability is available, a test will not be required.

The Fitzgerald's hull, one of the first of its kind to be welded rather than riveted, was built to the maximum length allowed for passage through the St. Lawrence Seaway. During the hearings the Coast Guard spent hours interviewing naval architects and engineers about the vessel's state-of-the-art construction. Courtesy of Great Lakes Maritime Institute.

Q. Have you done stability calculations on the Fitzgerald *or a vessel like the* Fitzgerald, *in spite of the fact that you have a statement in a policy letter that says that stability tests are not required?*
Yes, sir, we have.

Q. And can you summarize the general results of those calculations?
What happened is the previous branch chief and myself both arrived in a six-month period. We questioned the absence of a criterion on a letter file stating that no stability test was required. At that time there were two self-unloading vessels being built. We took the stability criterion set in that, [and] applied them against the self-unloading vessels. Those vessels have a higher center of gravity due to the unloading equipment. We took a series of straight deck vessels, using their length, breadth, depth, and known hydrostatics in assuming a center of gravity at one-half the depth of the vessel and found out in all cases the vessels which ranged in length from 630 feet up to 820 feet far exceeded the stated criterion. We concluded that vessels built known as Great Lakes straight-deck vessels, due to their proportions and arrangements, far exceeded the Coast Guard stability criteria.

Q. Do you have any information on the load line statement for the Fitzgerald, *particularly in the load line statement which was recently changed in the 1973 regulations?*
Yes, I do.

Q. How did your office get involved?
Under the 1973 load line regulations, the Coast Guard became involved in approving the loading manuals for the vessel and insuring that stability and loading information was available on each of the ships to be issued in 1973. . . . We did calculations relating to the longitudinal strength of the vessel in accordance with the Interim Great Lakes Strength Standard. The results of the calculations showed that the vessel, as built, met the Interim Great Lakes Strength Standard.

RICHARD STERN *Naval Architect*

Q. Do you know whether your organization or any other has ever performed a stability test on the Fitzgerald?
I know that we didn't, our organization didn't, and I don't know if any other organization ever did.

Q. No stability test of any form, including a dead-weight survey? Nothing?
A dead-weight survey, as such, is not a stability test. We conducted a dead-weight survey on the vessel in preparation of the loading manual, but we did not conduct a stability test.

Q. All right. When did you conduct the dead-weight survey?
At some time prior to the preparation of the manual. I don't know when it was.

Q. Very briefly, what did the dead-weight survey consist of?
Well, I can give you our general procedure for the dead-weight survey: that is to board the ship, sound all the tanks, [and] note any cargo aboard. Preferably we make a dead-weight survey with no cargo aboard because it's very difficult to determine the amount of cargo, and we generally try to have the tanks pumped out so that we won't have to estimate the amount of ballast water.

We check the amount of fuel aboard, other consumables, and note anything that's aboard that is not normal. [We] check the drafts, and if we don't have complete plans on the vessel, check the general distribution and locations of major weight items and this sort of thing. In the case of the *Fitzgerald,* we would have accurate drawings for the engines, and anything necessary for us to make a weight-distribution diagram.

Q. I realize you didn't design the vessel, but you did design the loading manual to still water bending. What would be your best estimate of what the total state of stress would be in a normal seaway?
When you say "a normal seaway," are you referring to something less than a sea that we have been talking [about] in this hearing?

Q. I am really asking for a professional judgment. I guess what I am after is, you certainly must have thought about what the total stress would be on the vessel when you designed that loading manual, in spite of the fact that it's designed for still water bending. I wonder if you had a feel for what the total stress would be, or the maximum stress, I guess, is a better way to put it.

We show a loaded still water bending stress of about 2 tons per square inch. The [stress] allowable by the American Bureau of Shipping is 4 tons. We had run a calculation on this ship according to the Matthews method of 5.8 tons per square inch allowable still water bending stress.

Q. To your knowledge, have you ever done a calculation which would evaluate the state of stress during a loading, simultaneously deballasting and, conversely, an unloading and ballasting?

I don't believe we ever ran one. We considered the various possible combinations, and the combinations are practically infinite. It has been very difficult. If I may just talk about [this] a little bit, it's been very difficult to get loading manuals prepared that are practical because we have sixty or seventy years of ship personnel loading these ships. The loading procedures are passed down from generation to generation, and they worked up a very practical and evidently relatively safe method.

Now, when we try to analyze the optimum loading, we have the computer program that we feed all the data into, and because it's a fairly lengthy calculation to determine what the bending stresses are, even on a single calculation—for instance, dumping one pile into a ship, it's a very lengthy calculation because the ship changes trim, and you have a different water loading on the hull for each one of the cargo loadings.

We try to optimize the method of loading these vessels, and in the early stages we came up with what we thought was a very good loading, low stresses, and give it out to the mates, and they practically disregard it, for several reasons: They couldn't pump out water quite as fast as they were supposed to, to keep the trim that would be required for the particular loading sequence we showed, and any number of [other] reasons.

So, what we gradually did—and we did it in the case of the *Fitzgerald* —was to get the actual loading sequences that these mates have used,

Taconite pellets stream into the cargo hold, circa late 1960s. The Marine Board of Investigation meticulously questioned witnesses on whether the Fitzgerald *was loaded according to proper procedure before departing from Superior, Wisconsin, on November 9.* Courtesy of Great Lakes Shipwreck Museum.

and then we fed that data into our computer program. We check the actual stresses. If they are reasonable, we try to improve on them some, but not to any drastic degree. We try to get the best stress we can without diverting so far from what they consider a practical loading method that it would be thrown out when they went to use it.

So, for this reason I shudder to think of attempting, let's say, to control the deballasting of the vessel except in very broad generalities, which they have from past practices.

Now, we do state in here, along those same lines, that in general stresses [it] will be very safe if they maintain a straight keel line. We know this is the general practice and is a good backup for any type of loading.

Q. You said if the stresses were reasonable you would try to improve. What is reasonable?
I would consider during a loading operation a bending stress up to 6 or 7 tons would be quite reasonable.

Q. What would you consider unreasonable?
I would say 10 or 11 tons, in a calculated condition, would be unreasonable, because that doesn't leave much leeway for error.

ROBERT MASON

The condition of the loading manual is strictly related to strength. The conditions of the 1973 load line regulations stated that the Coast Guard would also be responsible to insure that the master had on board information relating to the stability of the vessel.

Although the vessel's guidance manual for loading is generally referred to as a loading manual, it basically refers to the strength of the vessel in still water, when underway. As to why the Coast Guard has not required a sequence loading or unloading manual, I cannot say.

Q. It does require one for loading, though, right?
No, sir. It requires one for its relationship upon still water bending. As a matter of fact, the different companies sometimes refer to it just as a guidance manual for loading, and others as a loading manual, but the basic strength criteria that is taken out of it only relates to underway still water strength.

Q. Underway still water strength? Is it possible to have such a thing when you have a ship dynamically moving through the water?

What we say when we say underway still water strength, the Matthews' criteria, which is set up in a joint agreement between the Coast Guard for the United States, the Administrative Transportation Department for Canada, Industry and Operators' Technical Committee, which establishes a wave theory which divides the loading of a vessel into wave action, some springing motion in still water. We take that still water portion of the maximum, the effect that the vessel will see, and use that for the criteria in the loading manual, and such design is that if the vessel keeps its stress below the still water, it will also keep its stress under the maximum underway.

WILLIAM CLEARY

The idea behind the loading manual is to give the skipper of the vessel the information that he needs to be certain that his vessel does not leave port in a condition of stress. We call that still water stress. That is really the only part of the entire examination of the strength of the vessel which you can be certain of, and by controlling that part of it, you hopefully make sure that the skipper will not leave port with his vessel stressed too highly.

There are a number of things which go along with that, the limiting stress value for harbor conditions, still water bending movement, and this is set low enough that there is a considerable reserve before you would expect anything that occurs out on the ocean or in a storm on the Great Lakes to cause a ship any harm.

The loading manual then is insurance for the master that he ought to have that reserve, if his ship is fully sound, that he can make it safely through the conditions that he has on his voyage.

It is expected that the calculations will cover all of the normal loading conditions, which the ship will normally use and that includes valid conditions.

He should have information on the other half of the voyage, round trip.

Water is pumped from the forward ballast tanks as the
Fitzgerald *prepares to leave port with a full load of cargo, 1960s.*

Q. *Can you be more specific of what the manual is to contain?*
Well, in cases of present ship, it is an iron ore carrier. It needs to know
how to load the full cargo of iron ore. It needs to have another page that
tells you how to load the ballast tanks for the return voyage. If any special
voyages are contemplated, or different cargoes are contemplated, they
are supposed to be covered by the separate conditions.

Q. *How specific should this "how to load" be?*
It has to be very specific. I know of one case up in Canada where I was
told that the vessel had broke in half because instead of moving—that
was right out of the dock, while they were loading the cargo.

The normal procedure is to load in balance along the length of the
vessel, so you don't load the middle over the ends too much at one time.

Then you often shift the vessel slightly to get other hatches in line

with the loading chutes, and then you continue the process trying to keep it as uniform as possible while you are loading.

When we put this regulation into effect, the working group and all of the Joint Technical Conditions group were aware that for many years the equivalent of a loading manual has been carried on most Great Lakes ships.

This is usually in the first mate's back pocket, a little black book which tells him how he is to load and how he is to ballast the vessel.

RICHARD STEARN

Q. Are you called upon frequently by Oglebay Norton to do work in connection with their vessels?
Oh, yes, quite frequently.

Q. How many years have you been associated with them?
I know at least since 1958.

Q. Do you find them to be a company that is concerned about the maintenance and the repair of their vessels?
Very much so.

Q. What other companies do you do similar work for?
Well, we do work for some other ship operators here: Huron Portland Cement, American Steamship Company, U.S. Steel Company.

Q. Did you have anything to do with the work in connection to the lengthening of the Anderson?
Yes. We laid out the contract drawings on that job.

Q. Did you have anything to do with the preparation of the loading plans for the Anderson?
Yes. We prepared the one that was used for the lengthening of the ship.

Q. Is that the one in use at the present time?
That's correct.

Q. Have you prepared other loading manuals for other vessels?
Oh, yes. We have prepared quite a few in the last six or eight years.

Q. Would you be good enough to enumerate those that you prepared— not all, just name a few.
All of Columbia, some Pickands Mather ships. . . . I can't give you the specific ship names of that company.

Q. Any U.S. Steel ships in addition to the Anderson?
Yes, U.S. Steel ships.

RICHARD FELDTZ

Q. Does the company, Oglebay Norton, periodically spot-check to see how the cargo is being loaded?
Yes, sir, I do.

Q. Does that come under you?
I do it as a point of doing it. Yes, sir.

Q. Do you know when the last time you may have made such an evaluation on the Fitzgerald?

Yes, sir. That was one of my reasons for riding the vessel on 6/18 of '74, which was to witness and also discuss the loading manual with the captain. It was also to witness that he was loading in principle in accordance with the loading manual.

Q. What was the nature of the discussion?

I asked him if he had—when I first put the loading manual aboard, I asked him to review it. I asked him to try to adhere to it and if he had any dissatisfaction or anything that he had disagreed with in regard to the loading manual to come back to us, and I asked him to review it and he read it. As you saw, it was lengthy. I wrote him, but I didn't hear from him. He said that he was familiar with the loading manual. We tried different ballasting conditions. I did not make notes, unfortunately, on the cargo that was loaded. I did review the mate's book.

I was aboard the vessel and made the comparison with the conditions as specified in the manual and was quite surprised that we were very close, I mean in tonnage here and there.

Q. Did you make a report of that?

No, I didn't, because I was satisfied that they were adhering to the manual, so I didn't see any need to make records at that point.

Q. Do you think, given the information that was in the loading manual, that the people aboard could properly load the vessel in proper sequence?

Yes, sir, in essence, I think the conditions in the loading manual were conditions followed for years with minor alterations.

The Hatches

Did the *Fitzgerald* Take On Water through Her Hatches?

The hatches are the weakest point of an ore carrier, and if the hatch covers aren't properly fastened, water from boarding seas can enter the cargo hold. The *Fitzgerald* began taking on water well before she sank. That much was known from conversations between the *Fitzgerald* and the *Anderson*. The Marine Board of Investigation focused much of its hearings on how the water might have boarded the *Fitz*. Was it the result of damage below the water-line? Or had water rushed in through missing or improperly fastened hatch covers? Given the length of time passing between the *Fitzgerald*'s reporting a list and her sinking, it was logical to assume that the vessel was taking on water at a volume too great for the pumps to control. It was also critical to know, from inspection records, the condition of the hatches at the time of the boat's departure from Superior.

RICHARD FELDTZ

Q. How do you check a hatch? How do you tell whether a hatch fits right or not?
I let the hatch sit without the hatch clamps and see if I have any irregularities. If she sits flush on the coamings, I figure, well, by the time you put the dogs on her, she will be fairly tight. The American Bureau does go around with a feeler gauge, and periodically they will see if they can run it through the coamings in the gasket with the hatch dog down.

Q. How does a crew know whether they are supposed to take care of the hatch covers, or how does that work out?

What I have is an inspection form that I have devised, and what I do is list all these items in detail—spar deck, side shell, hatches, hatch coamings, underdeck spaces—and it is pretty detailed, about eight pages. What I do is make the inspection either in port or ride the vessel with one of the mates, preferably the first mate, list the conditions that I have found, and then make a recommendation of what I would like the mate to do.

EDGAR M. JACOBSEN

Q. Captain Jacobsen, to your knowledge, has it ever been a practice of the Fitzgerald *to sail on any of the lakes with hatches open?*

It has probably happened at one time or another when they were painting coamings, at a time when the weather is good.

Q. To sail with hatch covers on?

With a cover off, to paint a hatch coaming.

Q. Would it be a practice to sail with hatch covers on, but not secured?

I would think, in any event, there would be some clamps on. I am not saying that they would all be on. As I pointed out earlier, it would be every other one or they would, maybe, skip two. . . . When the ship is loaded with cargo, all of the clamps would be on. In a lake condition, you could have 50 percent on, possibly, unless the weather report was such that a prudent master would require all the clamps to be put on.

ROY ANDERSON

After we have loaded the vessel, well, we make sure our vents are closed, and we batten down all the hatches and check the boat throughout and see that all the ports are closed, any openings that will take on water are checked. Then you know your ship is secure for sea or for the lake.

THOMAS GARCIA

Q. How were [hatch clamps] adjusted?

They had a set screw on the top, and you could adjust them with a 12- or

Two cargo hatches in view of the pilothouse and officers' quarters, circa 1970. During the hearings the Coast Guard pursued a controversial theory that the hatches were not secured properly, ultimately allowing water to flood the cargo hold. Courtesy of Detroit Historical Society.

13-inch crutcheon wrench. I am not sure what it was, but I never had to adjust the thing.

Q. How did you check to see if they needed adjustment?
Just by the looseness of the nuts on top of the clamp itself.

Q. That's how you would check to see if they needed adjustment?
Yes, but I guess you would just use your own discretion on that.

Q. And did the hatch clamps ever get damaged from any cause?
Not to my knowledge, no, sir.

Q. Did you go around and check hatch clamps and covers when you start getting a little weather?
Yes, sir. They tell us to check the clamps, check the boat and make sure everything is secure.

Q. Secure any loose gear on deck?
Yes, sir. Ladders, any oil barrels. I mean empty oil barrels that are on the boat decks—make sure they are fastened down. Port holes were dogged down below the spar deck, and you would report that back to the mate.

Storm Damage to the *Fitzgerald*

Was It Enough to Sink the Vessel?

There was no disputing that the *Fitzgerald* had been seriously damaged at some point during the storm. She had lost her radar and was relying on the *Arthur M. Anderson* to act as her eyes in the tempest. Captain McSorley had reported a fence rail down and two lost vents. The *Fitzgerald* had also taken on a list, beginning somewhere near Caribou and Michipicoten Islands on Lake Superior's far eastern side. Water was entering the vessel at such a volume that McSorley ordered the pumps to be used.

All of this was serious, but was it enough to sink the *Fitz*? The board directed its questions in a manner that addressed the workings of each damaged piece of equipment.

SIDNEY SPINNER

Q. The captain reports to the ship astern that they lost some vents. What vents might they be?

It could have been vents from the spar deck into the ballast tanks, or it could have been vents from the spar deck into the side tunnels.

EDGAR M. JACOBSEN

Q. Captain, I would like to direct some questions about the ballasting system on the Fitzgerald. *I wonder if you could describe that for me to the best of your knowledge.*

There are eight tanks per side; a total of sixteen ballast tanks, and each tank has a pipe going into it.

Q. Do you know what size?
I believe on the *Fitzgerald* it is an 8-inch pipe.

Q. How many pumps do you have that can be utilized on the ballast system?
Four.

Q. Do you know their capacity?
The main pumps are 6,000 [per minute]. There are two of those, and there are two smaller stripping pumps. I don't really know the capacity of those.

The Edmund Fitzgerald *was equipped with four ballast pumps, seen here circa 1960. They were used to stabilize the vessel during loading and unloading by pumping water into the ballast tanks.*
Courtesy of Detroit Historical Society.

Q. You have two main ballast pumps and two stripping pumps?
Right.

Q. Is that total or on one side?
That's total.

Q. How about the vents on those ballast tanks? Can you describe those for the board, please?
I believe it is an 8-inch pipe going from the top of the ballast tank, which comes up the side of the ship and terminates above the spar deck.

Q. With a screw-down cap cover.
That is right.

Q. What is the purpose of that cover on a vent line?
To keep the water out and the seas out.

Q. How high are they off the spar deck?
14 inches.

Q. Is that the top of the 8-inch pipe, or is it the top of the cover cap?
The cover of the pipe.

Q. In other words, let's take a hypothetical situation: if we had water more than 14 inches above the spar deck and that cover was off, water would enter through that opening. Is that correct?
Right.

Q. You say it had a screw cover. Would you describe that for me and tell us how that operated?
It is turned on by hand and screwed on with a right-hand pipe thread. It is like a mushroom.

Q. What is the normal procedure for opening and closing these vent caps when you ballast and deballast?
They have to be open when you ballast.

Q. Why is that?
You have got to have a place for the air to go.

Q. The air is displaced by the—
The incoming water.

Q. Do you know how fast that water could be pumped in?
2,000 gallons per minute if you are working on one particular tank.

Q. That would raise quite a bit of pressure within the tank, wouldn't it?
Yes.

Q. We have some preliminary indication that the Fitzgerald *may have been taking on water through the vents shortly before the casualty. What vents do you think this may have been?*
I assume they are talking about the cargo or ballasting tank vents.

Q. Could you give us a guess: would these vents have been damaged, would they have been opened . . . what circumstances could have existed that created a problem?
I have been trying to figure that out for seven days. I really don't know, if it was the case, how they came off or broke off or whatever happened. I really don't know.

Q. Could it have been possible that these vents could have been sheared off under certain rough sea conditions?
I can't imagine the sea doing that.

Q. They are sturdy, then?
Right.

Q. Is it possible that the caps could have been dislodged by rough sea conditions?
I can't see how it is possible.

Q. Is it possible that they could have been left open while the vessel was underway?
It is possible, but the cap would still be on. It could have been open, but the cap would have been on, which would not permit much water to get in.

RICHARD FELDTZ

Q. The reports that we have or the testimony before this board indicates that Captain McSorley indicated that he had lost some vents, that the fence rail either laid over or [was] damaged and he was developing a list and he had his pumps on. Given those facts, what could have caused the list in your estimation?

I question very much that they came from the vents, sir. They are 8-inch vents, and if they say two of them were missing, I would have to assume that they were two adjacent vents, which is a vent from, say, the after end of one hold and the forward end of the other. I can't see, if he is going to lose twenty vents, that he would lose one within 2 feet of the other and lose the other one on the other side of the tank in some manner.

The white-capped vent covers can be seen next to the fence rails on the spar deck of the Fitzgerald *in this photograph from 1974. The Marine Board considered the possibility that a wave or flying object could have knocked one of the vent covers off, allowing water to flood the ballast tanks.*

Kenneth Thro Collection, Lake Superior Maritime Collections, University of Wisconsin–Superior.

So, I would assume, from what I have heard in past testimony, that he would lose two vents, one in each tank. It is hard to believe that those 8-inch vents, which have a surface area of 50 square inches, would not be able to be handled with a suction of the four pumps, each rated at 7,000 gallons per hour, and could handle it without any problems whatsoever, without even creating a list.

I really can't visualize in my mind, and I have spent a lot of sleepless nights trying to visualize this, and I can't come up with that. I keep getting in discussions with myself and contradicting myself.

BERNIE COOPER

There is a good possibility of something that was adrift in the sea would come along and slap one of those [vent covers] and take it off. This is a possibility. I can't foresee how the sea could knock one of them off, the way they are built, because they are round already and you have a natural cushion on it. It would almost be a physical impossibility for a sea to knock it off.

EDGAR M. JACOBSEN

Q. There are preliminary indications, Captain, that the fence may have been damaged. When they talk about fence, what part of the vessel are they referring to?
They are apparently referring to the wire cables that are stretched through these stanchions, as these photographs show here.

Q. Would you describe that for the record, please?
The stanchions are three-quarter or one inch by four, and they fit into sockets on the gunwale, and they have holes, two holes or three, in which a cable is stretched from one end of the ship to the other.

Q. What is the purpose of this fence, Captain?
Safety, to keep one from falling off the side. It is just like a handrail.

Q. Is this for loading and discharging and so forth?
At all times.

Q. In rough weather, would a crew member be transiting the main deck, normally?
Normally, no.

Q. How would he get from one end to the other?
From the side tunnels, which are at the main deck level. There are passageways from one end of the ship to the other.

Q. On either side of the vessel?
Right.

Q. So when they say the fence was broken, that would be the railing, that protective railing?
As you know, that is hearsay.

Q. Could a sea condition damage this fencing?
I can't figure out how it could, really.

BERNIE COOPER

A hogging situation would cause the fence rail to break.

In all the years I have been sailing, I have never known anybody to lose a fence rail in a seaway, and I have been out in some pretty good-sized seas, actually or probably bigger than these. A fence rail is a series of stanchions with three cables running through them. They are set in slots in the deck, and there is no buoyancy to them. A sea wouldn't get underneath it and lift it. It might bend them, possibly, because the stanchions are about 3 inches wide. The only solution that I can have to a fence rail breaking is—you can't break one by sagging a ship, but you would have to bend the ship, hog it up in the middle, to put such a tension on the fence rail that you would break it.

Q. Let's say something hit the fence rail. Would that cause it to break?
That is five-eighths wire rope with three strands running in through there. You might break one, but you can't conceivably think of breaking three.

Lifesaving Equipment

Was It Effective?

The Board of Investigation was extremely troubled by the fact that there had been no survivors of the accident, and that no bodies had been recovered. This was inconsistent with the two most recent accidents on the lakes, the wrecks of the *Carl D. Bradley* and the *Daniel J. Morrell*, vessels that broke apart on the surface and sank quickly. In both cases, bodies of most of the victims had been recovered, all wearing life jackets and, by all indications, all having had the time to abandon ship. In each case, four crewmen managed to climb aboard a life raft, with two surviving the *Bradley* sinking, and one surviving the *Morrell*. Lifeboats had not been deployed in either case.

In its investigation of the *Fitzgerald*, the board was interested in learning everything it could about the vessel's lifesaving equipment, as well as whether the crew underwent lifeboat drills, and, ultimately, if a lifeboat or raft could have been launched in the type of seas that were tossing the *Fitzgerald* around.

RICHARD FELDTZ

Q. Mr. Feldtz, what can you tell me about the inflatable life rafts on this vessel?
There are two twenty-five-person life rafts. One was located by the pilothouse, starboard aft, and the other one was located by the afterside of the poop deck or boat deck and after stern, astern of the vessel behind the hull structure. . . . They are both identical. The launching mechanisms

are float-free stanchions, and there is a regulation in the Federal Register or the Coast Guard requirement—we did away with or replaced these float-free stanchions from the hydrostatically released devices, and this was approved by the U.S. Coast Guard at that time.

NORMAN LEMLEY *Chief of Survival Systems Branch, Coast Guard*

Q. What do your duties as Chief of the Survival Systems Branch encompass?
Basically to direct the Coast Guard approval for lifesaving and fire protection equipment, from the commercial vessel program and the boating safety program.

Q. Could you tell us what the present requirements for primary lifesaving equipment were for the SS Edmund Fitzgerald?
Currently required is 200 percent lifesaving appliance or primary lifesaving appliance, 100 percent of which is in lifeboats. The other 100 percent is in inflatable life rafts that float free.

We have indicated to the Ninth Coast Guard District and various shipbuilding concerns that under the equivalency provisions of the regulations we would permit 100 percent davit launch inflatable life rafts on each side, plus a motorized rescue boat that could be easily and quickly launched for man-overboard situations as a substitute for required light boatage.

Q. Do you have any feel, or has your research indicated how long it would take to launch a boat from a vessel such as the Fitzgerald?
We did an evaluation on the *Vhores,* an ore carrier, and the *Vhores* had a slide evacuation system similar to an aircraft slide system. It had problems, but it shows that the ideas are feasible, and Canada is looking at it for passenger vessel escape systems in Vancouver.

The other one was the davit launch inflatable raft, which we did an actual exercise, and the other was existing lifeboat systems, the *Frantz,* Manila Falls, but it did about ten minutes in an actual trial from start of the alarm until the boat was ready, and that was on a perfect calm day.

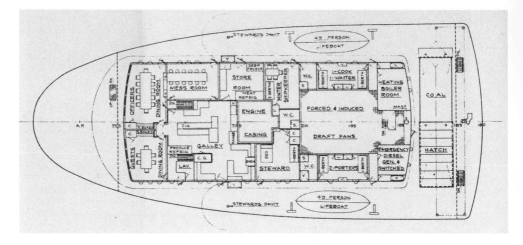

This detailed view of the deck plans shows the positions of the two lifeboats on either side of the aft cabin housing. An inflatable life raft was located behind the pilothouse on the forward side of the vessel. Historical Collections of the Great Lakes, Center for Archival Collections, Bowling Green State University.

Q. What vessel was this on?
The *Joseph Frantz.*

Q. Do you have any feel, or do you have any information concerning time to launch in a seaway?
In good weather, it could be ten to fifteen minutes, assuming everything worked right, but it could extend, I am sure, depending on the weather and time of day [or] night; so the absolute minimum of ten minutes, if everything works perfect, and this parent system would require someone to stay on board or the whole group to crawl down. So the time is varied, but it takes quite a bit of time.

CHESTER WALTER *Hull Inspector, Coast Guard*

The last time I was on board the *Fitzgerald* was on the 19th of March of this year [1975], and that was to conduct part of the annual inspection for certification. . . . I inspected the life jackets on the vessel, the ring buoys and the water lights for the green buoys, the fire axes and all the flares and the Very pistols. I looked at the two boxes on the boat deck used to store the life jackets that were kept back there.

There were a total of ninety-five [life jackets] when I went on board. Some of them were kapok-filled life jackets, and some were the old cork type. I rejected six life jackets. A couple of the jackets had been torn severely where the fabric is worn over the wearer's shoulder. These were cork jackets, I believe.

Q. You indicated that vessel was fitted with some carbide lights.
Do you recall how many carbide lights were attached to the life rings?
No, sir.

Q. What kind of an inspection did you perform on the carbide
water lights?
On the carbide water lights, I examined all the seams to see if there were any obvious discrepancies, and I would look at the pin on both ends of the water light, and I also would shake the water light to see if the

This official U.S. Coast Guard photograph showing life vests that had been stamped and cleared for service in April 1969 is one of the most haunting images related to the Fitzgerald's *sinking.* Frederick Stonehouse Collection.

carbide gave any indication that water had entered the light. If the light gave off a dull sound when shaken, like there were a large number of semi-soft objects in it, that would indicate to me that water had entered the light.

Q. If they were not good, what would have been your procedure?
If they were carbide water lights, I would have them destroyed and removed from the vessel.

Q. Did you write a requirement for any change aboard the Fitzgerald?
I did not write a requirement, but I indicated in the book that the vessel needed two more water lights. As I recall there were two water lights or more which were condemned.

Q. What was your entry read for that inspection visit: would you read that into the record, please?
"Toledo, 12 March 1975. Boarded vessel to continue inspection. Stamped eighty-nine life jackets, rejected six. Vessel needs two more ring buoy water lights and two ring buoys with line. All fire axes and flares and Very pistols for boats were okay. Inspection to continue," and then I signed my name.

PETER PULCER

We had two lifeboats and inflated life rafts on each end, and all your ring buoys. You always had your life jackets in every room. To meet the inspections and specifications, everything was right up to date.

NORMAN LEMLEY

Q. In talking about the Fitzgerald, *are you familiar with what type of davits the* Fitzgerald *had?*
Mechanical. They had wire, a hand-cranking device. The difference, I think, may have made it faster, but I would guess the time—the difference primarily would be that it had wire falls, and that should make it a quicker operation and a more simple operation as opposed to a manual operation, but I wouldn't guess that the time would be significantly different. They used the whole system starting with the alarm. A

lot of times the problem is not necessarily the equipment, but general familiarization.

The problem would be, in that type of weather, an open boat would be a problem no matter how you launch it.

RICHARD ORGEL

Even if they had time, trying to launch lifeboats in those sea conditions, it would be almost impossible. When you break your boat loose from its lashings, she goes all over the place. . . . You want to remember now that the only people familiar at all with those lifeboats are a couple of AB's and the mates. . . . Then, with that type of equipment, you can imagine what it is like in a 25-foot sea.

All these lifeboat drills and all this is always done on a nice sunny day in daylight in a harbor. It is a long way from the real thing. . . . I think all of these ships have had boat and fire drills while they are under way, but they are not going to put the boat in the water.

ANDREW RAJNER

[On abandoning ship and why no bodies had been recovered]: The only thing I can say, sir, was that they were all trapped. Because she certainly had enough lifesaving equipment on board her, as far as life jackets were concerned and life rings and buoys. She was well equipped as far as lifesaving equipment and everything.

Q. Do you think, given those circumstances, that you could have launched the lifeboats on the **Fitzgerald?**
That would be really tough, I think. The seas would be coming up on the boat all the way up to the boat deck.

MORGAN CLARK

With the seas that we had, I would say it was impossible to get a lifeboat off. Your only chance would have been inflating a life raft and trying to get in. I would say you couldn't throw one over the side to inflate it with the idea of getting in it after you got in the water. Myself, I think you would have had to take the chance of inflating it at some spot in the

*November gale-force winds were strong enough to rip apart
the* Fitzgerald's *lifeboats. Coast Guard investigators found that the
bow of lifeboat No. 2 was split down the middle.* Kenneth Thro Collection,
Lake Superior Maritime Collections, University of Wisconsin–Superior.

position that it was in and just taking a chance of riding it off, because
the waves were so big, if you threw the raft over and tried to get in the
raft, it might be 2,000 feet away from you by the time you decided that
you were going to jump into it.

ROBERT MAY

When you are out there, the ship is rocking. I think it would be impossible to launch a lifeboat, and this new setup, the inflatable raft, they are
closed, and again, I think in my opinion, and I think I said this: you had
a better chance.

   If you could, where the lifeboats are fixed, have a platform with those inflatable rafts where they would inflate, you could inflate them and stay, go down with the ship, and come back up. I think that would be safer than trying to launch a lifeboat under heavy seas.

BERNIE COOPER

In rough weather, I don't think I would attempt to launch one [lifeboat]. In the first place, the way the lifeboats are set up, they would be extremely dangerous in any kind of seaway. You would have to be lucky. With ours, maybe it would be a little quicker and easier because we do have the one in the bottom. We can release both at the same time, but even when it got into the water, if there was any sea running, I am sure it would be slamming into the superstructure of your ship. I don't know. I just somehow or another, I guess I have lost faith in lifeboats because of all the times I can remember, and all the casualties I have read about on the Great Lakes, any time there has been a seaway, that particular boat in trouble has never been able to get a [life]boat off.

Q. What would you use in an emergency then?
If I was one of the gang and if I heard the lifeboat drill, I think I would run for the nearest life raft and inflate it on deck and let it sink under me.

THOMAS GARCIA

I think it would be impossible to launch a lifeboat in rough weather. I don't think I would go for the lifeboat. I would go for the life raft behind the pilothouse. I would inflate it there on the deck behind the pilothouse.

Q. If you had to get off the Fitzgerald, *how would you do it? What piece of equipment would you want to use?*
The life raft, sir.

Q. Why?
It is more safe, and you are protected by it. You have a canopy. It encloses you, and you zip it up, and the water and wind won't get to your body.

RICHARD FELDTZ

Q. Does the company have any instructions on lifeboat drills?
The Coast Guard has instructions, sir, and I believe they say they should
be conducted once a week and logged in the logbook.

WILLIAM R. PAUL

Q. As you know or may not know, Mr. Paul, on the Fitzgerald,
*the boats are now at the Soo. They have been recovered, one boat
intact and the other, the half boat has been recovered. And the
question of the condition of the boats is very important. Can you
give us any indication or idea of how you inspected the lifeboats,
the hull structure, and what you did? Are they fitted with air tanks,
and if so, how did you test those?*
Yes, sir, generally the initial inspection is done in the fall layup to see if
there are any repairs, to see they are taken care of prior to fitting out in
the spring.

The final inspection prior to the vessel fitting up and getting underway, it's examined again physically to make sure the equipment is there,
make sure something else hasn't happened and if there are any other
requirements, making sure they have been taken care of. I might check the
equipment again, spot-check it to make sure that things are as indicated
previously. Then you have your weight test if it's indicated, your boat drill.

Q. Did you hold a boat drill on the Fitzgerald?
Yes, sir.

Q. What date did you hold it?
I think it was on the 9th of April, 1975.

Q. Which boat or boats did you launch, if any?
No. 1 boat.

Q. Is there an indication that the crew went to the boat and—
I made an entry, the number of the crew exercising in boat, eight.

Q. How many?
Eight.

Q. Eight.
No. 2 boat being on dockside wasn't lowered to the water but swung out.

Q. Did you personally witness the launching of No. 1 boat?
Yes, sir.

Q. Did you have a chance—who launched? Who was actually launching the boat? Do you recall what ship's officer did this?
I don't recall if the second mate or the third mate, one of the two, because I think the chief was in charge of the operation, or first mate.

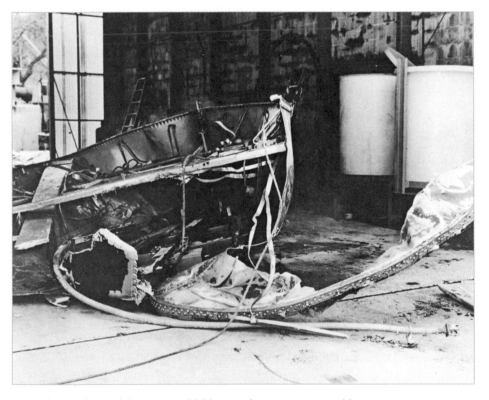

The wreckage of the recovered lifeboats, almost unrecognizable after the storm, was brought to the Coast Guard field office at Sault Ste. Marie, where the condition of the lifeboats was thoroughly documented by investigators. Kenneth Thro Collection, Lake Superior Maritime Collections, University of Wisconsin–Superior.

Q. During the course of the drill did you participate in any way?
Were you an observer or how did that work out?
I sometimes participate, you know, talk to people, ask them questions and so forth.

Q. But in the actual—
Observing the boat drill and seeing if it's resting properly.

Q. Do you recall how long it may have taken to launch this boat?
Well, I—generally they take it fairly loose as a rule, they aren't underway I don't think with any speed involved.

Q. Speed is not the objective, is that the idea?
No, sir.

Q. Did the swing out method by which the crew launched the boat;
does it show that they were familiar with their duties? Is that your
recollection?
Yes. I recollect that; yes, sir. They have done more than one drill before. If they haven't, it is not proper.

Q. If it is unsatisfactory, you hold it again?
Yes, sir.

Q. That was unnecessary for the Fitzgerald?
I made no entry to that effect. I don't think—I don't recall anything of that nature.

Q. If I understand the entry correctly then, the Fitzgerald *had a crew*
of twenty-nine, and eight were exercised at oars at this particular drill?
Yes, sir.

Q. On the inflatable life rafts, there were two aboard, and the procedure
was that they were inspected in Cleveland and you satisfied yourself.
How about the stowage of those? Did they have a float-free arrange-
ment, or were they arranged with hydrostatic release? Do you recall?
I don't recall specifically, but I know which is which. I don't recall which type they had on this vessel, but I would make sure that the painter was attached to make sure they would operate automatically, if they were required to.

Q. Ring buoys: there were a lot of ring buoys on the Fitzgerald, *is that right? How many ring buoys does she require?*
Twenty-four ring life buoys.

Q. Twenty-four ring life buoys. How many of those would be fitted with lights, if any?
Let's see—at least—

Q. Would there be an indication in your inspection book?
I think it is in the inspection book, yes, sir.

Q. Okay, here you are. (hands book to witness)
In the entry here it states that, two—this is my writing, but I think what I meant to say was a need for two more water lights and lines and two ring buoys.

Q. Do you know if there was a requirement for this?
I believe this was on the work list. Since the vessel wasn't underway, a requirement wasn't really indicated, and this would have been something I would be sure was completed prior to departure.

Q. How would you be sure?
Visually inspect it.

JOHN LARSON

Q. How often did you have lifeboat drills on the Fitzgerald?
Geez, I know when [Pulcer] was there we had them maybe every five days, and McSorley was very lenient on it. We didn't have them very often.

One offshoot of the discussion about lifeboats and rafts was the question: What would happen to any crew member who found himself either in the water or on a raft in heavy seas? One new area of study was the survival suit, which was being designed to protect the wearer at least minimally from hypothermia.

NORMAN LEMLEY

There is no current requirement [for exposure suits], but there have been studies, and there are continuing studies as part of the Great Lakes program. A study was done on the analysis of exposure suits, a method of evaluating exposure suits, and the process was that they purchased several of them. Cranked into the actual problem of exposure suits was the maintenance and the whole problem of activity coming from aboard the ship. At that time those that were commercially available didn't meet the requirements that you would even need to have a minimum requirement and make it a meaningful requirement. The tool is there to evaluate suits. As part of the study that has just begun, on hypothermia, we have funded the University of Victoria, Dr. [John S.] Hayward to look into hypothermia and what areas of the body are most sensitive to cold. He has already been doing work on it. He is one of the experts in the world. We have with the Navy a contract to develop a suit, a potential suit, to see whether it would be useful. That contract should near completion the first of this year where a suit then would be evaluated. It is along the lines of the Canadian suit. There are manufacturers in this country that are making suits that surely would be useful to have. They may or may not be good enough that you could put a Federal requirement on it to say that it is justified requiring it, but it would be good advice to say that if you are going to be involved in very, very cold weather, it would be good to have a course on it.

What Happened?

The Experts Weigh In

WILLIAM R. PAUL

*Q. We have a ship with twenty-nine people and a certificated vessel
in compliance with the regulations, according to your testimony,
except for one item, and it was fully in compliance with the regulations.
It is lost. We recover all lifesaving equipment or at least in some condition, and we save all the lifeboats and the life rafts, many life jackets,
and yet we don't save one soul or don't recover any bodies, and no one
wearing a life jacket. Given these facts, what is your opinion?*
I don't really think I can come up with that, Captain. I really don't know.
I don't think anything I could offer would add anything to this investigation. I have really no idea.

Q. Well—
I could speculate like anybody else, but I don't know.

*Q. I think you have a lot to offer this investigation. I disagree,
Mr. Paul. You were the last inspector at the last Coast Guard annual
inspection. You looked at these things and reported entries in your
books, and you looked at it personally, subject to recollection, which
I am not going to fault you for not remembering exact details because
there were many, many items that you looked at. But I feel that you
do have something to offer this investigation, and I would like you
to think on it a minute and give me your best opinion of why no one
was saved or no bodies were recovered.*

Well, I would have to assume that all of the bodies, I mean all of the personnel involved, were inside the fore or the aft end. I would have to also assume that the hatches were dogged.

Q. Trapped inside?
I would assume that whatever happened, happened in a hurry, and it was probably too rough to be outside. Even if they had an indication of an impending failure or something, it would be pretty hard to be outside on the weather deck. That is my best idea of whatever happened.

Q. Whatever happened, happened very suddenly.
The personnel were inside the cabins and the bridge and the after compartments.

RICHARD FELDTZ

Q. What do you think could have gone wrong?
Well, I'll tell you, sir. It is my opinion and in the evaluation of the different items that have been presented, going through the process of elimination of events and what have you, it does appear to me in my opinion that the vessel had struck an object. I don't know if it hit the bottom or something close to the bottom. It had to be something fixed causing damage to the lower part of the bilge, which is indicated on the drawing as a riveted connection. It could have possibly opened up the tank or two tanks, and it was in the way of a division bulkhead. This has happened, ripping—unfortunately I haven't gotten into talking with anyone who knew or knows, and I do not actually know what the bottom configuration is in that area of a possible shoal that hasn't been spoken of. It could have gone through there like a surge and ripped a hole. The tanks would have definitely flooded, and [that] would create the list that we are speaking of. [He] would more naturally [have] lost his buoyancy in that side tank or, say, the side tanks or possibly even more, which would then really take away from his upriding buoyancy or his upriding momentum and put him in a listed condition, which would create a slow response to a roll.

This is the thing that has been going through my mind in trying to visualize this. So taking that into consideration and the possibility of the vessel rolling, in that area, of course, from what I have gathered the rolls of the seas become closer, and it could have been hit with another sea while he was in his roll and was responding to a slow response of slow upriding movement due to his lack of upriding stability.

The tension area that was put on there from compression into this hole, or ripped or severed area, caused him to roll, which I can satisfy in my mind [is] why the crew never made it at least off of the vessel. There were no bodies found, no life jackets. The pilothouse had to be pretty well struck by water. The sounding buoy that was located on the aft part of the pilothouse was screwed to the marine bulkhead. The two screws, as you saw yesterday, were in this sounding board. This board was located on the after side of the pilothouse. So I do feel strongly that in my mind, on trying to evaluate this, and I am sure [that] I as well as our company wants to know more than anyone, as much as the board here, as to what just did happen, and this is what I would come up with.

The vessel rolled, at which time this area had begun to open up to an extent that caused her to sink or to begin to roll and not respond to her upriding stability or her lack of upriding stability with a starboard roll, assuming that that was the way she was listing. [She] then went over, possibly sideways or upside down, and then with the high shift or cargo, which would then put this area, which as we all realize was a very critical area, and that is why it is riveted—

Q. The bilge area?
The bilge area, the low bilge area, and with the transfer from the metric center of the buoyancy, it was a transfer of the center weight of the cargo to the top of the vessel, increasing the high stressed area in this area here, which would cause it to fracture or open up.

Q. I thought you said something about transfer of the metric center.
That is my own personal opinion.

Q. Do you think she capsized?
I do feel, yes, she capsized. This is my personal opinion of trying to evaluate it. Like I say, as was brought out, I am responsible for the structure

The Great Lakes Engineering Works hull plate for the Edmund Fitzgerald, *circa 1970. Throughout the hearings several witnesses testified that the* Fitz *was among the best boats in the fleet.* Courtesy of Great Lakes Shipwreck Museum.

of a vessel, and I do want to try to find out what possibly could have happened to the best vessel we had. In fact, up to a number of years, I would have considered it the best vessel on the Lakes. I have always said she was the last of the best-built boats, but this is what I think happened.

It has been indicated, and I was aboard the vessel at the sonar investigation, and it appears that there were two objects that were found in two pieces. "Can we assume she is in two pieces?" indicates my point. Is she broken? Did she break while in a roll while she was sinking? I really don't know, sir.

RICHARD STEARN

Q. We have a very tragic accident. We have lost twenty-nine people. The circumstances, as the board has developed them from the testimony, is that the vessel was underway, at sea, in seas of 20 to 30 feet high, the winds anywhere 50, 60, 70 knots, the master, sometime before the vessel was lost, notified another vessel that they had lost a couple of vent covers, was taking on water, was pumping the water, and that the vessel was developing a list. We have recovered the lifeboats, in some condition. We have recovered the life rafts and many jackets, life jackets, but we haven't recovered any survivors or any victims. Given these circumstances, I wonder if you could venture an opinion for the board as to what may have happened?

Well, number one, I am sure it was a sudden happening. The evidence all points to something that happened very fast. I can't believe that an open vent . . . even two or more vents, I don't think would create an influx of water situation that would be any hazard whatsoever. If there was a list, it must have been from a fracture in the hull caused by grounding or other means.

I can hardly believe that a fracture of the hull, a sudden breaking, would cause a sinking. It would be so fast that you would not get any radio message or at least attempt to get a couple of people aboard lifesaving equipment. I just can't think that would happen unless there was a simultaneous capsizing.

Q. Well, you are aware of the vessel's subdivision. You have worked with the vessel, and given the vessel's subdivision, let's assume she did break in two: how long do you think the ends would remain afloat, given the subdivision in a loaded condition?

I would think it should be at least a matter of five to ten minutes because her ballasts are intact unless, as I say, there is a fracture well down the side. On the other hand, if there is a capsizing caused by, let's say, a combination of free water, initial list, and possibly a cargo shift caused by the listing, and maybe in association with a large wave, a capsizing would blow the covers, the hatch covers, and create a very sudden sinking situation and put everybody in a position where they couldn't get out of the cabins.

Coast Guard naval architect William Cleary's testimony indicates how intense (and borderline testy) the questioning could be. The usual protocol for questioning was one board member at a time. This was not the case with Cleary.

WILLIAM CLEARY

Q. Mr. Cleary, we have here a fully loaded ship going along in a very bad storm, reported 20 feet on up to 21 to 27 feet, winds blowing 50 to 70 knots is what witnesses testified to. We have 29 people aboard. The vessel has apparently been lost. The major concern is the fact that we found the lifeboats, damaged, but nevertheless, we found the lifeboats, life rafts, many life rafts, life rings, but we have not recovered any survivors or any victims as a result of this casualty. Given these facts, could you give us any idea or opinion as to what might have gone wrong?

Captain, the information that I have had coming here today, it consists mostly of what I either heard on the radio or read in the newspaper, and I have heard that there was a list on the vessel in one newspaper, that the hatch cover might have come loose, or a vent might have come loose. I believe all three of those were reported in newspapers, anyway. Whether these are true or not is yet to be seen. Taking those three instances, if a hatch cover did come loose in a storm like that, the entire cargo hold would fill with water after a matter of time.

THOMAS O. MURPHY *Attorney, Oglebay Norton*

Based on the hypothetical question, Mr. Chairman, that was propounded by the questioner, there is no indication or any evidence, either before this hearing or anywhere else, that there has ever been any loss, or reported loss of a hatch cover. There was one news broadcast where the girl who was making the broadcast misinterpreted the report of the loss of the two vents to a loss of a hatch cover, but that is the only place to my knowledge that has been heard, and this hypothetical question that was placed by Captain Zabinski does not include that assumption. For that reason, I object to any such opinion going into this record on that basis.

ADAM ZABINSKI

I pose the question.

W. W. BARROW

I think just for the record that the customary question we have been asking the witnesses has been generally that the vessel has gone down, it's gone down without recovery of inflatables, without recovery of people, but with life jackets, but with lifeboats, life rafts, and no people, no bodies, and I think at this point we have asked generally is the experience of the people who are testifying what went wrong, and I think—may we state it in [those] terms?

CAPTAIN ZABINSKI

That is fine.

W. W. BARROW

Is that satisfactory?

THOMAS O. MURPHY

That's satisfactory with me as long as it's not one of the assumptions that the witness is making from the question that the questioner was putting.

W. W. BARROW

Go ahead, Mr. Cleary.

WILLIAM CLEARY

Yes, sir. From the way you have restated it, Admiral, I think the first assumption that must be made is that the tragedy occurred very suddenly. As to what the tragedy was, I can think of two possibilities: One is a capsizing, and the other is a breaking in half, which would destroy all power on the vessel and probably sink in a matter of seconds and people would not have the opportunity to get out.

I consider the possibility of capsizing to be much less of a possibility than the possibility of a structural failure.

From what I have heard of the sea state and the actions of the other vessels in that storm, I find it hard to believe that a structural—that some single wave that came along, that the stress to the hold girder was to the extent it failed unless there was some weak spot which was undetected by either the ship's crew or the inspectors from either the Bureau or ourselves.

Beyond that, I think it's getting into real guesswork.

ADAM ZABINSKI

What about the degrees of water you indicated previously?

WILLIAM CLEARY

In the ballast tank? While that would cause a list, it would not cause structural problems which may lead to structural failure.

THOMAS O. MURPHY

Mr. Cleary, there also has been some indication in the testimony here and at least a suggestion that this vessel passed very close to some shoal areas, one as shallow as 6 fathoms, which then also raises the possibility of a grounding. Would you not have to then include that possibility, with that information, in your opinion as to one of the potential causes as long as it's based solely on speculation?

WILLIAM CLEARY

Yes, sir, I would have to include that as a possibility.

W. W. BARROW

Mr. Cleary, that does raise another point I think we have discussed with other witnesses, and that would be the impact on the hull structure of a vessel such as the *Fitzgerald* passing within very close proximity to the bottom. Would you talk about that for a few minutes?

WILLIAM CLEARY

Yes, sir. The point that comes immediately to mind is the scope of—is the wide scope of possible damage and the reaction in the ship's girder. If it were just a glancing blow, it might turn out to be something that might not cause any problem for a while. This could be—well, let's say that the ship passed the edge of a reef and some part of the bilge were exposed instantaneously or hit, whether it was grounding, and that would open up a ballast tank and cause the list, and it might take several minutes or perhaps a little longer, depending on degree of the hit, to fill that ballast tank.

If the ship grounded even instantaneously along the keel, either at the bow or the stern, with all of the dynamic heaving up and in and out and up and down of the seaway, having its own speed involved, I would consider it would fracture right then and there and leave it on or next to that reef.

I don't know where to go from there, Admiral.

W. W. BARROW

With a situation where the vessel did not actually strike but [did] come very close to the bottom, 6 inches or so, would this create a stress problem for the hull structure?

WILLIAM CLEARY

In two or three minutes' thinking, one thinks of all sorts of things.

I think what that would—let's say it came over a sandbar instead of a reef and came close to the bottom. If there was an instantaneously hydrodynamic pressure right directly underneath the ship while it was in, let's say, a sagged condition, there is a possibility of either opening up a seam or some local damage somewhere, which would fill at a rather slow rate.

If that—you have to make one assumption right on top of another— this occurred [in] only one area and then this filled a ballast tank which caused a list, which caused problems, whatever time it was—

W. W. BARROW

I guess the next question would be whether or not you would consider this to be a good possibility of a sudden increase in hydrodynamic pressure in a situation such as that.

WILIAM CLEARY

Along with that, would it be enough to break open a seam? I really don't know, Admiral.

ADAM ZABINSKI

Would there be any additional vibration experienced by a vessel passing over shoal water, hull vibrational forces?

WILLIAM CLEARY

This is known to occur, Captain. It's one of the sources of springing, although not a significant source of high springing, but we have had masters tell us their ships spring in the Saint Marais River when they get in very shallow waters. We can probably say it's not waves but pressure differential underneath the ship.

ADAM ZABINSKI

Would this be a continuous vibration or just a one-shot deal in your estimation?

WILLIAM CLEARY

If it were going on the shoal area, being carried over a wave, or two or three series of waves, I would expect it to be more in the nature of a one-shot, although it takes vessels two or three waves to get over the shoal. It might be two or three simple shots which would cause an introduction of vibratory stress into the ship's girders, and this might be a shocking or slamming stress, although it's not exactly the same thing, that type of stress decays, the shock stress which decays very quickly.

Final
Remarks

W. W. BARROW

At this specific time, we have no knowledge of witnesses who are apparent to us and whose testimony would be useful to this board.

I would like to announce for the record, however, that I have requested the Commandant U.S. Coast Guard Authority, and prior to opening this opening session, to conduct an underwater visual survey of the *Edmund Fitzgerald.* I have not received a formal agreement to that. I have orally been advised by the Commandant that my request for that was approved. This survey is tentatively scheduled for April the 15th, 1976, or thereabouts, depending upon the weather. The underwater survey is to be conducted with an unmanned television and still camera-equipped submersible vehicle, called CURV III. It is owned by the U.S. Navy and it will be leased by us to be flown into the area from San Diego.

In arriving at our decision to delay the underwater visual survey, we considered very carefully the typical weather which is available in the eastern Lake Superior and the ice conditions, and these were the primary considerations in waiting until spring to conduct the survey.

I might point out that the survey that we have in mind is one which cannot be accomplished in a single day or two days. It is a rather detailed survey that we have in mind, and that may [be] very difficult to accomplish during midwinter season.

Between now and April, members of the board are going to review and conduct a detailed analysis of the evidence and the testimony which we have received thus far. One member of the board is scheduled next week to ride a Great Lakes ore carrier as an observer for the end of this shipping season. The remainder of the board members will also ride ore carriers between now and the time that the underwater visual survey is accomplished.

We also intend to ask for soundings to be taken between Caribou Island and Michipicoten Island and eastern Lake Superior.

One additional matter that I might ask at this point is that we certainly at this time have indicated that we have talked to all of the witnesses who are apparent to us at this time, and we are always open to any indication of additional witnesses who may appear or may become apparent by a review of the testimony that we have, and that anyone having information which is pertinent to this board should contact the Chairman or the Marine Board of Investigation, to the Commissioner Ninth Coast Station.

Postscript

The Board of Investigation felt no obligation to rush the release of its report on its findings, not with nearly six months' wait for the first opportunity to positively identify the discovered wreckage as the *Edmund Fitzgerald* and explore it with a cable-controlled underwater research vehicle (CURV). There was no telling what the CURV III television and 35mm camera might determine. In addition, new soundings planned for the Caribou and Michipicoten Islands might reveal previously uncharted shallows the *Fitzgerald* might have passed over.

This was not a time for avoidable educated guesses on the part of the Coast Guard. Lawsuits were inevitable, and the hearings had been attended by attorneys representing the victims' families, those testifying at the hearings, and various commercial interests, all listening carefully for information that might prove to be useful in legal proceedings. Bernie Cooper's attorney might have been the norm when he advised Cooper to avoid any kind of conjecture and testify solely on what he knew for certain.

On May 20, 1976, just over six months after the loss of the *Edmund Fitzgerald,* the CURV III was lowered into the frigid Lake Superior water. The Coast Guard cutter *Woodrush,* a vessel involved in the initial search for *Fitzgerald* wreckage and survivors, later deployed to search for the wreckage, commanded by Captain Jimmy Hobaugh, had no difficulty in conducting a side-scan sonar search and locating the wreckage. The *Woodrush,* modified to accommodate the CURV's requirements, served as the command post vessel. Admiral Barrow from the Board of Investigation was on board to witness the exploration of the wreckage.

*The Coast Guard leased the unmanned submersible CURV III
from the U.S. Navy for use in locating and documenting the wreck.
The craft was lowered into Lake Superior from the* Woodrush *on
May 20, 1976.* Courtesy of the U.S. Naval Undersea Museum in Keyport, Washington.

The CURV III found the wreckage in the dark, murky water and worked its way around one massive section until, to the surprise of those aboard the *Woodrush,* the camera revealed the section to be the stern portion, upside down in the depths of Lake Superior, with the words "Edmund Fitzgerald" and "Milwaukee" inverted to the camera's eye. The positive identification of the wreckage left the Coast Guard explorers with conflicting emotions: the elation of the determination that the wreckage was indeed the *Fitzgerald* was offset by the depressing sight of the incredible damage to the freighter and the knowledge that most, if not all, of the *Fitzgerald's* twenty-nine crew members were probably entombed in the wreckage.

Evidence of the *Fitzgerald*'s violent last moments cluttered the area. Hatch covers, broken loose during the sinking, lay around the wreckage. Tons of taconite were scattered throughout the area. The *Fitzgerald* had gouged the floor of Lake Superior as she plowed ahead before coming to a stop. The bow portion, terribly damaged, the pilothouse windows blown out, had come to rest in an upright position, listing slightly, deep in mud. The CURV III took hundreds of photographs—nearly nine hundred—between May 20 and May 28, and more than 43,000 feet of television footage. The images were less than perfect, and all they offered definitely were the identification of the wreckage and proof that the *Fitzgerald* was in two pieces.

The CURV III measured the two sections. The bow measured 276 feet, and the stern 258 feet, leaving almost exactly 200 feet of the *Fitzgerald*'s midsection unaccounted for. The Marine Board reasoned that the missing portion broke off when the bow struck bottom at tremendous

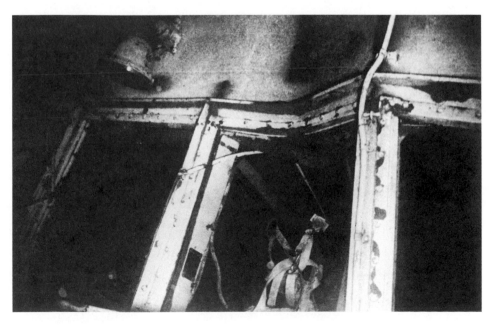

The shattered windows and twisted metal framing of the pilothouse as captured by the camera on CURV III in May 1976. Copyright 1976 The Associated Press.

force while the stern, still operating under its own power, was still near or at the surface. It added up. The *Fitzgerald*, at 529 feet, came to rest in 530 feet of water, leaving 200 feet of its midsection with nowhere to go. The board rejected its earlier belief that the *Fitzgerald* had probably split on the surface. The question now was what caused it to sink.

The board debated the possibilities. Its members already knew that the *Fitz* was filling with water, but had it been to such an extent that she lost her freeboard? If one could judge by Captain McSorley's final conversation with Morgan Clark just minutes before the *Fitzgerald* disappeared from the *Anderson*'s radar, McSorley didn't think so. Had the cargo hold, instead of or in addition to the ballast tanks, filled with water? With no way of taking an accurate sounding in the stormy weather conditions, there was no way of telling. If it had, the water, along with the taconite pellets, would have placed the *Fitzgerald* in grave peril of capsizing if hit by a gigantic rogue wave. And since the *Fitzgerald* was being punished by a following sea that entered in the stern and rolled up the spar deck, there was good reason to believe that the seas pounding the back of the pilothouse might have ripped away a hatch cover or two, or pushed the bow beneath the surface, initiating a dive from which the *Fitzgerald* could not recover.

The board's report, released on July 26, 1977, immediately fired up a controversy. After intense discussion and disagreement, the board decided to stand behind the theory that the *Edmund Fitzgerald* had lost buoyancy after flooding water entered the cargo hold through the hatch covers. The vessel had plunged so suddenly that no one had been able to escape. The *Fitz* broke in two either on the way down or when her bow plowed into the lake floor.

The controversy gathered more fuel when the National Transportation Safety Board rejected the Coast Guard's findings. David E. Trimble, president of the Lake Carriers' Association, had written a letter of dissent to the NTSB arguing against the Marine Board's conclusion. It was more likely, Trimble asserted, that the *Fitzgerald* had ground somewhere near the Six Fathom Shoal, ruptured hull plates, and lost buoyancy when her pumps were unable to pump out water faster than it was boarding the freighter. The NTSB took Trimble's views under advisement, but after poring over the evidence and the Coast Guard report, issued its own findings on May 4, 1978. The NTSB endorsed the Marine Board's conclusion that the *Fitzgerald*'s cargo hold had filled from massive topside flooding, rather than water entering the *Fitzgerald* from beneath the waterline. The Safety Board differed, however, in its assessment of *how* the water entered the cargo hold: it was more likely, the NTSB said, that the fatal flooding occurred due to the *Fitzgerald*'s losing one or more hatch covers.

The disagreement between the two authoritative bodies all but guaranteed that the *Fitzgerald* would remain one of the biggest mysteries in Great Lakes history. Gordon Lightfoot's song "The Wreck of the *Edmund Fitzgerald*," an enormously popular depiction of the *Fitzgerald*'s sinking, had already guaranteed the vessel's place in the public's memory; the Marine Board and National Transportation Safety Board reports signaled a beginning to a debate that would last for decades.

Further exploration of the wreckage was probably inevitable, though it was far from a simple matter. The *Fitzgerald* had come to rest in water too deep for casual divers or even experienced underwater explorers. Visiting the site demanded special advanced equipment. In addition, the *Fitzgerald* was just inside Canadian waters, and visiting her required permits from the government. The families of the victims were not pleased by the prospects of having anyone boarding a deepwater grave site, and Canadian officials, sympathetic to these concerns, insisted that potential explorers demonstrate good reason for visiting the wreck.

Some did. Jacques Cousteau, internationally renowned for his underwater innovations and adventures, in Canada to film a documentary on the early French explorers of the St. Lawrence River, received permission, although he did not take part in a dive to the *Fitzgerald*. His son and another seaman commanded a two-person submarine that visited the wreck on September 24, 1980. Their conclusion only stoked the continuing controversy. The *Fitzgerald*, they announced, broke apart on the surface and sank very slowly, remaining on the surface much longer than anyone had previously believed. This theory was dismissed by many of those studying the accident. The *Fitzgerald* had been equipped with battery-operated communications equipment, and personnel in the pilothouse most certainly would have transmitted a "Mayday" call if the boat had broken up and they had the opportunity.

Two additional expeditions commenced a few weeks apart in July 1994, with no new conclusions, other than an examination of the inverted stern portion indicating no damage consistent with the *Fitzgerald*'s grounding on a shoal; if a grounding had occurred, it had to have been on the bow portion, but since that section was buried in mud, no definitive exploration was possible. New photographs, taken by an unmanned vessel not unlike the CURV III, offered much clearer images of the wreckage, but no clues of what might have happened.

One of the dives stirred up a major controversy when the explorers found and photographed human remains outside the *Fitzgerald,* near the bow. To that point, no one had reported seeing any remains, including inside the pilothouse. The victims' families, tolerant of the explorers prior to the discovery, petitioned the Canadian government to declare the wreckage off-limits to further exploration.

In July 1995, nearly twenty years after the sinking of the *Edmund Fitzgerald,* a team of divers spent several days removing the *Fitzgerald*'s bell and replacing it with a new bell, into which the names of the victims were engraved. Michigan State University restored the bell to its original shiny luster, and it was placed on deposit at the Great Lakes Shipwreck Museum near Whitefish Point, Michigan, not far from where the *Fitzgerald* had come to rest.

The families of the *Fitzgerald* victims persisted in their petitioning that the Canadian government declare the wreckage a grave site off-limits to further exploration, photographing, and even locating with side-scan sonar. Canada was reluctant to do so. Underwater archaeology was a growing science. Declaring some wrecks to be off-limits to exploration had the potential of creating a slippery slope for underwater archaeologists. Would a statute of limitations be involved? If so, how long would a wreck have to exist before it could be explored? Would there be problems of ownership with older vessels? Old wrecks with remains on board had been respectfully explored—more so than ever as diving equipment evolved. These and other questions were pondered by the Canadian authorities, but they were resistant to creating laws to answer them.

Finally, in April 2005, nearly thirty years after the *Fitzgerald*'s sinking, the Ontario government amended the Ontario Heritage law that required strict licensing on dives. The amendment included side-scanning sonar, exploration by mini-subs and other submersibles, and even underwater photography. The government went one step further in January 2006, when it banned exploration of specific wrecks, including the *Edmund Fitzgerald*. Under the new law, explorations of these declared grave sites were prohibited within 500 meters of the wreckage.

The board's investigation led to important changes in the shipping industry, including changes in late-season load lines and a requirement for survival suits for each crew member aboard a vessel. The *Fitzgerald* story never slipped from memory. Bell-ringing memorials take place around the lakes every year, and the *Fitzgerald* continues to be the largest, most expensive loss in Great Lakes history. As Gordon Lightfoot sang, "the legend lives on."

III. The Documents

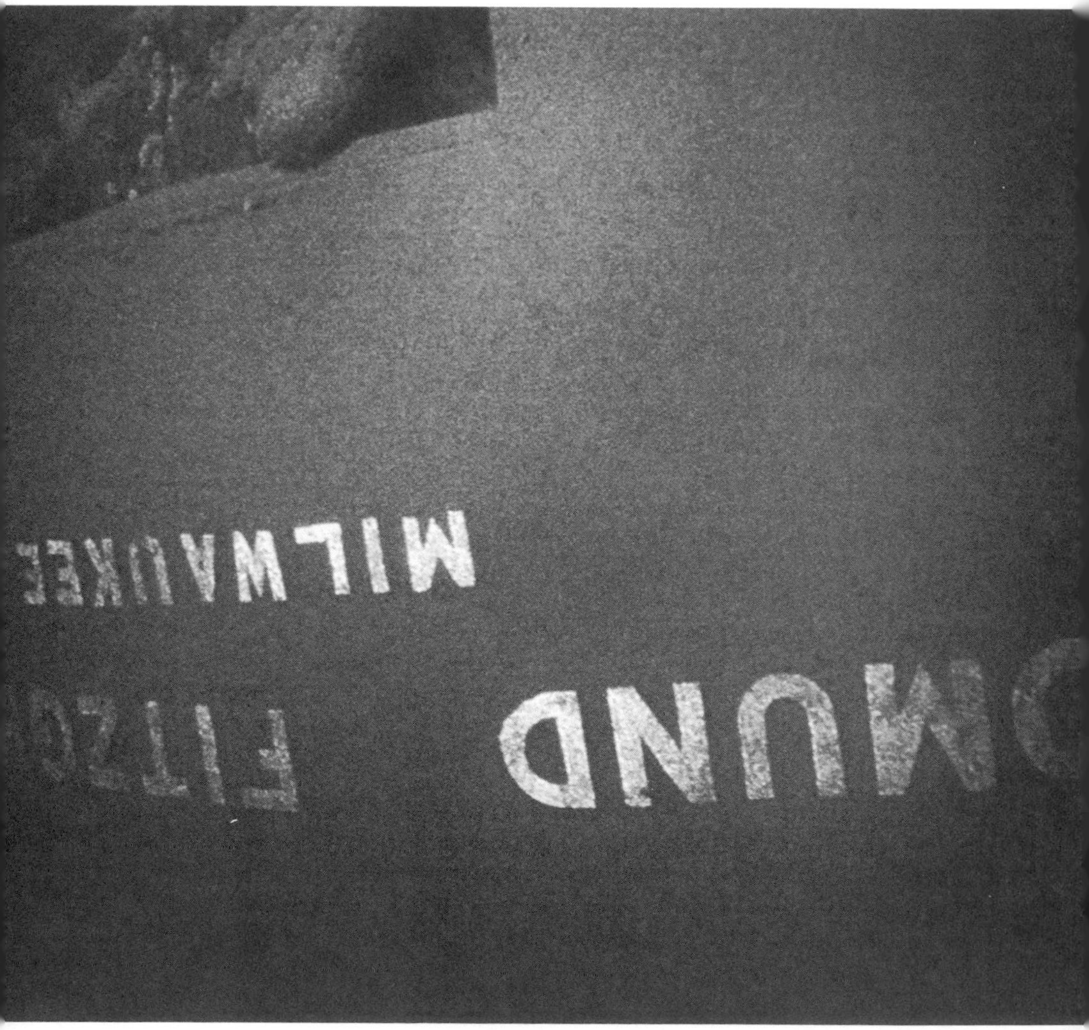
MILWAUKEE

DEPARTMENT OF TRANSPORTATION

COAST GUARD

MARINE CASUALTY REPORT

SS EDMUND FITZGERALD; SINKING IN LAKE SUPERIOR ON 10 NOVEMBER 1975 WITH LOSS OF LIFE

U.S. COAST GUARD

MARINE BOARD OF INVESTIGATION REPORT

AND

COMMANDANT'S ACTION

REPORT NO. USCG 16732/64216

DEPARTMENT OF TRANSPORTATION

UNITED STATES COAST GUARD

MAILING ADDRESS:

U. S. COAST GUARD (G-MMI/83)

400 SEVENTH STREET SW

WASHINGTON DC 205M

PHONE (202) 426–1455

26 JUL 1977

COMMANDANT'S ACTION

ON

The Marine Board of Investigation convened to investigate
the circumstances surrounding the sinking of the
SS EDMUND FITZGERALD
in Lake Superior on 10 November 1975 with loss of life.

The record of the Marine Board of Investigation convened to investigate the subject casualty has been reviewed; and the record, including the findings of fact, conclusions, and recommendations, is approved subject to the following comments.

◀ *The inverted stern of the* Edmund Fitzgerald, *photographed by divers in 1994.*

Courtesy of Great Lakes Shipwreck Museum.

REMARKS

1. This casualty presented the Board unique investigative challenges which delayed the submission of the report. Since there were no survivors or witnesses to be questioned, the Board went to considerable lengths to examine wreckage located soon after the casualty. In the spring of 1976, an underwater examination of the wreckage, utilizing highly sophisticated remotely controlled TV and photographic equipment, positively identified the wreck of the SS EDMUND FITZGERALD. The equipment was used to develop a detailed survey and photographic record of the structural damage and position of the wreckage. The sketches of the wreckage in the Board's report, showing the inverted stern section, loose hatch covers, and bow section, were made from this video tape and photographic record.

   A further delay in the completion of the final report was due to the time needed to complete the sounding survey, conducted by Canadian authorities, of the water between Michipicoten Island and Caribou Island and adjacent waters.

2. The Commandant concurs with the Board that the most probable cause of the sinking was the loss of buoyancy resulting from massive flooding of the cargo hold. This flooding most likely took place through ineffective hatch closures. As the boarding seas rolled over the spar deck, the flooding was probably concentrated forward. The vessel dove into a wall of water and never recovered, with the breaking up of the ship occurring as it plunged or as the ship struck the bottom. The sinking was so rapid and unexpected that no one was able to successfully abandon ship.

   With regard to opinions as to the causes of damage and the final sequence of events, an analysis has been made which demonstrates a possibility of capsizing and/or foundering. The analysis of various stages of flooding indicates that bending moment magnitudes and distribution would not support a conclusion of general structural failure as a primary cause of the casualty.

ACTION CONCERNING THE RECOMMENDATIONS

1. The following Board recommendations relate to load line regulations and weathertight integrity and are addressed jointly.

   Recommendation 1: That Part 45 of Title 46 of the United States Code of Federal Regulations (Great Lakes Load Lines) be amended immediately to rescind the reduction in minimum freeboard brought about by the 1969, 1971, and 1973 changes to the Load Line Regulations.

Recommendation 3: That the owners and operators of Great Lakes ore carrying vessels undertake a positive and continuing program of repair and maintenance to insure that all closures for openings above the freeboard deck are weathertight, that is, capable of preventing the penetration of water into the ship in any sea condition. This program should include frequent adjustment of hatch clamping devices and vent closures and prompt repair of all hatches, coamings, covers, and clamping devices found damaged or deteriorated.

Recommendation 4: That Part 45 of Title 46 of the United States Code of Federal Regulations be amended to require closing and securing of hatches when underway in open waters and closing of vent caps when underway in a loaded condition. A visual inspection of the closure of hatch covers and vent caps should be conducted and logged by a licensed officer prior to sailing in a loaded condition.

Recommendation 5: That the Coast Guard undertake a program to evaluate hatch closures presently used on Great Lakes ore carriers with a view toward requiring a more effective means of closure of such deck fittings.

Action: Assignments of freeboard are based upon, among other things, a presumption of the ability to achieve the weathertight integrity necessary to prevent significant flooding.

The mutually dependent areas of safety which are an integral part of all Load Line Regulations are:

a. That the hull is strong enough for all anticipated seaways;
b. That the ship is designed and operated with proper stability;
c. That the hull is watertight to the freeboard deck;
d. That the hull has sufficient reserve buoyancy for seaworthiness;
e. That the topside area is properly fitted so as to be capable of being made weathertight for all anticipated seaways; and,
f. That protection for the movement of the crew on the weather decks at sea is provided.

None of these can be eliminated by additions to freeboard within practical limits. Freeboard, or its increase, is not by itself an adequate substitute for properly designed, maintained and operated hatches, coamings, gaskets, and securing attachments. Such substitution unduly penalizes good design, maintenance, and operations. Since the fall season of 1976, the Coast Guard has been conducting a Great Lakes Coast Guard ship-rider program to evaluate the overall effectiveness of the combination of freeboard, hatch closure, and ventilator closure effectiveness during the Intermediate (Oct 1–31) and Winter

(November 1–March 31) freeboard seasons. This program has confirmed the evidence found by the Board of Investigation indicating that it is not a singular occurrence that the hatch covers on the EDMUND FITZGERALD may not have been properly secured. Several ships have been found to suffer in varying degrees from a lack of weathertight integrity due to the inability to make hatch covers weathertight and due to the inattention to ventilator covers prior to a winter season voyage.

Accordingly, the Commandant is initiating action to:

a. Continue the ship-rider program in 1977 and in succeeding years as necessary in order to prevent sailing or severely restrict the voyage weather limits of any ship found to lack sufficient weathertight integrity. Extra seasonal freeboard requirements may also be assigned to supplement weather limitations by the Commander, Ninth Coast Guard District to vessels on an individual basis.

b. Bring to the attention of the owners and operators the fact that weathertight closures which are not effective when battened down void both the LOAD LINE CERTIFICATE and the CERTIFICATE of INSPECTION.

c. Firmly bring to the attention of ships' masters their operational responsibilities for weathertight integrity before and during weather conditions as outlined in operational regulations in 46 CFR 97.

d. Direct the Merchant Marine Technical Division at Coast Guard Headquarters, in cooperation with Commander, Ninth Coast Guard District, to immediately undertake a critical evaluation of the effectiveness of those hatch closures presently in use on Great Lakes bulk carriers utilizing information from the shipboard Coast Guard inspections. If this evaluation shows the present designs to be either not effective or requiring such maintenance as to be difficult to assure weathertight integrity, regulatory notices will be published stating their design or maintenance shortcomings and including a requirement that ships modify or change hatch covers to correct the deficiencies.

e. Direct the Merchant Marine Technical Division to reassess the existing INTERMEDIATE and WINTER Season freeboard corrections utilizing wave analysis information on Great Lakes wave spectra to be gathered during an ongoing research program (1977–1979).

2. The following recommendation concerns vessel subdivision and is relevant to the preceding Action.

Recommendation 2: That any subsequent amendments to the Great Lakes Load Line Regulations, as they apply to ore carriers such as FITZGERALD, reflect full consideration of the necessity for a means of detecting and removing flooding water from the cargo hold and for watertight subdivision of the cargo hold spaces. Such an appraisal should take due cognizance of:

a. The severe weather and sea conditions encountered by these vessels and the resulting high degree of deck wetness; and,

b. The inherent difficulty in meeting and maintaining a weather-tight standard with the system of hatches, coamings, covers, gaskets, and clamps used on FITZGERALD and many other Great Lakes vessels.

Action: The Commandant intends to develop a federal regulation establishing a minimum level of subdivision for inspected Great Lakes cargo ships for two reasons directly related to this casualty. First, the sudden catastrophic foundering of the vessel apparently allowed no time for radio messages nor for individual survival. Second, the SS EDMUND FITZGERALD survived for several hours **after** indicating by radio message that some damage had occurred and the ship was about one hour from a safe harbor when it sank.

It is possible that even a minimum degree of watertight subdivision within the cargo hold could have effected a great change on the ultimate fate of both the ship and her crew. It is possible that the flooding, which is presumed to have occurred through ineffective hatch covers, might have occurred through only 1 or 2 hatches, but the subsequent flooding was able to penetrate the entire cargo hold. Subdivision bulkheads in the cargo space would have limited this flooding, possibly enough to allow the ship to make it to safe harbor. If they had realized the extent of damage, the provision of subdivision calculations and damage control instructions might have at the least allowed the crew more time to escape prior to the sinking.

An additional concern is raised by the report of minor side damage incidents. Bulk carriers are now being built which do not have the crew passage, ballast tank combination at the sides which provided some protection in cases of minor penetration. The arrangements on these new vessels are such that a penetration of the hull near the waterline might cause flooding over 90% of the ship's length. An incident could occur such that little chance of preventing sinking of the vessel would exist and the crew might have a very short time to escape. Subdivision standards will be directed toward this type of casualty. As the benefits of subdivision apply also to oceangoing cargo ships, international discussions toward an increase of subdivision safety for all cargo ships will be further pursued.

3. The following recommendations concern lifesaving equipment and crew training and are addressed jointly.

Recommendation 6: That the owners and operators of Great Lakes vessels, in cooperation with the maritime unions and training schools, undertake a program to improve the level of crew training in the use of lifesaving equipment installed on board the vessels and in other emergency procedures. This program should specifically include training in the use of inflatable life rafts and afford crews of vessels the opportunity to see a raft inflated.

Recommendation 7: That Part 97 of Title 46 of the United States Code of Federal Regulations be amended to require crew training in launching, inflation and operation of inflatable life rafts.

Recommendation 8: That the Coast Guard institute a continuing program of inspections and drills for Great Lakes vessels prior to each severe weather season. The severe weather season should correspond to the Winter Load Line season, i.e., 1 November through 31 March. Under this program, just before the severe weather season began, there would be an inspection to verify that the crew had been trained in the use of the lifesaving equipment and drills would be conducted with the crew then on board the vessel. There would be a physical inspection of the spar deck and all critical structural and non-structural members exposed to damage from cargo loading and off-loading equipment including, but not limited to, hatch coamings, hatch covers, vent covers, tank tops, side slopes, hatch-end girders, arches, spar deck stringers, and spar deck plating. Additionally, all emergency drills would be witnessed, and alarms, watertight closures, navigation equipment, and required logs would be inspected.

Recommendation 10: That the Coast Guard complete, as soon as possible, the studies currently underway, which concern primary lifesaving equipment, its launching, and disembarkation from stricken vessels. And, that the measure be implemented promptly to improve the entire abandon ship system, including equipping and training personnel, automatic launching of equipment, and alerting rescue forces.

Recommendation 13: That the Coast Guard promulgate regulations which require vessels operating on the Great Lakes during the severe weather season to have, for each person on board, a suit designed to protect the wearer from exposure and hypothermia.

Recommendation 15: That the Coast Guard foster and support programs dedicated to increasing awareness, on the part of all concerned with vessel operations, inspection, and maintenance, of the hazards faced by vessels in Great Lakes service, particularly during the severe weather season. The programs should make maximum use of company safety programs, safety bulletins, publications, and trade journals.

Action: The intent of these recommendations is concurred with and the need for improved and periodic meaningful training in the use of lifesaving equipment and a vessel readiness inspection program prior to severe weather sailing is supported. The following action has been taken or will be taken relative to these recommendations:

a. In October 1976, the Coast Guard instituted a continuing program of inspections and drills for Great Lakes vessels prior to the severe weather season. The scope of the program includes the specific items listed in Recommendation 8 and the inspections are conducted while the vessels are underway and under actual operational conditions.

   The requirements for conducting emergency drills and crew training are contained in 46 CFR Parts 97.15–35 and 97.13–20. Emergency fire and boat drills are required at least once every week and the master is responsible to assure that they are conducted. Assuring adequate drills are conducted is not unique to Great Lakes vessels, therefore the operations sections of 46 CFR, Parts 35, 78, 167, 168, and 185 will be amended to incorporate crew training in the launching, inflation, and operation of inflatable life rafts. The Coast Guard recognizes this lack of training is of international magnitude and is working within IMCO in the preliminary stages of such a program.

b. Owners, operators, labor organizations, and training schools will be encouraged to develop a training program of the type indicated in Recommendation 6. To support this effort, the Merchant Vessel Personnel Division will work with the Maritime Administration to develop such training programs. The Coast Guard will set qualification standards requiring all licensed officers and able seamen be trained in the operation of inflatable life rafts as well as other lifesaving equipment. Input from the owners and operators of Great Lakes vessels, along with their crews' labor organizations and training schools, will be solicited.

c.   The Coast Guard is expanding its public awareness program to provide useful information to seamen and aid operators and unions in the conduct of their training programs. In September 1975, a pamphlet on hypothermia, CG-473, was published and distributed on the Great Lakes and other areas where cold weather survival could be a problem. A proposal has been submitted within the Coast Guard to the Office of Research and Development to develop a means by which the public, specifically those on board commercial vessels, will be made aware of various safety factors, regulations, and safe operating procedures that apply to their particular commercial operation. For example, pamphlets may be developed and distributed (i.e., via labor unions, commercial fisherman organizations, vessel documentation officers, professional and business organizations) for each class of commercial operation. Great Lakes vessels would be an appropriate area for such a public awareness program.

A summary of the Board's report and an article, directed at increasing the mariner's awareness of the hazards of the Great Lakes, will be prepared for publication in the Proceedings of the Marine Safety Council.

Concerning Recommendations 10 and 13, a Notice of Proposed Rulemaking based on an Advance Notice of Proposed Rulemaking, published 7 June 1976 in the Federal Register, is being prepared for Great Lakes cargo, tank, and passenger vessels which will propose that:

a.   All lifeboats on vessels be totally enclosed to provide protection from exposure and to lessen the danger of swamping and subsequent capsizing.

b.   All lifeboats be diesel engine driven with the ability to start the engine in temperatures as low as -22°F.

c.   Sufficient lifeboats be provided to accommodate 100% of the persons on board the ship with additional lifeboats and life rafts provided and located so as to provide accommodation for an additional 100% in the event that a casualty renders the other lifeboats unusable.

d.   All survival craft be provided with launching devices which will be launched from their stowed positions with all persons onboard, eliminating the need for lengthy pre-launch preparation, a deck crew to stay aboard to control the launch, and in the case of life rafts, the need to enter the water before boarding.

e. Automatic float-free launching be required for life rafts.

f. An exposure suit be required for each person on board that will protect the wearer from exposure and hypothermia.

One lifeboat manufacturer is developing a float-free launching system for lifeboats which are also launched conventionally. This will be given further consideration as a requirement upon completion of a prototype system and an evaluation of its feasibility.

The remainder of the Board's recommendations are addressed individually.

4. **Recommendation 9:** That the Coast Guard take positive steps to insure that the Masters of Great Lakes vessels are provided with information, as is required by the regulations, concerning loading and ballasting of Great Lakes vessels, and that the information provided include not only normal loaded and ballasted conditions, but also details on the sequences of loading, unloading, ballasting, deballasting, and intermediate stages thereof, as well as information on the effect upon the vessel of accidental flooding from damage of other sources.

    Action: The Coast Guard will develop performance criteria for loading manuals which will cover all the items in this recommendation except flooding conditions. Flooding conditions will be addressed in conjunction with the casualty control efforts discussed in the action on Recommendation 2.

5. **Recommendation 11:** That the Coast Guard schedule maintenance status for buoy tenders and icebreakers located in the Great Lakes so as to maximize surface search and rescue capability during the severe weather season, consistent with their primary missions.

    Action: Commander, Ninth Coast Guard District has implemented this recommendation by issuing a District Directive on 9 September 1976. This Directive contains the requirements and guidelines for scheduling maintenance and underway periods of Coast Guard vessels on the Great Lakes.

6. **Recommendation 12:** That Subpart 94.60 of Title 46 of the United States Code of Federal Regulations, which requires emergency position indicating radio beacons (EPIRB), be amended to include requirements for such beacons on vessels operating on the Great Lakes during the severe weather season.

    Action: Action is being taken to permit the operation of EPIRB's in the VHF-FM marine band. There is at present virtually complete shore station coverage on the Great Lakes on this band and constant monitoring of Channel 16 by stations in both the United States and Canada. A prototype EPIRB for testing is now being developed by the Transportation Systems Center. When the VHF-FM EPIRB's become available, regulations will be proposed requiring that they be installed on board inspected Great Lakes vessels during all seasons.

7.   **Recommendation 14:** That navigation charts, showing the area immediately north of Caribou Island, be modified to show the extent of the shoals north of the island and that this modification be given the widest possible dissemination, including Notices to Mariners.

Action: A copy of the completed marine casualty report will be forwarded to the U.S. Department of Commerce, National Oceanic and Atmospheric Administration, with a request that they coordinate the correction of the applicable charts with their counterparts in the Canadian Government.

O. W. Siler
Admiral, U. S. Coast Guard Commandant

DEPARTMENT OF TRANSPORTATION

UNITED STATES COAST GUARD

MAILING ADDRESS:
U.S. COAST GUARD
400 SEVENTH STREET SW.
WASHINGTON, D.C 20590

16732/S.S. EDMUND FITZGERALD
15 APRIL 1977

FROM: MARINE BOARD OF INVESTIGATION
TO: COMMANDANT (G-MMI)

SUBJ: S. S. EDMUND FITZGERALD, O.N. 277437;
SINKING IN LAKE SUPERIOR ON 10 NOVEMBER 1975, WITH LOSS OF LIFE

1. FINDINGS OF FACT

In the early evening on 10 November 1975, the S. S. EDMUND FITZGER-ALD, while in a severe storm, with a full cargo of taconite pellets, sank in eastern Lake Superior at 46°59.9'N, 85°06.6'W, approximately 17 miles from the entrance to Whitefish Bay, MI. FITZGERALD had left Superior, WI, on the afternoon of 9 November enroute Detroit, MI, and was in communication with other vessels periodically throughout the voyage. At approximately 1530, 10 November, FITZGERALD reported some topside damage and a list but did not say what caused this damage or express any urgency in the report. The Master of FITZGERALD did request that the Steamer ARTHUR M. ANDER-SON, which was following, provide navigational information to FITZGER-ALD and as the two vessels proceeded towards Whitefish Bay, FITZGERALD disappeared from ANDERSON's radar screen.

No distress message was received from FITZGERALD. The notification from ANDERSON of the suspected loss precipitated an extensive air and surface search. A large quantity of debris, including lifeboats, life rafts and other flotsam, was found, but no survivors or bodies were recovered. All of the twenty-nine crewmen on board at the time are missing.

After taking testimony, members of the Marine Board observed the underwater survey of the wreckage, which was conducted during late May 1976. Since FITZGERALD had passed between Michipicoten Island and Caribou Island in eastern Lake Superior and since charts of this area indicated that soundings last were taken in 1919, the Marine Board requested that Canadian authorities conduct a hydrographic survey of the area between Michipicoten Island and Caribou Island in eastern Lake Superior. The final field report of this survey was received on 25 March 1977.

2. VESSEL DATA

Name:	EDMUND FITZGERALD
Official Number:	277437
Service:	Freight
Gross Tons:	13,632
Net Tons:	8,686
Length (bp):	711 ft.
Length (oa):	729 ft.
Breadth:	75 ft.
Depth:	39 ft.
Propulsion:	Steam Turbine
Horsepower:	7,500
Home Port:	Milwaukee, WI
Owner:	Northwestern Mutual Life Insurance Company, 720 East Wisconsin Ave., Milwaukee, WI 53202
Operator:	Columbia Transportation Div., Oglebay Norton Co., 1210 Hanna Bldg., Cleveland, OH 44115
Master:	Ernest M. McSorley Bk 004418 License 398 598, Master and First Class Pilot Steam and Motor Vessels any GT, Master Great Lakes, Connecting and Tributary Waters, First Class Pilot between Duluth, Gary, Buffalo, North Tonawanda and Ogdensburg, Issue 7, 9, 29 Oct 1973, Toledo, OH.
Last Inspection for Certification:	9 April 1975, Toledo, OH
Last Spar Deck Inspection:	31 Oct 1975, Toledo, OH
Cargo:	Taconite Pellets, 26,116 long tons
Draft (at departure on last voyage)	27'02" forward / 27'06" aft
Propeller	
Diameter:	19'6"
Pitch (on .7 radius):	15.86'

FITZGERALD was a conventional "straight decker" Great Lakes ore carrier. The vessel was arranged with cargo holds in the center of the ship, and ballast tanks outboard of and below the holds. There was a forward deckhouse containing accommodations and the pilothouse and an after deckhouse above the engine room with accommodations and messing facilities. The weather deck between the deckhouses was called the Spar Deck. Above the Spar Deck, forward, were the Forecastle Deck, which contained the Captain's office and stateroom and two additional staterooms, and, above that, the Texas Deck. The navigating bridge and chart room were in the elevated pilothouse with a void separating it from the Texas Deck. Above the Spar Deck, aft, was the Poop Deck with a lifeboat port and starboard, and the galley, mess room, dining rooms and accommodations within the house. Access between forward and aft could be accomplished topside or through "tunnels" located port and starboard, outboard, immediately below the Spar Deck. FITZGERALD was fitted with a collision bulkhead separating the forepeak from the No. 1 ballast tank and with watertight bulkheads forward and aft of the engine room. Figures (1) through (4) show the general arrangement and midships section of the vessel.

Cargo was loaded and discharged through twenty-one cargo hatch openings, each eleven feet longitudinally and forty-eight feet transversely, arranged on twenty-four foot centers along the Spar Deck. The cargo hatches were numbered from No. 1 forward to No. 21 aft. The total molded volume of 860,950 cubic feet of cargo space was divided into three cargo holds by non-watertight screen bulkheads located between hatches No. 7 and No. 8 (frame 69) and between No. 13 and No. 14 (frame 117). The No. 1, or forward cargo hold, was 177'0" long, No. 2 (amidships) was 144'0" long and No. 3 (aft) was 198'0" long.

Each cargo hatch was fitted with a vertical coaming all around the opening, the top of which measured 24 inches above the Spar Deck. The Spar Deck had 18 inches of camber, thus the coaming at the centerline was 3'6" above the deck at the side. The longitudinal sections of the coamings were located three feet outboard of the hatch openings, providing a vestibule at each side of each hatch. Each cargo hatch was closed by a single piece (11'7"×54'0") $^5/_{16}$" stiffened steel hatch cover, with a gasket all around the underside of its perimeter. The gasket landed on a 3"×3"×9.4# angle iron which was welded all around the top of the coaming. Hatch covers for hatches No. 4, 10 and 17 had 18 inch circular, bolted scuttles in the middle of the covers. Each hatch cover was secured by sixty-eight manually positioned "Kestner clamps," i.e., double pivot, adjustable, tension clamps, which were arranged on approximately two-foot centers around the coaming. Each Kestner clamp had an adjustment bolt, one end of which landed on a dished "button" on the hatch cover. Thus, there were sixty-eight "buttons" around the perimeter of each hatch cover. Adjusting the bolts increased or decreased the force required to position the clamps and this determined the deflection of the hatch cover, the compression of the gasket and the tightness of the closure. There was no company requirement concerning routine maintenance of the clamps or gaskets.

Hatch covers were removed and replaced by use of an electrically powered hatch crane which straddled the hatches and traveled fore and aft on tracks located outboard of the hatch coamings, port and starboard.

In addition to the twenty-one cargo hatches, access from the Spar Deck to the cargo holds was provided through two 30" by 60" access hatches, each with a 24" coaming on the Spar Deck. One access hatch was located between hatches Nos. 7 and 8, immediately forward of the forward screen bulkhead on the starboard side providing access to the No. 1 hold. The other was located between hatches Nos. 13 and 14, immediately aft of the after screen bulkhead on the port side providing access to the No. 3 hold. Each screen bulkhead was fitted with a door at the Main Deck which provided access to the No. 2 cargo hold from either access hatch and there was also a door providing access to or from the tunnel at these locations. Access to the cargo holds was also provided through a door in the forward bulkhead of the No. 1 hold, port side, Main Deck, and through a door at the after bulkhead of No. 3 hold, port side, Main Deck.

Outboard of and below the cargo holds were eight ballast tanks, divided at the centerline into port and starboard tanks. Each ballast tank was fitted with two eight-inch vent pipes, one at each end of each tank. Each vent extended 18 inches above the Spar Deck and was fitted with a screw-down, "mushroom" closure cap, 14½" in diameter and 9¼" high, over the top of the 8" vent pipe. Rotating the cap by use of the handle on top of it caused the cap to ride up or down on threads on the top of the vent pipe, opening or closing the vent. There was no external indicator to show whether the cover was in the open or closed position. The port and starboard access tunnels were provided with similar covered vents, one forward and one aft, extending thirty inches above the Spar Deck. Ballast tanks were sounded through sounding tubes terminating on the Spar Deck and the soundings were recorded on chalk boards called "sounding boards" located in the pilothouse and the engine room. Remote reading gauges (King Gauges) in the lower engine room near the ballast pumps also provided a check on ballast tank water levels. There were neither sounding tubes nor remote reading gauges for the cargo holds.

The ballast tanks were filled and drained by four electrically driven 7000-gpm main ballast pumps and two electrically driven 2000-gpm auxiliary ballast pumps. The pumps, valves and manifolds and the remote reading level indicators for the ballast tanks were located in the forward section of the lower engine room. Any ballast pump could be used to drain No. 3 cargo hold through the ballast manifold and through the single suction well ("rose box") located aft in No. 3 cargo hold, although it was common practice to use the 2000-gpm auxiliary pumps for this purpose. There were no suction wells in the No. 1 or No. 2 cargo holds. Water in these holds drained aft along the length of the holds and through sluices fitted in the lower portions of the screen bulkheads separating the holds, to the suction well at the after end of No. 3 hold. When the vessel was loaded with cargo, water entering the hold would have to filter through the cargo before it could be pumped. Experienced Great Lakes mariners testified that the cargo would restrict the flow and that the holds could not be pumped when loaded with cargo. Coast Guard regulations require a bilge pumping plant capable of pumping from or draining any watertight compartment. As an antipollution measure, the discharge from the engine room bilges was pumped onto the cargo.

FITZGERALD was fitted with two 400-KW ship's service steam turbo generators, and one 200-KW auxiliary diesel generator, located in the engine room. A 30-KW emergency diesel generator located on the Poop Deck, starboard side, forward, was fitted with an automatic starting mechanism, and provided power only for emergency lighting.

Radiotelephone equipment on board FITZGERALD was located in the pilothouse and chart room and consisted of the following:

(1) VH F/FM, 12-channel, 25-watt radiotelephone, Model RF-457, Serial No. 5825, installed May 17, 1974. This set operated from ship's power.

(2) VH F/FM, 12-channel, 25-watt radiotelephone, Model RF-457, Serial No. 6273, installed October 22, 1974. This set operated from rechargeable battery power, with the batteries installed in the pilothouse.

(3) Automatic, 12-channel, 25-watt, full duplex, Model RF-150-D, Serial No. 3850, VHF/FM dial radiotelephone, installed September 13, 1975. This set operated from ship's power.

(4) AM medium frequency and high frequency, eightchannel, 100-watt, Model LC-100-M8CL. This set had channel 51 (2182 Khz) capability and operated from ship's power.

(5) AM 50-watt, medium frequency, emergency radiotelephone, Model
KR-102, included channel 51 (2182 Khz). This set operated from
rechargeable battery power.

It had been the practice on FITZGERALD to use the battery powered
radiotelephones regularly.

The FCC station license was issued on September 30, 1971, expiring September 30, 1976. The call sign WJ9721 was assigned to FITZGERALD. The
last FCC inspection certificate was issued by the Detroit Office of the Federal
Communications Commission on April 9, 1975.

On 10 November, FITZGERALD had requested a radio serviceman to
meet the vessel on arrival in Detroit. The service contractor believed that this
request was for service on the duplex dial radiotelephone which had been
recently installed.

FITZGERALD was also fitted with a McKay type 4003A radio direction
finder.

FITZGERALD was not required to have a fathometer and none was
installed. Soundings, if needed, would have been taken by a hand lead.

FITZGERALD was fitted with two surface scan radar sets, one a Sperry
Mark 3 and the other a Sperry Mark 16. Maintenance records for 1975 indicated only routine maintenance on each radar set. There is no evidence that
the radar sets were not operating properly when FITZGERALD left Superior,
WI, on 9 November.

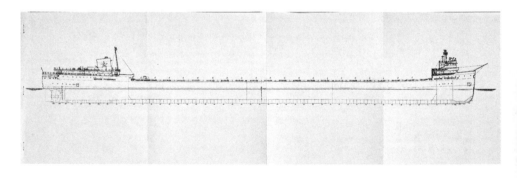

Figure 1. Edmund Fitzgerald, *outboard profile, Great Lakes Engineering Works, 1958.*
Historical Collections of the Great Lakes, Center for Archival Collections, Bowling Green State University.

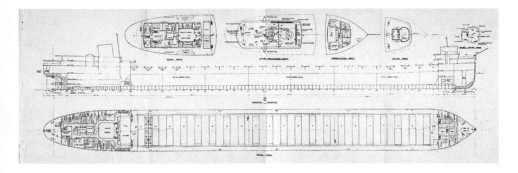

Figure 2. Edmund Fitzgerald, *spar deck and inboard profile, Great Lakes Engineering Works, 1958.* Historical Collections of the Great Lakes, Center for Archival Collections, Bowling Green State University.

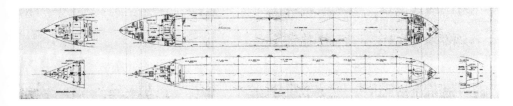

Figure 3. Edmund Fitzgerald, *tank top and main deck, Great Lakes Engineering Works, 1958.* Courtesy of Detroit Historical Society.

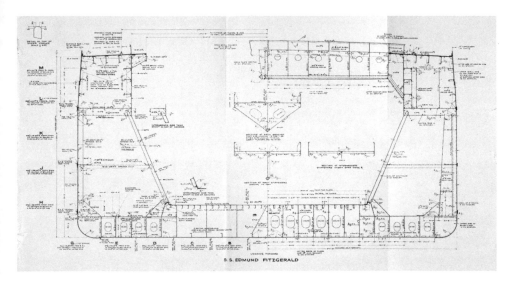

Figure 4. Edmund Fitzgerald, *mid-ship section, Great Lakes Engineering Works, 1958.* Historical Collections of the Great Lakes, Center for Archival Collections, Bowling Green State University.

3. RECORD OF MISSING CREWMEN

a. The following crewmembers are missing:

McSORLEY, Ernest M.
Address: Toledo, OH
Next of Kin: Wife, same address
Master

McCARTHY, John H.
Address: Bay Village, OH
Next of Kin: Wife, same address
First Mate

PRATT, James A.
Address: Lakewood, OH
Next of Kin: Wife, same address
Second Mate

ARMAGOST, Michael E.
Address: Iron River, WI
Next of Kin: Wife, same address
Third Mate

HOLL, George J.
Address: Cabot, PA
Next of Kin: Brother, Wilmer
Holl, Berea, OH
Chief Engineer

BINDON, Edward F.
Address: Fairport Harbor, OH
Next of Kin: Wife, same address
First Asst. Engineer

EDWARDS, Thomas E.
Address: Oregon, OH
Next of Kin: Wife, same address
Second Asst. Engineer

HASKELL, Russell G.
Address: Millbury, OH
Next of Kin: Wife, same address
Second Asst. Engineer

CHAMPEAU, Oliver J.
Address: Milwaukee, WI
Next of Kin: Daughter, Deborah
Champeau, Milwaukee, WI
Third Asst. Engineer

BEETCHER, Frederick J.
Address: Superior, WI
Next of Kin: Son, Gene
Beetcher, Superior, WI
Porter

BENTSEN, Thomas
Address: St. Joseph, MI
Next of Kin: Parents: Harold
and Florence Bentsen,
same address
Oiler

BORGESON, Thomas D.
Address: Duluth, MN
Next of Kin: Children, Mary
Beth, Bradley, Theresa, Jack, and
Robin Borgeson, Duluth MN
AB Maintenance Man

CHURCH, Nolan F.
Address: Silver Bay, MN
Next of Kin: Wife, same address
Porter

CUNDY, Ransom E.
Address: Superior, WI
Next of Kin: Wife, same address
Watchman

HUDSON, Bruce L.
Address: North Olmsted, OH
Next of Kin: Parents, Oddis A.
and Ruth G. Hudson, North
Olmsted, OH
Deckhand

KALMON, Allen G.
Address: Washburn, WI
Next of Kin: Wife, same address
Second Cook

MacLELLAN, Gordon F.
Address: Clearwater, FL
Next of Kin: Parents, Donald
and Sadonia MacLellan,
Clearwater, FL
Wiper

MAZES, Joseph W.
Address: Ashland, WI
Next of Kin: Brother, John
Mazes, Ashland, WI
Special Maintenance Man

O'BRIEN, Eugene W.
Address: St. Paul, MN
Next of Kin: Son, John O'Brien,
Toledo, OH
Wheelsman

PECKOL, Karl A.
Address: Ashtabula, OH
Next of Kin: Parents,
William and Elinor Peckol,
Ashtabula, OH
Watchman

POVIACH, John J.
Address: Bradenton, FL
Next of Kin: Wife, same address
Wheelsman

RAFFERTY, Robert C.
Address: Toledo, OH
Next of Kin: Wife, same address
Steward

RIIPPA, Paul M.
Address: Ashtabula, OH
Next of Kin: Mother,
Ashtabula, OH
Deckhand

SIMMONS, John D.
Address: Ashland, WI
Next of Kin: Wife, same address
Wheelsman

SPENGLER, William J.
Address: Toledo, OH
Next of Kin: Wife, same address
Watchman

THOMAS, Mark A.
Address: Richmond Heights, OH
Next of Kin: Father, Richard A.
Thomas, Richmond Heights, OH
Deckhand

WALTON, Ralph G.
Address: Freemont, OH
Next of Kin: Wife, same address
Oiler

WILHELM, Blaine H.
Address: Moquah, WI
Next of Kin: Wife, same address
Oiler

WEISS, David E.
Address: Agoura, CA
Next of Kin: Father, Aaron W.
Weiss, Canoga Park, CA
Cadet (Deck)

4. WEATHER

A storm, which was described by a National Weather Service forecaster as "a typical November storm," was generated over the Oklahoma Panhandle on 8 November (all dates referred to hereafter in this report will assume the year 1975 and all times referred to will be Eastern Standard Time unless specifically identified otherwise), and by 0700, on 9 November, this well-defined storm was located over south-central Kansas, moving to the northeast, with a minimum barometric pressure of 29.53" Hg. The National Weather Service issued 12-, 24- and 36-hour Surface Weather Forecasts at 0700, on 9 November, predicting that the storm center would travel in a northeasterly direction and pass just south of Lake Superior by 1900 on 10 November.

The storm was centered over the northeast corner of Kansas by 1300 on 9 November with a minimum barometric pressure of 29.40" Hg and an average speed of advance of 19 knots. The National Weather Service issued 12- and 24-hour Surface Weather Forecasts Maps at this time which predicted that the storm would shift to a more northerly direction, pass over Lake Superior east of Michipicoten Island and increase in speed. The storm center was predicted to be over James Bay, Canada, by 1900 on 10 November.

The storm intensified rapidly as it passed over east central Iowa and, by 1900 on 9 November, it had a minimum barometric pressure of 29.33" Hg and an average speed of advance of 37 knots. At this time, the National Weather Service issued Gale Warnings for all of Lake Superior. Winds in the eastern half of the lake were predicted to be "East to Northeast, increasing to 25 to 37 knots during the night, and Northeasterly 28 to 38 knots, shifting to Northwest to Northerly 30 to 40 knots by Monday (10 November) afternoon, waves 5 to 10 feet.

The National Weather Service revised the forecast at 2239 on 9 November, the next scheduled broadcast, predicting "Easterly winds 32 to 42 knots becoming Southeasterly Monday morning, and West to Southwest 35 to 45 knots Monday afternoon, rain and thunderstorms, waves 5 to 10 feet increasing to 8 to 15 feet Monday."

Wave heights in National Weather Service forecasts refer to the distance from peak to trough and are "significant wave height." Significant wave height is a statistical evaluation, roughly equivalent to the average height of the highest one third of the waves. The actual distance from peak to trough of the highest wave could be as much as twice the significant wave height. Officials of the National Weather Service stated that significant wave height is very close to the wave height shipboard personnel report in weather observations.

The storm continued to intensify and to move to the northeast, and, as its center passed over central Wisconsin at 0100, 10 November, it had a minimum barometric pressure of 29.24" Hg and an average speed of advance of 29 knots. The Gale Warnings were increased to Storm Warnings at 0200 on 10 November, when a special warning was issued with a prediction of "Northeast winds 35 to 50 knots becoming Northwesterly 28 to 38 knots on Monday, waves 8 to 15 feet."

The storm continued on its northeasterly track and its center had passed over Marquette, MI, by 0700, 10 November, with a minimum barometric pressure of 29.00" Hg and an average speed of advance of 22 knots. The National Weather Service revised the forecast for Eastern Lake Superior at 1034, 10 November, predicting "North to Northwest winds 32 to 48 knots this afternoon becoming Northwesterly 25 to 48 knots tonight and Westerly 20 to 30 knots Tuesday, waves 8 to 16 feet decreasing Tuesday."

The storm center crossed Lake Superior to the west of Michipicoten Island and was over White River, ONT, at 1300, 10 November, with a minimum barometric pressure of 28.95" Hg and an average speed of advance of 21 knots. As predicted, a line of shifting winds followed the storm center, with winds hauling from the northeast, decreasing to less than 10 knots when out of the south, then continuing to haul and increasing rapidly to 35 to 50 knots from the northwest. The windshift line extended from north-northeast to south-southwest, and, at 1300, 10 November, was approximately 20 miles west of Caribou Island, ONT, moving eastward at 20 to 25 knots.

At the next regular broadcast, at 1639, the National Weather Service revised the forecast for Eastern Lake Superior, predicting "Northwest winds 38 to 52 knots with gusts to 60 knots early tonight and Northwesterly winds 25 to 35 knots diminishing Tuesday, waves 8 to 16 feet tonight decreasing Tuesday." The storm continued on its northeasterly track and by 1900 on 10 November its center had passed over the southern tip of James Bay, Canada, and by 0100, 11 November, the storm center was over eastern Hudson Bay as the effects of the severe storm abated on Lake Superior.

At 0100, 10 November, FITZGERALD was approximately 20 miles due south of Isle Royal and reported winds from 030°T at 52 knots, overcast, visibility two to five miles in continuous heavy rain, temperature 37°F, waves 10 feet. At 0700, FITZGERALD was approximately 35 miles north of Copper Harbor, MI, and reported winds from 050°T at 35 knots, overcast, visibility two to five miles in continuous moderate rain, temperature 41°F, waves 10 feet. The 0700 report was the last weather report received from FITZGERALD.

The SS ARTHUR M. ANDERSON filed 0100 and 0700 weather reports from approximately the same positions as reported by FITZGERALD and the reports from ANDERSON substantially agreed with those from FITZGER-ALD. At 1300, 10 November, ANDERSON was approximately 20 miles northwest of Michipicoten Island, near the center of the storm, and reported winds from 150°T at 20 knots, visibility 10 to 25 miles, no precipitation, and waves 12 feet. At 1900, ANDERSON reported winds from 300°T at 50 knots, visibility 10 to 25 miles in light rain and snow, and waves 16 feet.

The Motor Vessel SIMCOE (Canadian), approximately 15 miles to the southwest of the ANDERSON at 1300, 10 November, reported winds from 270°T at 44 knots, visibility 10 to 25 miles, no precipitation, and waves 7 feet. At this time, the remote weather reporting station at Stannard Rock was reporting winds from the WNW at 50 knots, gusting to 59 knots, and the station at Whitefish Point was reporting SSW at 19 knots, gusting to 34 knots. At 1900, Stannard Rock was reporting WNW at 40 knots, gusting to 65 knots, and the Whitefish Point Station was inoperative.

5. THE LAST VOYAGE

At approximately 0830, on 9 November, FITZGERALD commenced loading taconite at Burlington Northern Railroad Dock No. 1, in Superior, WI. Fuel was also taken on at this time. FITZGERALD completed loading and fueling at approximately 1415 and crewmembers were observed replacing the hatch covers. There were no unusual incidents or occurrences and this appeared to be a routine loading and departure.

FITZGERALD departed for Detroit immediately and proceeded at full speed of 99 r.p.m., approximately 16.3 mph. (It is conventional on the Great Lakes to describe distances in statute miles (mi) and speeds in statute miles per hour (mph), and distances and speeds referred to hereafter in this report will follow this convention unless specifically identified otherwise.) After about two hours, FITZGERALD reached the area near Two Harbors, MN. The SS ARTHUR M. ANDERSON, one of the vessels of the United States Steel Corp., had departed Two Harbors at 1630. ANDERSON, with a cargo similar to FITZGERALD's, was bound for Gary, IN, and the two vessels proceeded eastward on similar courses, separated by 10 to 20 miles.

FITZGERALD made routine radio weather reports at 0100 and at 0700, 10 November, and at 0720 made the normal radio morning report to the company office. This report indicated that the ETA at Sault Ste. Marie was indefinite due to weather.

Because of the storm, FITZGERALD departed from the recommended Great Lakes shipping lanes at the southern shore of the lake, and headed northeastward, approximately half way between Isle Royal and the Keewanaw Peninsula, turning eastward to parallel the northern shore of Lake Superior and then southeastward along the eastern shore. By 1300, 10 November, FITZGERALD was approximately 11 miles northwest of Michipicoten Island.

FITZGERALD passed to the west of Michipicoten West End Light, and changed course to pass north and east of Caribou Island, heading generally southeastward towards Whitefish Bay, MI. FITZGERALD sank sometime after 1915 at a position of 46°59.9'N, 85°06.6'W, near the International Boundary Line.

Figure (5) is a chart of Lake Superior, showing Michipicoten and Caribou Islands, Whitefish Bay and the position where the wreckage of FITZGERALD was located.

The SS ARTHUR M. ANDERSON, making turns for a speed of 14.6 mph, which it maintained during the entire transit of Lake Superior, joined FITZGERALD at approximately 1700, 9 November. Shortly thereafter, ANDERSON received notice of Gale Warnings. Sometime after 0200 on 10 November, CAPT Cooper, Master of ANDERSON, contacted CAPT McSorley, Master of FITZGERALD, on VHF-FM radiotelephone. CAPT Cooper had just received the notification of Storm Warnings which predicted northeast winds to 50 knots. During this conversation, both Captains expressed concern over the deteriorating weather. They agreed to depart from the normal shipping lanes which are at the southern shore of the lake and proceed on a more northeasterly course in order to be in the lee of the Canadian shore.

At 0300, ANDERSON changed course to 055°T and logged winds from 034°T at 42 knots while FITZGERALD headed 060°T. Up until now, FITZGERALD had been close behind ANDERSON, now she was pulling ahead slightly because of her faster speed.

At 0400, the First Mate, Morgan Clark, came on watch on ANDERSON, and the two vessels proceeded along together throughout his watch. The First Mate was relieved for the 8–12 watch by the Third Mate, Bernard Dorobek. At 0953, Dorobek changed course and headed due east, and at 1030, when approximately 25 miles from shore, he changed course to 125°T, heading southeastward along the Canadian shore. Watch officers on board ANDER-SON observed that FITZGERALD went closer toward the shore before heading south. Because ANDERSON was, in effect, cutting corners, it was able to keep up with the faster FITZGERALD.

At 1152, the Third Mate changed course to 149°T. The weather recorded at this time was overcast with winds from 158°T at 30 knots. The barometer had dropped rapidly and was now 28.84, waves 10 to 12 feet.

The Second Mate, Roy Anderson, assumed the 1200–1600 watch on board ANDERSON and sent the 1800Z weather report at 1240 (weather reports were made in Greenwich Mean Time, designated Z; 1800Z corresponds to 1300 Eastern Standard Time).

At 1252, the Second Mate, steering 148° to make 149°T, recorded a beam bearing 10.8 miles off Otterhead. He changed course at this time to 154°T, intending to clear Michipicoten Island West End Light by 2 to 2½ miles. At this time, FITZGERALD was 7 or 8 miles ahead and to the east of ANDERSON's heading, and the two vessels appeared to be on slightly converging courses. At approximately 1340, CAPT Cooper talked with CAPT McSorley and said that he anticipated that the wind would shift to the northwest. He told CAPT McSorley that he intended to "haul" (i.e., change course) to the west, before passing Michipicoten Island, in order to insure that the seas were astern. CAPT McSorley, whose vessel was just past Michipicoten, indicated that he would continue on, although his vessel was "rolling some." CAPT Cooper observed that FITZGERALD changed course after passing Michipicoten Island. Since no plot of FITZGERALD was maintained, this was the only course change that the Master or Watch Officers of ANDERSON were sure that FITZGER-ALD made after passing Michipicoten. At 1350, ANDERSON logged a course change to 230°T and steered it without "holding up" any for the wind. The Second Mate observed that just before this course change, FITZGERALD was about 9 or 10 miles ahead and slightly to the starboard. He assumed that FITZGERALD was steering a course of 141°, and estimated that FITZGER-ALD would have passed off the western end of Michipicoten Island at a distance of 3 miles. CAPT Cooper estimated the distance to be approximately 2½ miles. The weather was logged as overcast, winds 5 knots from 304°T, visibility fair.

After ten minutes on the new course of 230°T, at 1400, the Second Mate took a radar range and bearing which he did not record in the ship's log. This placed ANDERSON on the trackline drawn for 230°T. At 1425, the Second Mate took another "fix" by radar, which again he did not log. This one placed the vessel on the trackline, 3.9 miles beyond the 1400 position.

At 1445, ANDERSON logged a course change to 130°T. The Second Mate "held up" one degree for wind, and ordered the Wheelsman to steer 131°. This course was set in order to pass clear of the 6-fathom shoal approximately four miles north of Caribou Island. By the time ANDERSON was steady on the new course, FITZGERALD was observed to be approximately 16 miles ahead, winds had increased to 42 knots from 315°T, and it had started snowing. As a result, ANDERSON lost sight of FITZGERALD and it was never seen again.

At 1520, the Second Mate logged ANDERSON abeam of Michipicoten Island West End Light at a distance of 7.7 miles. The seas were beginning to build rapidly from the northwest and on the 130° course, CAPT Cooper thought this ship was being set down too close to Caribou so the course was changed to 125°T. This new course was "shaped up" to clear the 6-fathom shoal north of Caribou Island and to reach a point 6 miles off the island. After ANDERSON steadied on the 125° course, the Mate on watch observed that FITZGERALD was a little over 16 miles ahead of ANDERSON and a "shade" to the right of dead ahead. CAPT Cooper estimated the angle as a point to a point and a half to the right. FITZGERALD's position then was observed to open further to the right of ANDERSON's heading flasher. Watch officers on ANDERSON stated that no plot of FITZGERALD was maintained and they did not know whether the change in the relative position of FITZGERALD resulted from the divergent courses of the two vessels or whether FITZGERALD had made another course change. While ANDERSON was on this course, FITZGER-ALD was observed to have passed north and east of Caribou Island. CAPT Cooper testified that he estimated that FITZGERALD had passed close to the six-fathom shoal north of Caribou Island. He also testified that he told the Mate on watch on ANDERSON that FITZGERALD was closer to this shoal than he wanted ANDERSON to be. At 1520, ANDERSON recorded steady winds of 43 knots from the northwest and it was still snowing. The seas were 12 to 16 feet, and ANDERSON was shipping a considerable quantity of water on deck.

The First Mate relieved the Second Mate of the watch at 1520, and between 1530 and 1535, while the Second Mate was still in the pilothouse and at a time when the Captain was there also, FITZGERALD called ANDER-SON. CAPT Cooper, on ANDERSON, answered the call and the two watch officers listened. Reports of this conversation varied, but it was generally agreed that FITZGERALD reported a fence rail down, two vents lost or damaged, and a list. Both the Master and the Mates who heard this report testified that they understood this to mean the loss of ballast tank vents and a small list. FITZGERALD told ANDERSON that she would "check down," i.e., reduce speed, to allow ANDERSON to close the distance between them. Whoever it was that was speaking on FITZGERALD did not identify himself, although everyone on the bridge of ANDERSON believed that it was CAPT McSorley. CAPT Cooper asked CAPT McSorley if he had "his pumps going" and the reply was: "Yes, both of them." CAPT Cooper noted that at this time the radar indicated that FITZGERALD was approximately 17 miles ahead of ANDERSON and a point to a point and a half to the right of ANDERSON's heading. CAPT Cooper agreed to keep track of FITZGERALD. None of the officers on ANDERSON who heard this conversation felt that it indicated any real concern about the welfare of FITZGERALD.

Shortly after this, ANDERSON received a Coast Guard broadcast that the Sault Ste. Marie locks had been closed and that all ships should seek a safe anchorage.

Between 1610 and 1615, ANDERSON was informed by FITZGERALD that her "radars weren't working." CAPT Cooper was not in the wheelhouse at this time. FITZGERALD asked if ANDERSON would keep track of them and provide navigational assistance, and the First Mate on watch on ANDERSON agreed.

At a time that CAPT Cooper estimated to be between 1600 and 1630, FITZGERALD was observed to pass approximately three to five miles east of Caribou Island, its closest point of approach to the island.

At 1620, on ANDERSON, the Second Mate relieved the First Mate for dinner. At 1630, it grew dark and the Second Mate noted that the radar showed FITZGERALD was approximately 16 miles ahead and "possibly between one to two degrees, maybe" to the right of ANDERSON's heading. At 1652, the Mate on ANDERSON logged a position abeam of the north tip of Caribou Island at a distance of 6 miles, and the course was changed to 141°T. The wheelsman was ordered to steer 142° because of the expected eastward drift. The 1652 position was not plotted on the chart in use in the pilothouse of ANDERSON. CAPT Cooper later testified that the course change was made at a point northnortheast of the northern tip of Caribou Island at a distance of approximately 7½ miles, and that five minutes later, at 1652, ANDERSON passed abeam of Caribou on the 141° course at a distance of 6 miles. On the chart he plotted during his testimony, the point of the course change and the point of passing abeam of Caribou are 4 miles apart. On the new course, FITZGERALD was observed to be about one mile to the right of ANDERSON's heading flasher and 14 to 15 miles ahead. At the time of this course change, ANDERSON logged winds of 58 knots from 304°T, the highest winds recorded during the voyage. It was still snowing lightly, limiting visibility, and seas were 12 to 18 feet.

The First Mate returned from the dinner relief and resumed the watch just as the course was being changed. Sometime later, FITZGERALD called ANDERSON and requested a position. The First Mate took a radar range and bearing which showed that ANDERSON was 10.5 miles on a bearing of 088°T from Caribou Island Light. The First Mate testified that he received the call from FITZGERALD and took the fix at 1701. He also noted that the radar showed FITZGERALD was 15 miles ahead of ANDERSON and "just a shade" to the left of the heading marker. He informed FITZGERALD that Whitefish Point was 35 miles on a bearing of 144°T from FITZGERALD's position. FITZGERALD replied, "Thanks," and that (they) "wanted to be 2 to 2½ miles off of Whitefish Point." The Mate on ANDERSON estimated that with the drift, FITZGERALD was probably headed for that point.

CAPT Cooper testified that at around 1800, when approximately 15 southeast of Caribou Island, and just out of its lee, ANDERSON encountered heavy seas with some waves which were as high as 25 feet. At 1810, CAPT Cooper left the wheelhouse and went below. At 1820, the First Mate called FITZGERALD again and asked what course they were steering because they appeared to be working to the left of ANDERSON. They replied they were steering 141°T. At 1849, the First Mate sent the 0000Z weather to the Coast Guard at Grand Marais. ANDERSON's position on the weather report was approximately two miles to the west of the trackline presented when the Master and Mates testified.

At 1900, the Mate informed FITZGERALD that they were 10 miles ahead and 1½ to 2 miles to the left of ANDERSON'S heading flasher, and that FITZGERALD was thus 15 miles from the Highlands at Crisp Point. At 1910, the Mate called FITZGERALD again and told them, "There is a target 19 miles ahead of us, so the target is nine miles on ahead." FITZGERALD asked, "Well, am I going to clear?" and the Mate said, "Yes, he is going to pass to the west of you." FITZGERALD replied, "Well, fine." As the Mate started to sign off, he asked, "Oh, by the way, how are you making out with your problems?" and FITZGERALD replied, "We are holding our own." The Mate replied, "Okay, fine, I will be talking to you later." This was the last transmission heard from FITZGERALD. Just as this conversation ended, at around 1910,

CAPT Cooper returned to the pilothouse, and he testified that at that time ANDERSON was 25 miles northnorthwest of Whitefish Point, with the radar showing FITZGERALD 9 miles ahead and a mile to a mile and a half to the east of the heading flasher. This was the last time that anyone on ANDERSON observed a target on the radar that they were certain was FITZGERALD.

Shortly thereafter, it stopped snowing and visibility improved considerably. At this time the Wheelsman on ANDERSON thought that he saw a red and a white light on the port bow, with the white one forward of the red one. He concluded that the red light was on the shore and then mentioned the white light to the rest of the bridge watch, but no one else was able to see it. The Mate could now see lights which he believed to be those of one of the upbound, saltwater ships, NANFRI, BENFRI and AVAFORS, which were 17 to 18 miles ahead. Because FITZGERALD should have been closer, he was surprised that he could not see her lights. CAPT Cooper thought that FITZGERALD might have had a blackout and told everyone on the bridge to look for a silhouette on the horizon. At this time the First Mate believed that FITZGERALD should have been 13 to 14 miles due west of Coppermine Point. CAPT Cooper recalled it as 15 miles north of Crisp Point and 14 miles west of Coppermine Point.

At 1920, after adjusting the radar, ANDERSON had three distinct targets, but none was FITZGERALD. CAPT Cooper then tried to call FITZGERALD on VHF-FM, and there was no response. The Mate then tried to call FITZGER-ALD, and then one of the saltwater vessels, without success. He then called the SS WILLIAM CLAY FORD, which was anchored in Whitefish Bay. FORD replied to ANDERSON that his signal was good. CAPT Cooper stated he then tried to call the Coast Guard at Sault Ste. Marie on Channel 16 and was told to shift to Channel 12, but received no follow-up. CAPT Cooper then called NANFRI, which was upbound near Whitefish Point, and talked with the Great Lakes Registered Pilot, CAPT Jacovetti. CAPT Jacovetti told CAPT Cooper that he had no contacts on his radar which could be FITZGERALD. CAPT Jacovetti stated that this call was at 2000 or later. CAPT Cooper then called the Coast Guard again and expressed concern for the FITZGERALD. CAPT Cooper stated that the Coast Guardsman told him to watch for a lost 16-foot boat. Approximately ten minutes later, he called the Coast Guard at Sault Ste. Marie again, feeling that by this time it was "pretty evident that the FITZGERALD was gone." This time the Coast Guard tried calling FITZGERALD. CAPT Cooper later stated that he was down around Whitefish Point before he "got to thinking for sure that FITZGERALD was gone." ANDERSON was abeam of Whitefish Point at 2059 and at that time logged winds of 48 knots.

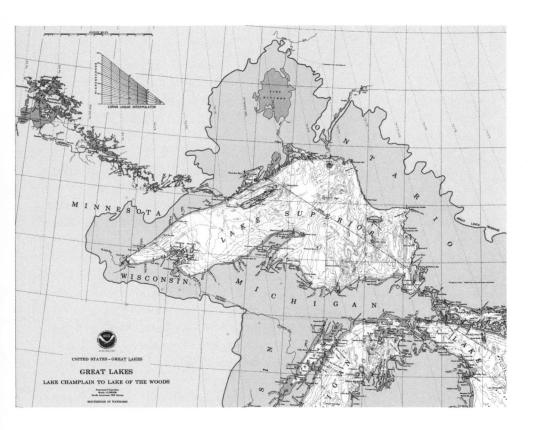

United States - Great Lakes

GREAT LAKES
LAKE CHAMPLAIN TO LAKE OF THE WOODS

Coast Guard Group Sault Ste. Marie logged a call from the ARTHUR M. ANDERSON on Channel 22 at 2032 in which CAPT said, "I am very concerned with the welfare of the Steamer EDMUND FITZGERALD. He was right in front of us experiencing a little difficulty. He was taking on a small amount of water and none of the upbound ships have passed him. I can see no lights as before and don't have him on radar. I just hope he didn't take a nose dive." This is the first recorded call from ANDERSON and the station log makes no mention of a broadcast concerning a lost 16-foot boat.

At approximately 1639, the coast Guard Station at Grand Marais, MI, received a call from FITZGERALD asking if Whitefish Point radio beacon was operating. The watch-stander at Grand Marais called Group Sault Ste. Marie on the teletype asking if the radio beacon was out. Group Sault Ste. Marie told him that there had been a power failure and that the equipment showed that Whitefish Radio beacon was not operating. Grand Marais called FITZGERALD back immediately and told them the beacon was not operating.

Some time between 1600 and 1630, CAPT Cedric C. Woodard, a Great Lakes Registered Pilot on board the Swedish vessel AVAFORS, upbound near

Whitefish Point, answered a call from FITZGERALD for any vessel in the vicinity of Whitefish Point. FITZGERALD asked if Whitefish Point beacon or light was on. CAPT Woodard replied that he could neither see the light nor receive the beacon. Somewhat later, CAPT Woodard overheard FITZGERALD call the Coast Guard at Sault Ste. Marie and then at Grand Marais. He did not hear whether or not the Coast Guard answered.

Approximately one hour after his first conversation, CAPT Woodard called FITZGERALD and, after confirming that he was speaking to CAPT McSorley, told him that Whitefish Point Light was on but the beacon was still off. At one point in this conversation, CAPT McSorley paused and, apparently in response to a question by someone on his ship, said, "Don't allow nobody on deck," and something else about a vent which CAPT Woodard was unable to understand. He then returned to his conversation with CAPT Woodard, saying that FITZGERALD had a "bad list," had lost both radars, and was taking heavy seas over the deck in one of the worst seas he had ever been in.

CAPT Woodard stated that during the time between his two conversations with FITZGERALD he overheard two conversations between FITZGERALD and ANDERSON. He did not recall the subject of the first conversation, but in the second one ANDERSON told FITZGERALD that it was about 20 miles above Whitefish "as near as he could tell," and ANDERSON was "about 10 miles behind you and gaining about a mile and a half an hour on you."

6. SEARCH EFFORT

Following CAPT Cooper's call at about 2025, expressing his concern about FITZGERALD, the Coast Guard radio watchstander attempted to contact FITZGERALD on VHF/FM and requested that the commercial radio station, WLC, at Rogers City, MI, attempt to contact FITZGERALD. Neither attempt was successful. At 2040, Coast Guard Station Sault Ste. Marie informed the CG Rescue Coordination Center (rcc) in Cleveland, which coordinates search and rescue efforts for the Great Lakes, that there was an uncertainty concerning FITZGERALD.

At 2103, ANDERSON called CG Station Sault Ste. Marie again, and this time reported that FITZGERALD was missing. This was relayed to RCC Cleveland at 2110, and, at 2115, RCC directed CG Air Station Traverse City, MI, to dispatch an aircraft. At 2116, the Canadian Rescue Center at Trenton, ONT, was advised. At 2125, RCC directed the Coast Guard Cutter NAUGATUCK (WYTM 92) to get underway from Sault Ste. Marie, MI, and, at 2130 the Coast Guard Cutter WOODRUSH (WLB 407) was also directed to get underway from its home port of Duluth, MN, approximately 300 miles from the scene.

Under the Search and Rescue Plan, Annex I to CCGDNine Operation Plan NRl-(FY), the Coast Guard Air Station at Traverse City, MI, provides fixed wing air coverage for all of the Great Lakes and rotary wing coverage for Lake Superior and the northern parts of Lake Huron and Lake Michigan. Under this plan, USCG Air Station Traverse City is required to have one HU-16 fixed wing search aircraft and one HH-52 helicopter in status Bravo-0 (capable of being launched in 30 minutes) or ALFA (airborne) at all times, and personnel on board immediately available and capable of launching either the HU-16 or the HH-52.

The first Coast Guard aircraft, an HU-16, was launched at 2206 after a minor delay to put flares on board, and was on scene at 2253. An HH-52, fitted with a Night Sun, an externally mounted, remote controlled, focusable, 3.8 million candlepower, Xenon arc searchlight, was launched at 2223, and was on scene at 0100, 11 November. A second HH-52 was launched at 2249 and was on scene at 0005, 11 November. A Canadian C-130 was launched at 0037.

Under the Vessel Employment Schedule then in effect, NAUGATUCK was in a maintenance status for the period 1 November through 16 November, but because of the bad weather it had been ordered to upgrade to a standby status at 1947, 10 November. This class of vessel is restricted from operating in open water when winds exceed 60 knots, and because of the severe weather and sea conditions which existed in eastern Lake Superior on the evening of 10 November, at 2125, when NAUGATUCK was directed to get underway it was also directed not to proceed beyond the entrance to Whitefish Bay. After the order to get underway was received, NAUGATUCK suffered a failure of a lube oil line and repairs were begun immediately. By the next morning, repairs were completed and the weather had moderated. NAUGATUCK got underway at approximately 0900 and was on scene at 1245.

The Coast Guard Cutter WOODRUSH had been in a BRAV0–6 Standby Status, i.e., ready to proceed within six hours. WOODRUSH got underway at 0008, 11 November, and arrived on scene approximately twenty-four hours later.

A Coast Guard 40-foot patrol boat (CG 40573) was directed to proceed from CG Base Sault Ste. Marie on the morning of the 11th and searched until late afternoon. The rescue coordination center evaluated the possibility of using the 36-foot motor lifeboat stationed at Grand Marais, MI, and concluded that it would not be effective due to the 35 to 40 mile distance, the slow speed of the boat and the severe weather. In addition, rcc concluded that the 40 foot patrol boats stationed at Marquette, MI, Bayfield, WI, and Duluth, MN, were too far from the scene to be effective.

The Coast Guard Icebreaker MACKINAW was at its home port of Cheboygan, MI, but was in a repair status preparing for its winter ice operations and was unable to get underway. The Coast Guard Buoy Tender SUNDEW was at its home port of Charlevoix, MI, also in a repair status.

The 40 foot patrol boat and 44 foot motor lifeboat at St. Ignace, MI, were evaluated as being too far from the scene to be effective.

There were no other Coast Guard SAR vessels available nearby in any of the adjacent Great Lakes which were evaluated as capable of responding in the weather conditions which existed.

The Canadian Coast Guard Vessel VERENDRYE was made available on 12 and 13 November and searched the area along the Canadian Shore.

At approximately 2100, 10 November, the Commanding Officer of the Coast Guard Group Sault Ste. Marie, MI, requested the Steamer ANDERSON, which by then had reached Whitefish Bay, to reverse course and assist in the search. ANDERSON turned around and was on scene at approximately 0200. At approximately 2230, the Commanding Officer of Coast Guard Group Sault Ste. Marie contacted the U. S. vessels WILLIAM CLAY FORD, WILLIAM R. ROESCH and BENJAMIN F. FAIRLESS and the Canadian vessels FRONTENAC, MURRAY BAY, HILDA MARJANNE and ALGOSOO, which were anchored in or near Whitefish Bay, and requested that they get underway to assist in the search. Of these, only the WILLIAM CLAY FORD (Ford Motor Co.) and the HILDA MARJANNE (Upper Lakes Shipping, Ltd.) responded that they would get underway. FORD got underway and proceeded to the area, arriving at approximately 0200, and searched throughout the night and into the next day. HILDA MARJANNE got underway but in approximately 20 or 30 minutes determined that the weather conditions were too severe for that vessel, and, accordingly, returned to anchorage in Whitefish Bay.

The Commanding Officer of the Coast Guard Group Sault Ste. Marie also called BENFRI, NANFRI and AVAFORS, foreign flag saltwater ships which were upbound, in or slightly beyond the area where FITZGERALD was lost, and asked them to reverse course and assist in the search. All three replied that they did not believe that they could reverse course without hazard to their vessels, because of the severe weather conditions. NANFRI did reduce speed, change course slightly to the north and maintain a lookout.

Coast Guard Station Sault Ste. Marie, MI, made Urgent Broadcasts on the Steamer FITZGERALD at 2145 and at 2200. An Urgent Broadcast was initiated by the Ninth Coast Guard District at 2238 and was rebroadcast regularly until 2127, 13 November, after the search was terminated.

In addition to the commercial vessels ANDERSON, FORD and HILDA

MARJANNE which undertook the search on the night of the 10th, the following vessels responded to the Urgent Broadcast and assisted in the search:

U. S. VESSELS

ARMCO (Columbia Transportation Div., Oglebay-Norton Co.)

ROGER BLOUGH (United States Steel Corp.)

RESERVE (Columbia Transportation Div., Oglebay-Norton Co.)

WILFRED SYKES (Inland Steel Co.)

WILLIAM R. ROESCH (Columbia Transportation Div., Oglebay-Norton Co.)

CANADIAN VESSELS

FRONTENAC (Canada Steamship Lines, Ltd.)

JOAN O. McKELLAR (Scott Misener Steamships, Ltd.)

MURRAY BAY (Canada Steamship Lines, Ltd.)

F/V JAMES D.

Throughout the night of the 10th the fixed-wing aircraft and helicopters and the vessels ANDERSON and FORD searched the area where FITZGERALD was reported lost and along the shoreline, utilizing lights and flares.

During the 11th, 12th and 13th, the search area consisted of the eastern end of Lake Superior from the eastern shore of the lake, westward to a north-south line approximately fifteen miles west of Crisp Point and from the southern shore of the lake, northward to an east-west line approximately at Caribou Island.

The search which began at daylight on the 11th utilized a C-130 from the Michigan Air National Guard, a Canadian C-130, a Coast Guard HU-16 and two HH-52 helicopters from Coast Guard Air Station Traverse City, and a Coast Guard C-130 from Coast Guard Air Station Elizabeth City, NC. The latter was designated On Scene Commander. All aircraft searched throughout the daylight hours on the 11th. During the 12th and 13th, the search continued, utilizing the Coast Guard C-130, the National Guard C-130, the Coast Guard HU-16, the Canadian C-130 and the Coast Guard helicopters. On the 12th, the launching of the aircraft was delayed because of the low ceiling. Helicopters were able to proceed first at a low altitude and later in the afternoon the ceiling rose and the HU-16 joined the search. During this same period, the Coast Guard Cutter NAUGATUCK and the Coast Guard Cutter WOODRUSH conducted various surface searches coordinated with the aircraft.

Active search was suspended at 2212, on November 13th, although Coast Guard Air Station Traverse City was directed to conduct daily flights over the area, and this was done for approximately one more week. After that, Coast Guard Air Station Traverse City conducted weekly flights over the area until the end of the year.

On 14 November, a U. S. Navy aircraft joined the search, and utilizing MAD (Magnetic Anomaly Detection) equipment located a strong single magnetic contact at 47°00.S'N, 85°06'W. A slight oil slick was observed at the contact position. This contact was later determined to be the sunken hulk of FITZGERALD.

Ontario Canadian Provincial Police conducted numerous shoreline searches during the active search period, and helicopters from CG Air Station Traverse City also searched the Michigan and Canadian Shores.

7. SEARCH RESULTS

Despite the intensive search, no survivors were found, nor were any bodies recovered. Only one lifeboat, one-half of another lifeboat, two inflatable life rafts, twenty-one life jackets or life jacket pieces and some miscellaneous flotsam identified as being from FITZGERALD were found.

One piece of a lifeboat was first sighted by ANDERSON at 0807, 11 November, at a location approximately nine miles east of where FITZGERALD sank. The other lifeboat was sighted by ANDERSON at 0905 approximately four miles south of the first one. The severely damaged piece of No. 1 lifeboat was recovered on 11 November by the Steamer WILLIAM R. ROESCH at a position approximately 2 miles northwest of Coppermine Point, Ontario. The No. 2 lifeboat, also severely damaged, was recovered on 11 November in the vicinity of Coppermine Point by the F/V JAMES D. Both lifeboats were delivered to the U. S. Coast Guard Base, Sault Ste. Marie, MI, where a survey of them was conducted on 25 November 1975.

The remains of the No. 1 lifeboat consisted of the forward sixteen feet of the boat with the starboard side badly damaged. The words "EDMUND FITZGERALD NO. 1" were painted in three-inch letters on both bows and the words "500 CU. FT. 50 PERSONS" were painted in one and one-half-inch letters below that. There was no name plate attached and there were no air tanks, buoyancy material, or boat equipment present, however, a substantial amount of this was found floating nearby. The plating was heavily buckled and holed over a four foot by four foot area, port side, forward. This damage was centered in the turn of the bilge area. The forward section of the port grab rail was torn free and sharply rolled back. The grab rail was missing from the starboard side. The life line and seine floats for this portion of the boat were present. There was a sharp indentation in the plating over a one foot by six inch area on the starboard side, forward, at the turn of bilge. The bow ring was missing and the thwarts and side benches were damaged throughout. The forward Rottmer Releasing gear, consisting of the hook, preventer bars, lock, upper and lower guide bearings, universal joints and the complete portion of the shafting to the after universal, was present. The shaft was twisted and distorted. The plate attachment to the stern was in place. The releasing lever was torn loose from its secured position and the hold-down brackets were severed. Data on the name plate for the Rottmer Releasing Gear was:

Marine Safety Equipment Corp., New Jersey,
Approval No. 160.033/52/0

The hook lock was in the position in which it would be with the boat stowed, that is, it was in the locked position. However, the base of the hook was not inside the hook lock and as a result, the hook was free to rotate about the horizontal pin.

The entire No. 2 lifeboat was recovered. The words "EDMUND FITZGER-ALD NO. 2" were painted in three-inch letters on both bows and the words "500 CU. FT. 50 PERSONS" were painted in one and one-half-inch letters below that. There was no name plate attached. The plating along the port side of the stem was split open from the gunwale to about 2 feet above the keel. The bow plating was buckled from gunwale to keel from the stem to 12 feet aft on the port side, and to 9 feet aft on the starboard side. The plating was holed on the port side forward, at the turn of the bilge, over an area of two and one-half by one and one-half feet. The rivets fastening the stern sheet to the port side of the boat were missing. The forward half of the grab rail was buckled and the forward shell fastening were pulled out (there were a total of 6 such fastenings). The starboard grab rail was distorted throughout its 12-foot length, and the third (from forward) of the six grab rail to shell connections was pulled out. The shell connection of the first thwart was torn loose on the starboard side. The first and third side bench brackets were torn loose at the upper connection to the gunwale. The forward and after air tanks on the port side were missing and the other four were distorted. The forward air tank on the starboard side was adrift and the other five tanks were in place. The thwarts and side benches were generally damaged. The Rottmer Releasing gear, consisting of the hook, preventer bars, lock, upper and lower guide bearings and universal joints, was intact at both ends. The plates securing the gear to the stem and stern were present. The shafting was twisted. The releasing lever was in the closed position. Legible data on the after releasing gear name plate stated:

Marine Safety Equipment Corp., New Jersey,
Approval No. 160.033/52/0

Both of the hook locks on boat No. 2 were in the same condition as the hook lock on boat No. 1, i.e., the hook lock was closed but the hook was outside of the lock and free to rotate about the horizontal pin. No boat equipment was found in No. 2 boat.

A SWITLIK, 25-man inflatable life raft, identified as being from FITZGERALD, was found inflated and floating upright, near the shore, in the vicinity of Coppermine Point. This raft was recovered by the M/V ROGER BLOUGH at 0942 on 11 November. The second SWITLIK, 25-man inflatable life raft from FITZGERALD was found south of Coppermine Point at 1100 on 11 November and was recovered, partially deflated, by an Ontario, Canada, Provincial Police Shore Party, later that day. Both rafts were delivered to the U. S. Coast Guard Base Sault Ste. Marie, MI, and a survey of them was conducted there, and at the U. S. Steel, Great Lakes Fleet Warehouse, Sault Ste. Marie, MI, on 24 November 1975, by U. S. Coast Guard Inspectors and a Canadian government Marine Surveyor.

The first raft inspected was the one recovered by the M/V ROGER BLOUGH. This raft was a SWITLIK inflatable life raft manufactured by the Switlik Parachute Co., Inc., Trenton, NJ., Approved by U.S.C.G. for 25 persons, Lot No. 3, Approval No. 160.051/20/1, Serial No. Spec. MM 13, Original Inspection: 12/5/67.

When first examined, it was in a deflated condition and it was fully inflated during the inspection. The raft and canopy were found to be in serviceable condition. There was a small tear in the after section of the floor, a slight air leak at the lower half of the separation buoyancy tube and a small tear in the forward part of the top of the canopy cover. The outside light was in operating order but the light cable had been cut. The submersible batteries were dated September, 1974. The after section of the inflatable floor was missing. The inflation bottle and all valves of the inflation system were operational. The full 100 foot painter was properly secured to the raft and to the C02 release wire. The weak link that secures the painter to the vessel was missing. The following equipment was found in the raft:

(1) Part of sea anchor line

(2) Heaving line

(3) Two paddles—one handle

(4) One hand pump

(5) Two spare flashlight batteries

(6) Patch kit and glue

(7) Two relief valve plugs

(8) Life Raft Instruction booklet

(9) Water storage bag

Boarding ladders and lifelines outside and inside the raft were in good condition.

The second raft inspected was the one recovered by the Ontario Provincial Police. This raft was also a SWITLIK inflatable life raft manufactured by the Switlik Parachute Co., Inc., Trenton, NJ., Approved by U.S.C.G. for 25 persons, Lot No. 2, Approval No. 160.051/20/1, Serial No. Spec. MM 47, Original Inspection 2/5/67.

The raft had a 12 inch gash in a flotation tube and the nylon straps were badly tangled around the rubber inflating tube leading to the CO_2 cylinder. The blue nylon cover was badly torn. The lower buoyancy chamber had three holes. These had been punched with a pocket knife by the Ontario Provincial Police shore party to allow the water in the raft to escape when the raft was recovered. The inflation bottle and valves were operational. Only 30 feet of the 100 foot painter remained and it appeared to have broken under tension. The painter was properly secured to the raft and to the CO_2 release wire. The inspection report stated that it appeared that the upper buoyancy chamber inflation valve had been torn from the fabric in an attempt to deflate the buoyancy chamber. The valve was in operating order. The nylon canopy covers were ripped off the starboard side and the covers were partially ripped off the upper chambers. Other than this damage, the condition of the material of the chambers and canopy was good. Both manually inflatable floor sections were found uninflated near the raft.

A CO_2 inflation cylinder was found in the water beside the raft. The only other equipment found was an orange nylon bag, 3' by 4" by 6" in size, found tangled in the nylon straps, which contained sodden flares and the life raft instruction booklet and patch kit. The lights for inside and outside were broken but the wiring was intact and in order. The submersible batteries were dated September, 1974. The raft was covered in several places with heavy bunker fuel. It was not possible to identify which raft had been stowed forward or which aft.

The additional items recovered consisted of the following:

(1) 20 cork float life preservers or life preserver pieces.

(2) Eight oars or oar pieces.

(3) One piece of a Sounding Board, identified as the type which had been on FITZGERALD. There were no chalk markings on the Sounding Board.

(4) Eight flotation tanks, identified as having come from the lifeboats.

(5) One large built-up wooden fender block with line.

(6) Two propane cylinders, one with valve cover. Propane was used for galley fuel on board FITZGERALD and tanks such as these were stowed on deck, aft on the Poop Deck.

(7) Thirteen life rings, with pieces of line attached. Two had carbide "water light" canisters attached and two other life rings had threaded circular plastic discs attached to the lines. These discs were identified as end caps of electrically operated water lights.

(8) One piece of a life ring.

(9) One piece of line approximately 8 feet long.

(10) Two 2" by 12" planks, one approximately 12 feet long, the other approximately 5 feet long. One 6" by 8" plank approximately 15 feet long.

(11) One wooden stool, identified as similar to the type used on FITZGERALD.

(12) One heaving line.

(13) One stepladder.

(14) One-half of a boat cover, identified as the type which had been on the lifeboats on FITZGERALD.

(15) One rudder from a lifeboat.

(16) One lifeboat boat box, empty.

(17) One floodlight, identified as the type that was installed on the pilothouse and after deck of FITZGERALD.

(18) One plastic spray bottle, white, marked "Pilothouse Window."

(19) One broken extension ladder.

(20) Pieces of assorted broken scrap wood.

The end caps of the electrically operated water lights had been separated from the lights without damage to the caps. The caps were examined at Coast Guard Headquarters and were identified as having come from lights manufactured by the Automatic Lite Company, Baltimore, MD. Representatives of Columbia Transportation Division, the operators of FITZGERALD, confirmed that the lights on FITZGERALD had been SAVE-U-LIGHTS, manufactured by the Automatic Lite Company under Approval No. 161.010/3/1. Records at Coast Guard Headquarters indicate that this approval number was superseded on 25 May 1976, when the manufacturer redesigned the water light cap attachment because the caps on the prior design loosened and fell out or pulled out too easily.

Once the flotsam had been examined, it was turned over to Columbia Transportation Div., Oglebay-Norton Co., the operator of FITZGERALD, for disposition.

One additional cork float life preserver was found on the beach, approximately 5 miles north of Coppermine Point on 20 April 1976. This life preserver was in the same general condition as those which had been found during the November search.

8. POLLUTION

On the morning of 11 November 1975, when it became apparent that there was some discharge of oil in the area where FITZGERALD was lost, the Commander, Ninth Coast Guard District, activated the Joint U.S.-Canadian Pollution Contingency Plan and the Joint Response Team (JRT), with U. S. and Canadian representatives on scene at Sault Ste. Marie that evening. A representative of the Coast Guard Atlantic Strike Team was also present. The JRT remained on scene in an observation and advisory capacity until Friday, 14 November 1975, at which time it was concluded that the diesel oil on board the vessel (bow thruster fuel) had vented and that the Bunker C (main propulsion fuel) had reached a sufficiently low temperature that the viscosity had increased enough to preclude further venting. Thus, it was determined that the pollution potential was negligible and the JRT was deactivated. The oil which had been observed on the surface had dissipated and there was no cleanup effort.

9. UNDERWATER SEARCH AND SURVEY

An extensive sequence of underwater search and survey activities was undertaken to locate and identify the wreckage of FITZGERALD. The first of these was a side-scan sonar search conducted using equipment and personnel from the U. S. Coast Guard Research and Development Center during the period 14 November through 16 November 1975. The equipment used was an Egerton, Germershansen and Greer (E.G.&G.) Model 250 side-scanning sonar deployed from the Coast Guard Cutter WOODRUSH. Wreckage, which was later proven to be FITZGERALD, was located within the first half day of the sonar search. Using a Coast Guard owned Mini-Ranger Navigation System, the center of the wreckage was shown to be located at a position 46°59.S'N, 85°06.7'W.

Continuing search activity disclosed two large objects lying close together on the lake floor in approximately 530 feet of water. Although bad weather in the area resulted in poor sonar trace quality, preliminary calculations showed that each of the objects was approximately 300 feet in length. In addition, a "sonically rough" area near these objects was observed and this was tentatively identified as spilled cargo.

Because the first side-scan sonar search was conducted under conditions of adverse weather and because the equipment used was not fully adapted to operations at the depth at which the wreckage of FITZGERALD was found, the Marine Board recommended that a second, more detailed side-scan sonar search be conducted.

The second side-scanning sonar search was conducted by a commercial contractor, Seaward, Inc., of Falls Church, VA, during the period from 22 November through 25 November. This survey was performed from the USCGC WOODRUSH, using equipment similar to that used in the first survey. During this survey, horizontal surface positioning was maintained by the use of the same Coast Guard Motorola Mini-Ranger Navigational System used in the first survey.

Sonar operations were conducted almost continuously during the three-day period under severe wind and sea conditions. A total of 80 sonar traces were made, each of which recorded a transit of several hundred yards of continuous sonar searching. In connection with these 80 runs, nearly 300 navigational fixes were obtained. The purpose of the numerous runs was to obtain the maximum amount of data from as many different sonar aspects as possible.

Initial interpretation of the sonar traces indicated that the wreckage found was probably that of FITZGERALD. The side-scan sonar traces were taken to Seaward's facility and subjected to an intensive analysis, including the construction of a small model of the wreckage which was used to verify the interpretation of the side-scan results. Based on this analysis, the Marine Board determined that the wreckage was very probably that of FITZGERALD but that positive identification was necessary, and that the configuration and arrangement of the wreckage and the bottom conditions were such that a detailed visual survey was both feasible and necessary.

During the period 12–16 May, a third side-scan sonar survey was made. The survey was conducted to reestablish the accurate position of the wreckage for the photographic survey and to define the planned mooring radius for anchor placement clear of the wreck. This survey, like the second one, was conducted by Seaward, Inc., using Seaward equipment, from the USCGC WOODRUSH. This survey resulted in good quality traces which were interpreted to contain information which, for all practical purposes, was identical to that obtained at the second survey, in November.

Immediately following the third side-scan sonar survey, a visual survey of the wreckage was conducted using the U. S. Navy CURV III system contracted for by the Coast Guard. The CURV III system is composed of an unmanned underwater vehicle, an umbilical control and power cable, and surface equipment operated from any suitable support ship. The vehicle is capable of making visual observations, recovering small objects, and performing other light work tasks at depths to 7,000 feet. The vehicle consists of a frame, approximately 6 feet by 6 feet by 15 feet, which supports two horizontal propulsion motors, one vertical propulsion motor, one 35 mm still camera, two black and white TV cameras, lights, a manipulator arm, and other machinery. The vehicle operates on electric power supplied from special generators placed on the support vessel and is operated from a control van also placed on the support vessel. In addition to the remote control mechanism and sonar presentation, the control van contains video tape recording equipment.

From 12 to 19 May 1976, while the third side-scan sonar survey was being conducted, the CURV III was being transported to Sault Ste. Marie, MI. The CURV III system and operating and observation personnel were loaded on board WOODRUSH on 18 and 19 May 1976, and underwater operations began on 20 May 1976. Between 20 and 28 May 1976, CURV III made twelve dives, logging a total of 56 hours, 5 minutes of "bottom time" and recording 43,255 feet of video tape and 895 color photographs.

The results of the three side-scan sonar surveys and of the CURV III visual (television and photographic) survey were assembled and reviewed by an independent research contractor. Based upon all the information available, this contractor prepared sketches of a plan of the wreckage, Fig. (6), and artists' conceptions of the wreckage from several different views, Fig. (7)–(11).

The wreckage of FITZGERALD lies at 46°59.9′N, 85°06.6′W, in 530 feet of water in eastern Lake Superior, approximately 17 miles northwest of Whitefish Point, MI, and just north of the International Boundary, in Canadian waters. The wreckage consists of an upright bow section, approximately 276 feet long, lying on a heading of 125°T, an inverted stern section approximately 253 feet long, lying on a heading of 075°T, and debris in between. At its closest point, the stern section is approximately 170 feet from the bow section, and the overall distance from the rudder post, at the end of the stern section, to the stem, at the opposite end of the bow section, is approximately 540 feet. An area of distorted metal lies between the two pieces and to both sides over a distance of some 200 feet. Both the bow and the stern sections and all of the wreckage appear to be settled into the bottom mud, and a great deal of mud covers the portion of the Spar deck attached to the bow section. The bottom mud in the area of the wreckage shows extensive disruption and, in some locations, the bottom mud is in large mounds. The mud appears to be plowed up both at the bow and stern sections. The mud which is against the hull shows no regular pattern. The presence of the mud hampered the visible survey considerably, both because it obscured the details of the wreckage and because the passage of the CURV III vehicle caused the mud to swirl up, reducing the visibility. The name of the vessel was clearly visible, both on the stern section and on the bow section, and the identity of this wreckage as that of the SS EDMUND FITZGERALD was thus positively confirmed. During the survey, no bodies were found, nor were any items seen which could be identified as personal effects of the crew.

The bow section is sitting nearly upright on the bottom, inclined approximately 15°. The Spar Deck of the bow section extends to a location between hatch No. 8 and No. 9. At the separation, the starboard side of the hull is bent in toward the centerline and is folded under the deck, while the deck is bent upward from a point approximately two hatches forward of the separation. Mud is spread and piled all over the Spar Deck area, and the deck edge on the port side is completely covered with mud. At some locations it is possible to distinguish taconite pellets, or the mud-covered outline of them. The hatch covers are missing from No. 1 and No. 2 hatches. The forward coaming of No. 1 hatch is severely damaged. The after coaming of No. 1, and the forward and after coamings of No. 2 hatch show less damage. No. 3 and No. 4 hatches are covered with mud. The hatch covers for hatches Nos. 5, 6, 7 and 8 are missing. The forward coaming of No. 5 hatch is laid down and damaged. The degree of damage to the deck and hatch coamings increases from No. 1 to the separation. The access hatch, located between cargo hatches Nos. 7 and 8, is present, with the cover on and dogged. No fence rail stanchions are present. The sockets into which the portable stanchions were fitted are undamaged. The 28-foot draft mark is visible just above the mud line, and the hull beneath that is buried in the mud. The bow above the mud is damaged on both sides immediately adjacent to the stem. On the starboard side, slightly aft of the stem, the hull immediately below the Spar Deck level is holed and badly distorted. The shell plating between the Spar Deck and Forecastle Deck is badly damaged and distorted, and aft on the starboard side this plating is badly bent and laid in towards the centerline. Throughout this area the plating is heavily wrinkled, and the white paint which had been on the hull in this area has broken away and the plating beneath it has rusted. The steering jib is bent completely back and the end of it lies up against the forward section of the Texas Deck bulwark. The plating of the bulkhead of the forward house between the Forecastle Deck and the Texas Deck is badly damaged. The forward section of the pilothouse is damaged on both the port and starboard sides and the forward section of the sunshade above the pilothouse windows is damaged on the port side. Most of the pilothouse windows are missing. The radar and r.d.f. antennas and the ship's bell, which had been installed on top of the pilothouse, are also missing. Foundations for the radar antennas are visible but no antennas can be seen.

The stern section is upside down, inclined approximately 10°. All of the bottom plating and the side shell plating which is visible above the mud line is intact. The separation is estimated to be at frame 155, which would correspond to the after end of hatch No. 18. At the separation, approximately 12 to 15 feet of the hull extends above the mud. At the after end, the overhead of the Spar Deck, i.e., the underside of the Poop Deck, is lying approximately even with the mud level. The aft superstructure is buried in the mud. The rudder and propeller are clearly visible and undamaged. The rudder appears to be at the midships position. There is no hole or rupture in the exposed stern section of the hull other than at the separation.

One dent was found slightly to port of centerline, approximately 50 feet forward of the rudder post. A large inward dent, which appears to be a buckle, was found on the starboard side of the stern section at a position approximately

20 feet from the separation, extending vertically from the mud line to the turn of the bilge and across the hull for 10 or 15 feet. There was no breach of the hull at either dent. At the separation on the starboard side, the plating is twisted outward from the hull, while on the port side, the plating is, in general, twisted inward.

Extending outward from the separation at the bow section and at the stern section is an extensive area of debris. For the most part, this debris cannot be identified as coming from a particular part of the vessel, although much of it appears to be pieces of interior structure. This debris is covered with mud and, in some cases, taconite pellets are visible within or on top of the mud. A set of three damaged but regularly spaced hatch coamings and a hatch cover are located adjacent to the inverted port side of the stern section. One of these coamings has the numeral "11" on it. Although a systematic survey of this debris was attempted, no regular order to it could be determined by visual examination.

All of the areas of the separations, which were examined in detail, show curving, twisted edges such as is associated with ductile failure. No separations were seen which appeared to be the sort of straight or flat separations common to brittle fracture. All of the hatch coamings found have hatch clamps attached, and the great majority of the hatch clamps observed appear to be undamaged. One coaming, which could not be identified by number, has a line of clamps, with one distorted and several completely undamaged clamps on either side. One distorted piece of structure, which was identified as a badly damaged corner of a hatch coaming, was observed to have undamaged hatch clamps attached to it. This general pattern, i.e., that nearly all of the hatch clamps found appeared to be undamaged and only a few were distorted, was seen at every location where a hatch coaming was found.

A few pieces of debris were found which were identified as hatch covers. One of these was folded to a right angle and another was protruding from the No. 6 hatch opening. There was no sign of scrape mark or other damage at the button on which the hatch clamps land on these covers.

A few deck vents were observed, primarily on the starboard side of the bow section. It was not possible to determine whether the vent covers were in the open or closed position. One vent was observed torn away from the deck, and an opening in the deck at the base of the vent pipe could be seen.

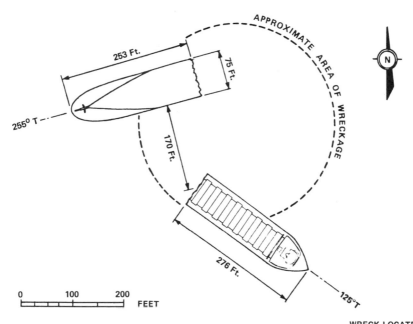

APPROXIMATE AREA OF WRECKAGE

253 Ft.

75 Ft.

255° T

170 Ft.

276 Ft.

125° T

N

0	100	200

FEET

WRECK LOCATED AT
LAT   46° 59.9′ N
LONG 85° 06.6′ W

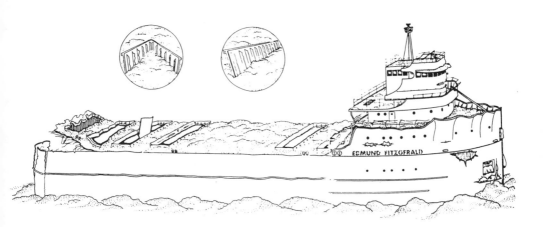

EDMUND FITZGERALD

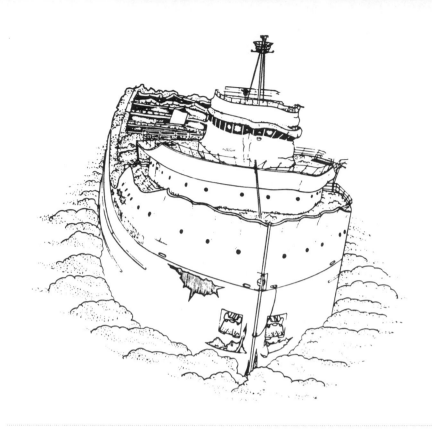

10. HISTORY AND MAINTENANCE

FITZGERALD was built in 1958 at Great Lakes Engineering Works, River Rouge, MI, Hull No. 301. Owned by Northwestern Mutual Life Insurance, of Milwaukee, WI, FITZGERALD was immediately chartered to the Columbia Transportation Division, Oglebay-Norton Corporation, and placed into service as a bulk carrier on the Great Lakes.

FITZGERALD continued in operation essentially unchanged until 1969, at which time a Byrd-Johnson, diesel powered bowthruster unit was installed. During the 1971–72 winter lay-up, while at Duluth, MN, FITZGERALD underwent a coal-to-oil conversion. All of the coal fuel equipment and accessories were removed, and the plant was converted to burn oil. Incidental to this conversion was the installation of two fuel tanks in the space previously occupied by the coal bunkers. A Bailey Meter Digital System for automatic control of the boiler combustion system was also installed. This system, a Bailey Type 762, which consisted of a complete pneumatic combustion and feedwater control system, operated without incident from the time it was installed. At the same time of the coal-to-oil conversion and automation, the vessel was equipped with a sewage holding tank and additional CO_2 firefighting equipment was installed.

No structural problems which were considered severe enough to cause the vessel to be removed from service during the operating season were reported by FITZGERALD during its 17 years of operation. The only notable structural modification, other than the conversion from coal to oil, took place during the 1969–70 winter lay-up. The vessel had experienced cracking at the keelson to shell connection and a naval architect recommended installing additional vertical stiffening on the keelsons. Following this modification, no further circumstances of this cracking were found until the 1973–1974 winter lay-up and drydocking, and these were of sufficiently reduced scope that no more than simple rewelding repairs were necessary. During the same 1969–70 lay-up, the crew discovered a fracture in the vertical section of the gunwale bounding angle, portside, adjacent to hatch No. 14. This fracture, which began at the top of a rivet hole and propagated vertically, was determined to have been caused by a fault in the original construction of the vessel. The fracture was repaired by rewelding and there was no recurrence. Prior to the 1973–74 winter lay-up, the vessel had experienced some minor cracking, described as "hairline cracks one to one and one-half inches in length," in the vertical welds joining the hatch end girder and the transverse hatch coaming, beneath the Spar Deck. Each hatch had four such welded joints and of the eighty-four joints on the vessel, twenty were found with cracks. During the 1973–74 winter lay-up, these cracks were repaired and the radius of the cutout above this connection was increased to two inches. During the 1974 and 1975 operating seasons, no repetition of this cracking was observed. Because cracks had been found at Hatch 14 in the vertical butt weld of the longitudinal hatch end girder channels, this connection was modified, during this same lay-up, at the butt, by sniping away the lower and upper flanges of the channel, rewelding the webb and riveting the upper flange. No recurrence of this cracking was observed after this modification.

The following is a list of hull structural casualties sustained by FITZGERALD since 1969. All structural damage was repaired. In most instances, this was accomplished by removing the damaged portions and replacing as original.

a. 6 September 1969. Grounding in the vicinity of the locks, Sault Ste. Marie, MI. Damaged areas were in the B and C strakes (hull strakes were lettered from A at the keel to M at the deck edge), frames 156 to 198 (hatches 19–21 and after house) in the D strake, frames 131–148 (hatches 16 and 17) and frames 181–198 (after house), and in the E strake frames 156–165 (hatch 19). The hull plating was set up heavily, scored and gouged and the associated internal stiffeners were also damaged.

b. 30 April 1970. Collision with the SS HOCHELAGA. Damaged areas were in the J, K, L and M strakes, frames 117–165 (hatches 18 and 19).

c. 4 September 1970. Striking a lock wall at the locks at Sault Ste. Marie, MI. Damaged areas were in the L strake, frame 145–162 (hatches 18 and 19).

d. May 1973. Striking a lock wall, Sault Ste. Marie, MI. Damaged areas were in the K, L and M strakes, frames 20–70 (hatches 2–7) and in the Main (tunnel) deck. Plating and associated internal stiffeners were set it.

e. 17 June 1974. Striking a lock wall at Sault Ste. Marie, MI. Damaged areas were in the L strake, frames 20–45 (hatches 2–4) and in the Main Deck and associated internal stiffeners.

In September 1974, the crew inadvertently started to lift the cover from No. 8 hatch without removing all of the hatch clamps. Four clamps, the coaming and the hatch cover and the stiffeners on the coaming and cover were damaged. Repairs were accomplished during the 1974–75 winter lay-up period.

Maintenance of the vessel during the operating season was the responsibility of the crew. The Master and Chief Engineer had the authority to contract for minor maintenance items as well as supplies. Repairs of a substantial nature, that is, those for which the cost would be more than a few hundred dollars, had to be approved by the company office. During winter lay-up, repairs and maintenance were accomplished by commercial contractors and by a winter standby crew which provided maintenance for several of the vessels operated by the company. During the fall preceding the loss of FITZGERALD, a company representative had performed an inspection of the vessel and had consulted with the crew concerning their requested work items. The detailed Winter Work List had not yet been developed. The company representative testified that there were no items on the list of work requested by the ship's crew for the 1975–76 lay-up or in the notes of his inspection which he considered anything other than routine maintenance. These lists did include items to "check all hatch covers and coamings and straighten as found necessary (No. 21 fwd. starboard side)" with estimated cost of $2100, and "V-out and weld all fractures in plating for tank top, side tank and bulkheads throughout cargo holds, as marked" with estimated cost of $6000. Identical work items appear on the 1974–75 work lists, with $1200 estimated for hatch cover and coaming repairs and approximately $3800 actually spent, and $2800 estimated for structural repairs and approximately $3200 actually spent.

11. LIFESAVING EQUIPMENT

FITZGERALD was required by Coast Guard Regulations to have primary lifesaving equipment for 200% of the persons authorized to be carried on board. Of this primary lifesaving equipment, one-half, or facilities for 100% of the persons to be carried on board, was required to be in the form of lifeboats, and the other half was required to be in the form of inflatable life rafts. Because FITZGERALD had crew berthing and working spaces "widely separated," at least two inflatable life rafts were required. Lifesaving equipment installed on board FITZGERALD consisted of two 50-person lifeboats and two 25-person inflatable life rafts. Each inflatable raft was installed in a rack from which it was designed to float free. Upon floating free, the raft would inflate automatically. One life raft was located aft of the forward house on the Texas Deck, starboard side, and the other raft was located aft of the after deckhouse on the Poop Deck.

Considerable testimony was received from both licensed and unlicensed Great Lakes Merchant Mariners concerning the use of primary lifesaving equipment. Without exception, the witnesses expressed considerable doubt that lifeboats could have been successfully launched by the crew of the vessel under the weather conditions which existed at the time FITZGERALD was lost. A Great Lakes Registered Pilot testified: "I have said that if the damn ship is going to go down, I would get in my bunk and pull the blankets over my head and say, 'Let her go,' because there was no way of launching the boats."

Drills, in good weather, at the dock, show that a conventional lifeboat could not be launched in less than 10 minutes and testimony indicated that as much as 30 minutes might be required to launch a lifeboat in a seaway. Most witnesses expressed more confidence in the inflatable life rafts than in the lifeboats, although very few of them had ever seen a life raft inflated or launched. Coast Guard Regulations require training and drills in the use of lifeboats, but do not address life rafts. Testimony indicated that Oglebay-Norton Co., the operator of FITZGERALD, had no training program in the use of life rafts.

The Coast Guard is involved in a research and development program dedicated toward improving lifesaving equipment and procedures. Much of this research is specifically directed toward Great Lakes shipping. The initial studies concluded that improvement is needed in launching and embarking into primary lifesaving equipment. This research is continuing.

Coast Guard research has also included the development of a method of evaluating exposure suits. There are no requirements for exposure suits on Great Lakes vessels, and no suits were provided on FITZGERALD on its last voyage on 9 November.

On 15 June 1976, the Coast Guard published an Advance Notice of Proposed Rulemaking concerning increases in the requirements for lifesaving equipment on vessels operating on the Great Lakes. This notice stated that the Coast Guard was considering amendments to the regulations for Great Lakes vessels in the following areas:

a. Lifeboat exposure protection.
b. Lifeboat maneuverability.
c. Survival craft availability.
d. Launching of survival craft from stowed position.
e. Lifeboat capability to float free automatically from a sinking vessel.
f. Personal exposure protection.
g. Communications equipment on survival craft.
h. Lights and reflectorized materials.
i. Standards for equipment substituted for required equipment.

Comments were requested to be submitted to the Coast Guard by 7 September 1976, and a Notice of Proposed Rulemaking is in preparation.

Coast Guard Regulations require that fire and boat drills be conducted at least once each week on a cargo vessel such as FITZGERALD. Testimony from licensed officers who had previously served on FITZGERALD indicated that drills were held on a regular basis. Testimony of unlicensed mariners who had served on FITZGERALD at various times during the 1973 and 1974 seasons indicated that drills were not held. The regulations also require that an entry be made in the vessel's Official Logbook concerning each drill conducted. Log-books for FITZGERALD were not available, having been lost with the ves-sel. Under a procedure established by the company which operated the vessel, extracts of the vessel's logbook and of the engineering logs were prepared and forwarded to the company office in Cleveland, OH. These extracts, known as Office Logs and Engineering Logs, respectively, were available from April 12, when the vessel began the 1975 season, through the end of October. These show a total of fourteen Fire and Boat Drills during that twenty-eight week period.

The Certificate of Inspection called for a total of eighty-three life preserv-ers: one for each of the forty-nine crew, twenty-five for the required 50% excess, two in each lifeboat, three for the bow watch, and two in the engine room. There were three types of life preservers on board FITZGERALD: Cork type, two in each boat and thirteen or fourteen in each lifejacket box near the boats; Horse-collar, foam type, in each stateroom; and several Kapok type.

FITZGERALD was required to have twenty-four 30-inch ring life buoys on board, twelve of which were provided with water lights. Testimony indicated that there were both electrical (battery) and chemical (carbide) water lights on board FITZGERALD at the time of the casualty. Although the Coast Guard approval for carbide water lights has been withdrawn, those on board were allowed to be retained as long as they were maintained in good and serviceable condition. Coast Guard Regulations require that ring buoys be placed so as to be readily accessible to persons on board and "capable of being cast loose" and "not permanently secured in any way." There is no requirement that either bat-tery or carbide water lights or the ring buoys to which they are attached be able to float free from the vessel in the event of sinking.

Coast Guard Regulations which require an Emergency Position Indicating Radiobeacon (EPIRB) for ocean vessels do not require such a device on vessels operating on the Great Lakes, and no EPIRB was installed on FITZGERALD.

12. LOAD LINE AND STABILITY

The requirements for load lines on merchant vessels engaged in voyages on the Great Lakes are based upon the Coastwise Load Line Act, as modified by agreements between the U. S. and Canadian governments. A comparison of the load line requirements for Great Lakes vessels and those for vessels operat-ing on the oceans shows that, for vessels of similar dimensions, the freeboard required for a Great Lakes load line and that required for ocean service would be approximately the same. However, the longitudinal strength required for the Great Lakes vessel would be approximately one-half of that required for a vessel on an ocean voyage.

FITZGERALD was built in 1958, and was issued a Load Line Certificate at that time. In 1967, a joint U. S.–Canadian committee undertook a reevaluation of the load line requirements for operation on the Great Lakes. This study resulted in extensive changes to the Great Lakes Load Line Regulations. The first of these changes was published in 1969 as an addition to the Load Line Regulations, which allowed "Reduced Freeboards for Steamers Having Superior Design and Operational Features Engaged on Great Lakes Voyages." In 1971, the regulations were amended by reducing the "factor for winter season," with the result that the minimum freeboard allowed during the winter season, i.e., after 1 November, was reduced. Finally, in 1973, the Great Lakes Load Line Regulations were completely revised. These revised regulations have become known as the 1973 Great Lakes Load Line Regulations.

The 1973 Great Lakes Load Line Regulations, which were in effect and applied to FITZGERALD at the time of the casualty, include requirements involving watertight integrity above the Freeboard Deck, details of hatch covers and doors, strength of superstructures, details of air pipes, ventilators, scuttles and manholes, and protection for the crew. Under the 1973 Great Lakes Load Line Regulations, for vessels with length in excess of 500 ft. greater length does not require a proportionally greater required freeboard. Also, under the 1973 Great Lakes Load Line Regulations, the winter penalty for Great Lakes Load Lines was reduced to be no greater than the winter penalty for a vessel operating on the oceans.

The following table shows the load lines assigned to FITZGERALD:

MINIMUM REQUIRED FREEBOARD

Date	Midsummer	Summer	Intermediate	Winter
Originally assigned when vessel was built	11 feet-10¾ inches	12 feet-6¾ inches	13 feet-6¾ inches	14 feet-9¼ inches
3 July 69	11 feet-4½ inches	12 feet-½ inch	13 feet-¾ inch	14 feet-3½ inches
17 Sept 71	11 feet-4½ inches	12 feet-½ inch	13 feet-¾ inch	13 feet-2 inches
13 Sept 73	10 feet-5½ inches	11 feet-2 inches	11 feet-2 inches	11 feet-6 inches

Before the 1973 load line was issued, minor modifications of the vessel were required. These included modification of watertight doors by adding stiffeners and deadlight covers, installing an additional course of railing on the Forecastle deck and Poop deck, increasing the freeing port area aft, increasing the height of the tunnel vents and installing covers on the windlass room chocks.

Under the 1973 Load Line Regulations, Midsummer load lines applied May 1 through September 15, Summer load lines applied April 16 through April 30 and September 16 through September 30, Intermediate load lines apply October 1 through October 31 and April 1 through April 15 and Winter load lines apply November 1 through March 31. Thus, the Winter load line applied to FITZGERALD at the time of her last loading.

The last Load Line Certificate for FITZGERALD was issued by the American Bureau of Shipping at New York City on 1 July 1974.

The last Load Line Survey was conducted in connection with the American Bureau of Shipping annual survey in Toledo, OH, on 9 April 1975.

One of the significant changes included in the 1973 Great Lakes Load Line Regulations was the requirement that a vessel must have on board, in a form approved by the Commandant of the Coast Guard, sufficient information to:

a. Enable the Master to load and ballast the vessel in a manner that avoids unacceptable stresses on the vessel's structure, and
b. Guide the Master as to the stability of the ship under varying conditions of service.

The first of these established a new requirement for a Loading Manual. Before this, a Loading Manual had not been required on Great Lakes vessels.

The regulations do not include particulars on what should be included in the Loading Manual. Testimony of Coast Guard naval architects indicated that it should include information on all normal cargo and ballast loading conditions, instructions on how to ballast and deballast the ship and information on the sequence of loading and unloading.

Other testimony indicated that first attempts to develop Loading Manual for vessels operated by Oglebay-Norton Company included detailed theoretical analysis of the loading and unloading of vessels. These theoretical studies resulted in loading plans which varied markedly from those used in the practice of loading these ore carrying vessels. Experience with these earliest loading plans showed that the Mates in charge of the loading of the vessels strongly preferred the loading procedures which they had been using. These procedures were analyzed by a naval architect employed by the operators of the vessels, and it was found that only small modifications were necessary to insure that stresses of the vessels as loaded were within acceptable limits. Based upon this analysis, the actual procedures were used to develop a new loading manual for FITZGERALD. This Manual was approved by the American Bureau of Shipping on 17 October 1973 and by the Coast Guard on 23 October 1973.

A detailed analysis of this Loading Manual for FITZGERALD shows:

a. The Manual contains information relating to the total load for each hatch, but there is no information provided on intermediate loads within the loading sequence or on any aspect of unloading.

b. The Manual was prepared for the two-belt loading system used at Silver Bay, MN, FITZGERALD's normal point of loading. It does not contain information directly applicable to a chute dock, such as the one at which FITZGERALD loaded on 9 November.

c. The Manual does not contain information on ballasting or deballasting or on fueling.

d. The Manual does not contain information on calculation of Stress Numeral.

Stability requirements for Great Lakes ore carriers of the straight deck type, such as FITZGERALD (i.e., not equipped with unloading machinery), are the same as those for ocean-going vessels; the Master of the vessel must be furnished with sufficient stability information to allow him, for any condition of loading, to obtain accurate guidance as to the stability of the vessel. However, detailed studies have indicated that the typical Great Lakes ore carrier has a very high level of inherent stability because the cargo is dense (with a stowage factor of 10 to 18 cubic feet per ton), it is carried low in the vessel and there is little free surface effect from the ballast tanks (the width of the upper portion of the tanks is small compared to the beam of the vessel). Because of this high level of inherent stability, it has been determined by the Coast Guard that neither stability tests nor stability calculations are required for vessels of this type. Accordingly, no inclining experiment had ever been performed on FITZGERALD, and no stability calculations were available.

Coast Guard regulations do not require general service cargo ships, operating on the ocean or on the Great Lakes, to meet any damage stability standard. Accordingly, FITZGERALD had not been subjected to a damage stability assessment.

The Great Lakes Load Line Regulations require that when an air pipe to any tank extends above the freeboard or superstructure deck, it must be of steel and of substantial construction, have a permanently attached means of closing, and have a height, from the deck to a point where water may obtain access below deck, of at least 30 inches above the freeboard deck, 24 inches above raised quarter decks and 12 inches above other superstructure decks. However, the regulations also state that if this height "interferes with working the ship, the Commandant may approve a lower height after considering the closing arrangements." Such approval had been granted in the case of the ballast tank vents on FITZGERALD, which, including the mushroom cap, extended only 18 in. above the spar deck. The vents for the fore and aft tunnels, located forward and aft on the Spar Deck, were of the same 8-inch pipe as the ballast tank vents, and had similar mushroom closures. The tunnel vents had been raised to 30 inches above the deck as part of the September 1973 load line assignment.

13. CARGO AND LOADING PROCEDURE

FITZGERALD sailed on its last voyage with a cargo of 26,116 long tons of taconite pellets. Taconite pellets, a very common cargo for Great Lakes ore carriers, are manufactured by a process known as "oxide pelletizing." This process begins with the mining of taconite, a form of iron ore. The taconite is crushed and ground and the iron it contains is then oxidized and the silicon and waste materials removed. The iron ore concentrate remaining is essentially a fine powder which is dewatered to about 10% moisture, and rolled into balls approximately one-half inch in diameter, which, after being heated to release more of the moisture, are fired in a kiln to a temperature of 2200°F to 2400°F. The results are dark, reddish-brown spheres, which are cooled to approximately 200°F and stockpiled awaiting shipment. Because of the natural insulative quality of the material, it is not uncommon to have the interior of a stockpile remain at a temperature above ambient. As a result, vessel operators have observed what they described as "steam" rising from the material after it has been loaded on board. There are no known instances of structural distortion resulting from this elevated temperature either on vessels or on rail cars carrying taconite. The spheres, or pellets as they are called, contain approximately 65% iron oxide, and have a bulk density on the order of 130 lbs. per cubic foot. This is equivalent to a stowage factor of 17 cubic feet per long ton. Because of the small size and generally spherical shape of the pellets, the commodity is easily handled on conveyor belts, in hopper-type railroad cars and in chutes. Taconite exhibits an angle of repose, the angle between the horizontal and the slope of a free-standing pile of the material, of between 26° and 30°. There is some evidence to indicate that a slightly higher angle of repose could be achieved if the material were stacked in high piles, due in part to the presence of a higher quantity of finer material. There is no evidence to indicate that the presence of surface or internal moisture significantly affects the angle of repose, nor are there any reported instances that any vessels have experienced shifting of taconite cargo in normal service. The compressive strength of taconite pellets is approximately five hundred to six hundred pounds per square inch. This strength, which results from the firing, is sufficient to withstand the weight of the material when stacked in open piles or in the holds of vessels. The pellets do not dissolve in water and they are essentially non-magnetic, i.e., they are not attracted to an ordinary magnet. They will absorb moisture up to about 7% by weight. Information on the surface friction characteristics of the material, either in the wet or dry condition, is not available.

Loading and unloading and the accompanying ballasting and deballasting of Great Lakes ore carriers is normally the responsibility of the Chief Mate, who is assisted by the regularly assigned deck watch officers and crew. The Chief Mate typically maintains a notebook which contains information on procedures used for loading and in which the exact amount of cargo and the loading sequence for each load is recorded. This notebook remains on board the vessel and is used as a guide for loading sequence and cargo quantity. This notebook is different from the Loading Manual required by the Load Line Regulations. (An officer who had served as Chief Mate on FITZGERALD during the 1973 and 1974 seasons testified that he had never seen the Loading Manual, and that he relied on the Chief Mate's notebook for loading information.)

Upbound voyages are made with water ballast used to obtain desired draft and trim. During a normal loading, the ballast water is pumped out at the same time the vessel is being loaded with cargo. Since the ballast tank suctions are located at the after bulkhead of each ballast tank, trim by the stern is necessary to deballast completely. During a normal loading, it is not unusual to interrupt cargo loading for an hour or so to maintain this trim while ballast water is discharged. When the vessel is fully loaded with cargo, no ballast water remains on board.

The final cargo profile of a normal load has approximately 28% of the cargo in the center half length of the cargo hold; the forward and aft quarter lengths, or the "shoulders of the ship," are loaded with the remaining 72%, or about 36% on each end. Hatch covers are put in place as the loading into the hatch is completed.

The closures for ballast tank vents on many Great Lakes ore carriers are customarily left open during all conditions of operation in the belief that with a vent closed, it would not be possible to obtain suction to dewater a ballast tank which might be making water.

During loading, draft readings are monitored by members of the ship's crew. Final draft and trim are adjusted by adding small amounts of cargo. An ideal loading would result in a few inches trim by the stern. Midships drafts are checked at the end of the loading by hanging a portable draft gauge over the side. Final cargo adjustments are made to achieve no hog, however, one inch of sag, or "belly," is considered acceptable and an even keel is the most desirable.

For the last several years, FITZGERALD had fueled at the loading dock at the same time as cargo was being loaded. There were two fuel tanks located in the space previously occupied by the coal bunker, immediately aft of the cargo holds. Total fuel capacity was 114,000 gallons. The vessel usually received approximately 50,000 gallons of fuel, which would be enough for the five-day round trip voyage.

FITZGERALD loaded its last cargo at the Burlington Northern Railroad Dock No. 1 East, in Superior, WI, on 9 November. The docks at Superior are equipped with storage bins, called "pockets," built into the dock, and chutes which are used to direct the cargo from the pockets into the hatches of the vessel being loaded. FITZGERALD usually loaded at the Reserve Mining Co. dock at Silver Bay, MN, where two conveyor belts are used to load ore vessels. During the 1975 season, FITZGERALD had loaded at the Burlington dock in Superior on two other trips.

The pockets on the dock were loaded prior to the arrival of the ship. Most of the pockets were loaded with approximately 300 tons of pellets, although there were a few 200-ton and 100-ton pockets which were used in the final phase of loading to trim the ship. Each ore pocket has its own chute, which was lowered to the hatch opening on the ship when the ship was ready for that pocket of ore. Communication between the Mate on the ship and the loading dock supervisor was accomplished by voice.

The vessel moored starboard side to, on the inner end of the eastern side of the dock. The forward hatch on the vessel was lined up with the furthest inshore pocket on the dock. Loading began at approximately 0730 CST, starting with Hatch No. 21 and working forward to Hatch No. 1. Each hatch received one pocket of ore, approximately 300 tons. Once each hatch had received one pocket, a "run" was completed. Upon completion of a run, the vessel had to shift its position along the dock to line up for the next run. The chutes on the dock are on 12-foot centers and the hatch openings on the ship were on 24-foot centers, so the vessel was shifted aft 12 feet to line up with the next set of chutes and received another complete run, again starting aft and working forward. Upon completion of the second run, the vessel shifted again and took 5 or 6 pockets in the hatches aft. This maintained the required trim by the stern. Loading proceeded in this manner until the total desired load was on board.

Loading was completed at approximately 1315 CST, on 9 November, and the Mate passed the final draft readings up to the loading dock personnel. The Bill of Lading shows these as 27'2" forward, 27'6" aft. The departure midships draft readings are not available. The Bill of Lading shows that 26,116 long tons of National Taconite pellets were received. This figure is, however, only approximate. About one-half of the cargo that FITZGERALD received was dumped into the pockets on the dock directly from ore cars. The exact amount of taconite in each ore car was not known. For purposes of cargo billing and the Bill of Lading, it was assumed that each car was loaded with the average load for that type of car, the average being based on the report from the taconite plant at which the ore was loaded into the cars. The other half of FITZGERALD's cargo was loaded into the pockets by conveyor belt, and for these pockets, the load was weighed before it reached the pockets. Details of the amount and distribution of cargo typically would have been entered in the Chief Mate's notebook but this was lost with the vessel. Little information is available on prior cargo loadings. Such information is in the Bills of Lading and in the Office Logs, and this consists of the total amount of cargo loaded and the fore and aft drafts at departure.

On 9 November, in addition to the taconite cargo, FITZGERALD took on 50,013 gallons of No. 6 fuel oil, delivered from a barge which came alongside while the cargo was being loaded.

No difficulty was experienced by cargo loading personnel nor was any report of difficulty from ships personnel received during this loading.

14. INSPECTIONS

The last inspection conducted on FITZGERALD was a Spar Deck Inspection which took place on 31 October 1975, in Toledo, OH, while the vessel was unloading. This inspection was conducted under guidelines set out in Commander Ninth Coast Guard District Instruction 5941.lC, 28 August 1970, which calls for an inspection during the operating season of the Spar Deck areas most susceptible to severe wastage and damage on those Great Lakes ore carriers which have a portion of the Spar Deck stringer enclosed within the hatch coaming. Inspections of Great Lakes vessels are normally performed during the winter lay-up period. However, during the winter lay-up, Great Lakes vessels are usually on shore power with only a watchman on board. Because it would be necessary to provide extra personnel and electrical power to remove the hatches and because the decks of the vessels are frequently covered with ice and snow during the winter lay-up, Spar Deck Inspections, which are considered part of the vessel's regular, annual inspection, are conducted during the operating season while a vessel is loading or unloading. In this way inspection can be performed while hatch covers are removed, allowing a detailed inspection of the deck and other structure within the hatch coaming. Typically, Spar Deck Inspections performed by the Coast Guard are coordinated with surveys performed by the classification society, and the 31 October inspection was conducted by a Coast Guard inspector, an ABS surveyor, an ABS surveyor trainee, and a representative of Oglebay-Norton Company, the operator of FITZGERALD.

The 31 October inspection disclosed discrepancies at No. 13 hatch, No. 15 hatch, No. 16 hatch, and at No. 21 hatch. The discrepancy in No. 13 hatch was a notch, less than one inch in depth, in the inboard edge of the Spar Deck inner stringer on the port side of the hatch opening, approximately 3 ft. aft of the forward coaming. The discrepancy in the No. 15 hatch was a gouge, less than one inch in depth, in the inboard edge of the Spar Deck inner stringer on the port side of the hatch opening approximately 3 ft. aft of the forward coaming. The inspector stated that a notch was a defect which had been made by a sharp edge, while a gouge was made by a side blow or scraping motion. The discrepancy in No. 16 hatch consisted of an indentation and a crack in the port hatch end girder. The hatch end girder was an 18-inch deep channel beam which constituted the port and starboard extremes of the hatch opening. On Figure (4) this structural member is designated 18" × 4.200 × 58#. [The Coast Guard inspector testified that the crack ran vertically and was eight to ten inches in length. He also testified that he believed that the channel, i.e., the hatch end girder, was 14 or 16 inches deep. The ABS surveyor thought that the indentation was approximately one and one-half inches deep and that the crack was more on the order of four to six inches in length. The discrepancy in No. 21 hatch was a crack in the weld at the intersection of the hatch coaming and the hatch end girder, on the starboard side, aft. This crack was approximately one inch in length. Both the Coast Guard inspector and the ABS surveyor testified that they believed that these four discrepancies were typical of damage noted on other ore carriers where dockside offloading equipment was used.

At the conclusion of this Spar Deck Inspection, the Coast Guard inspector telephoned the Marine Safety Office, Toledo, OH, and discussed the discrepancies with the Senior Inspector, Materiel. As a result of the telephone call, during the course of which the Commanding Officer was consulted concerning these discrepancies, the inspector obtained approval to prepare a Merchant Marine Inspection Requirement (Form CG-835) concerning these discrepancies, requiring that they be repaired prior to the beginning of the 1976 season. It was anticipated that the discrepancies listed on the Form CG-835 would be repaired as soon as the ship laid up at the conclusion of the 1975 season.

Following the Spar Deck Inspection, the vessel sailed, and, in follow-up, on 4 November, the Commanding Officer of the Marine Safety Office, Toledo, OH, sent a letter to the operators of the vessel concerning the results of the Spar Deck Inspection. This letter called for rewelding the discrepancies in hatches 13, 15 and 21, and for cropping and renewing the fractured section of the hatch end girder on the port side of hatch No. 16. It stated that FITZGERALD was authorized to operate until the repairs were made and that the repairs should be completed prior to 1 April 1976.

The Coast Guard Certificate of Inspection for the SS EDMUND FITZGERALD was issued in Toledo, OH, on 9 April 1975 to expire on 9 April 1976. The certificate was issued following an inspection which had been conducted during the period between 3 February 1975 and 9 April 1975 while the vessel was in winter lay-up in Toledo, OH. At the completion of this inspection, there were two requirements which remained outstanding. One of these involved lifting and setting safety valves and conducting operational tests of the automation safety devices on the auxiliary boiler. This requirement was completed on 18 July 1975. The other requirement called for posting a fire control plan in accordance with new regulations. The plan had not been posted prior to the loss of FITZGERALD, and the operator had anticipated that it would not be available during the 1975 operating season. The Spar Deck Inspection, completed on 17 October 1974, in Cleveland, OH, with the notation "Spar Deck was satisfactory," was considered part of the inspection for certification which took place in the Spring of 1975.

During the course of the inspection for certification, a weight test was performed on the No. 1 boat and the boat was launched and a boat drill was conducted with eight members of the crew being exercised at oars. Since the vessel was moored port side to during the lay-up period, the No. 2 boat was swung out but not put into the water.

The Certificate of Inspection calls for lifesaving equipment for 49 persons and requires a total of 83 adult life preservers. When the inspection for certification began, there were 95 life preservers on board. During the course of the inspection, 6 life preservers were rejected, leaving a total of 89 satisfactory life preservers on board, 6 in excess of the required 83.

The American Bureau of Shipping also conducted an Annual Survey of Hull, Machinery and Boilers, part of the Continuous Machinery Survey and an Annual Load Line Inspection during the 1974–75 winter lay-up. This survey was completed on 9 April 1975 with no outstanding requirements.

FITZGERALD was last drydocked in Cleveland, OH, in April 1974. At that time the accessible areas of the interior and exterior of the hull were inspected.

This inspection was completed on 20 April 1974, with the satisfactory repairs of damage to the sheer strake, and of cracking in the welds in the hatch end girders and keelsons (see paragraph 10).

15. OUTAGES TO AIDS TO NAVIGATION

At approximately 1630 on 10 November, the remote monitoring equipment (Moore Gear) at Coast Guard Station, Sault Ste. Marie, MI, which monitors the automated aids to navigation under the cognizance of Commanding Officer, Coast Guard Group, Sault Ste. Marie, indicated that the light and radio beacon at Whitefish Point were inoperative. Whitefish Point is an unmanned light, radio beacon, sound signal and weather collection station remotely controlled by Coast Guard Station Sault Ste. Marie. At 1639, FITZGERALD called Coast Guard Station, Grand Marais, MI, and asked if the radio beacon at Whitefish Point Light was operating. Grand Marais determined from the Coast Guard Station, Sault Ste. Marie, that the monitoring equipment indicated that the light and radio beacon were not operating and passed this on to FITZGERALD.

Several attempts were made to restore the Whitefish Point navigational aids, using the remote controls on the monitoring equipment at the Coast Guard Station, Sault Ste. Marie. The light was observed to be operating at approximately 1700, but, sometime after that, the monitoring equipment again indicated a failure. For a while it was thought possible that the navigational aids were operating properly, with the trouble indication due to the fact that the telephone lines used in the monitoring system were down as a result of the weather. Finally, however, it was concluded that the Whitefish Point light and radio beacon were not operating and could not be restored immediately, and, at 1905, Coast Guard Group Sault Ste. Marie sent out a Safety Broadcast to that effect.

As soon as the weather subsided the next morning, Coast Guard Group Sault Ste. Marie sent a repairman to Whitefish Point. He found the aids not operating. The emergency generator was not running, but the engine was warm, which indicated to him that the emergency generator had been running only a short time earlier. The relay which switches the aids from normal power to emergency power was found to be stuck in an intermediate position. In this position, there would have been no power to the navigational aids. It was believed that the relay became stuck while efforts were being made to restore the aids through the use of the remote monitoring equipment. The navigational aids at Whitefish Point were restored to full operation at 0930, 11 November.

The aids to navigation monitoring equipment at Sault Ste. Marie Coast Guard Station is fitted with a paper tape recording mechanism, but there are no indicator recordings for 10 November. There is no requirement that a permanent record of the monitoring equipment be maintained.

The records of the Commander, Ninth Coast Guard District, indicate that Whitefish Point Light was automated and unmanned on 11 June 1970. This was one of the first aids in the area to be automated. Immediately following the automation, several outages were experienced, however these were attributed to the newness and complexity of the automation equipment. Between 1 June 1973 and 15 November 1975, outages were:

Year	Light	Radio beacon	Fog horn
1976	6	11	7
1974	1	0	3
1975	2	3	5

The lighthouse at Whitefish Point is also fitted with a battery powered, auxiliary light, with a range of nine and one-half miles, which would come on automatically if both the normal power and emergency generator power for the main light should fail.

The only U. S. navigational aids in eastern Lake Superior north or west of Whitefish Bay which were inoperative on the afternoon or evening of the 10th of November were those at Whitefish Point. There were no Canadian aids in eastern Lake Superior which were inoperative.

16. HYDROGRAPHIC SURVEY

Testimony of the Master and Watch Officers of ANDERSON indicated that FITZGERALD had passed near the shoals north of Caribou Island. Charts of the area, U. S. Chart L.S. 9 (September 1973) and Canadian Chart 2310 (1972) showed a least sounding in this area, denoted "North Bank" on Chart 2310, of 6 fathoms. Chart 2310 indicates that the soundings are based on surveys of the Canadian Hydrographic Service in 1916 and 1919, while Chart L.S. 9 contains a notation: "Canadian Areas. For data concerning Canadian areas, Canadian authorities have been consulted."

Following the taking of testimony and review of the charts, the Marine Board requested, through the Commander of the Ninth Coast Guard District, that Canadian authorities conduct a hydrographic survey of the area north of Caribou Island.

The hydrographic survey, Canadian Hydrographic Service, Central Region, Project 76–2, was performed by CSS BAYFIELD during the period 19 May–8

FIELD SHEET 3908

Lake Superior, Canada
Project Number 76-2, 1976
Central Region
Canadian Hydrographic Service

Universal Transverse Mercator Projection
SOUNDINGS IN METERS
(Under 30 meters Soundings
are in Meters and Decimeters)
Reduced to a Soundings Datum which is
182.88 Meters I.G.L.D. (1955)

CARIBOU I.

47°30'N

47°25'N

47°20'N

88°55'W

88°50'W

88°45'W

.88

FIG. (12)

July 1976 and 7 August–30 September 1976. The area surveyed included the waters between Michipicoten Island and Caribou Island and all around Caribou Island and adjacent waters between 47°10′N and 47°45′N and between 85°33′W and 86°11′W. Soundings were obtained using an ATLAS DESO 10 Echo Sounder and horizontal positioning was obtained using a three-station Minifix system. Results were reduced to a datum of 182.88 meters (599.85 feet) above the International, Great Lakes Datum (IGLD) and plotted on Field Sheet 3908 (F.S. 3908), with soundings in meters. Chart L.S. 9 is plotted to a datum of 600.0 feet above IGLD, thus there is a difference of 0.15 feet between L.S. 9 and F.S. 3908. Canadian Chart 2310 is plotted to a datum based upon Mean Sea Level, and this datum is 0.53 feet above the datum used in plotting the BAYFIELD data on F.S. 3908. Figure (12) is a replica of a portion of F.S. 3908 which includes the waters surrounding Caribou Island and the shoals to the north of it.

L.S. 9 shows the 6 fathom (10.9 meters) sounding at 47°26.7′N, 85°50.8′W, while 2310 shows 6 fathoms at 47°26.8′N, 85°50.3′W. Analysis of F.S. 3908, Figure (12), shows two locations with soundings of 6 fathoms (10.9 meters) or less. These have been marked [1] and [2] on Figure (12).

[1] 47°26.B′N, B5°50.2′W / 9.5 m (5.2 fathoms)

[2] 47°26.B′N, 85°48.7′W / 9.7 m (5.3 fathoms)

Position [2] is slightly more than one mile due east of position [1] and Chart 2310 indicates soundings adjacent to this location of 8 and 9 fathoms.

F.S. 3908 shows two other soundings of less than six fathoms (10.9 meters) due north of and immediately adjacent to Caribou Island. These are marked [3] and (4] on Figure (12).

[3] 47°25.4′N, 85°48.6′W / 9.7 meters (5.3 fathoms)
   (Chart 2310 shows 6 fathoms at 47°25.6′N, 85°48.7′W.)

[4] 47°24.6′N, 85°47.6′W / 7.5 meters (4.1 fathoms)
   (Chart 2310 shows 4½ fathoms at 47°24.5′N, 85°47.7′W.)

CONCLUSIONS

1. **Preface**. The SS EDMUND FITZGERALD left Superior, WI, on the afternoon of 9 November 1975, enroute Detroit, MI, with a full cargo of taconite pellets. That evening, and the next day, FITZGERALD proceeded eastward in Lake Superior, on a course north of the charted lanes due to the weather, heading towards Whitefish Bay and the Locks at Sault Ste. Marie, MI. At the same time, a severe November storm was crossing Lake Superior and, as a

result, FITZGERALD encountered worsening weather throughout the early hours of the 10th of November, and by that afternoon, was experiencing winds in excess of 50 knots and seas approaching 16 feet. At approximately 1530, 10 November, FITZGERALD reported damage, but did not, at that time or in subsequent communications, indicate that it was of a serious nature or that there was any immediate concern for the safety of the vessel. No distress message was received. FITZGERALD sank sometime after 1910, 10 November 1975, at a position 46°59.9′N, 85°06.6′W, approximately 17 miles from the entrance to Whitefish Bay, MI.

There were no survivors and no witnesses to the casualty. Information available to the Marine Board consists of testimony of people who were on board other vessels in the area at the time FITZGERALD was lost, of people who had served on FITZGERALD prior to its last voyage, of employees of the company which operated the vessel, of other persons familiar with the vessel or similar vessels or its cargo, of personnel of the Coast Guard and of the American Bureau of Shipping who had conducted inspections and surveys on the vessel, of Coast Guard personnel who participated in the extensive search which followed the report of its loss, of personnel from the National Weather Service concerning weather at the time of the loss, of personnel at the facility where the vessel loaded its last cargo, and of information from the several underwater surveys which were conducted on the wreckage which was found on the bottom of Lake Superior. Information available is incomplete and inconsistent in the following particulars:

a. **Position.** The only information available on the position and trackline of FITZGERALD is in the weather reports sent by FITZGERALD and in testimony of the Master and Watch Officers of the SS ARTHUR M. ANDERSON, which was following FITZGERALD, in voice radio communication with it, and observing it visually and on radar. The weather reports from FITZGERALD scheduled at 1300 and 1900, 10 November, were not received.

The position of FITZGERALD relative to that of ANDERSON cannot be reconstructed. Information available is based on the recollections of the Master and Watch Officers on ANDERSON, since the relative position of FITZGERALD was observed intermittently on the radar, but not recorded. Testimony on these observations is inconsistent. For example, the Officer on watch on ANDERSON recalled that FITZGERALD was "a shade to the right of dead ahead," as FITZGERALD passed northeast of Caribou Island, while the Master thought it was a point to a point and a half to the right at that time.

The Master and the Watch Officers on ANDERSON testified at length as to the position and trackline of ANDERSON in the afternoon and evening of 10 November. Analysis of this testimony shows that the vessel was navigated by radar ranges and bearings, that, at times, positions were determined but not logged, that course changes were made without simultaneous determination of position, that positions were determined as much as twenty minutes from the time that course changes were made, and that the courses steered varied from the course logged because of the expected drift. The Marine Board attempted to reconstruct the trackline of ANDERSON and found that in order for the vessel to have steered the courses and have been at the positions at the times testified to, the speed of the vessel would have varied from a low of 5 mph to a high of 66 mph. But the Master testified, and the engineering log confirmed, that throughout the period, ANDERSON maintained a steady speed, turning for 14.6 mph. Accordingly, it is concluded that the times and positions reported by officers of ANDERSON were not sufficiently accurate to allow the trackline of either FITZGERALD or ANDERSON to be reconstructed.

b. **Difficulties Reported by FITZGERALD.** FITZGERALD reported the loss of two vents and some fence rail, indicating that topside damage had occurred to the vessel. The flooding which could be expected to result from the loss of any two tank or tunnel vents would not be serious enough, by itself, to cause the loss of the vessel.

FITZGERALD reported, at the same time, that it had developed a list. The existence of the list which would result from flooding of any two ballast tanks, a tunnel, or a tunnel and a ballast tank would not, of itself, indicate damage sufficiently serious to cause the loss of the vessel.

FITZGERALD reported that steps were being taken to deal with the flooding and the list, and that two pumps ("both of them") were being used. FITZGERALD had four 7000-gpm pumps and two 2000-gpm pumps available, indicating that the flooding was evaluated by personnel on board FITZGERALD as not sufficiently serious to create a danger of loss of the vessel.

FITZGERALD reported difficulties with its radars, and requested ANDERSON to provide navigational information.

FITZGERALD reported slowing down to allow ANDERSON to catch up. This action might have been taken because the Master of FITZGERALD knew or sensed that his problems were of a more serious nature than reported to ANDERSON.

c. **Underwater Survey**. The underwater survey showed that mud covered a majority of the wreckage, that the midships section of the hull was completely disrupted, and that the stern section was inverted. Movement of the survey vehicle disturbed the mud, which limited visibility and made it difficult to identify individual components of the wreckage. However, the survey provided the Marine Board valuable information with respect to the vessel's final condition and orientation.

2. In the absence of more definite information concerning the nature and extent of the difficulties reported and of problems other than those which were reported, and in the absence of any survivors or witnesses, the proximate cause of the loss of the SS EDMUND FITZGERALD cannot be determined.

3. The most probable cause of the sinking of the SS EDMUND FITZGERALD was the loss of buoyancy and stability which resulted from massive flooding of the cargo hold. The flooding of the cargo hold took place through ineffective hatch closures as boarding seas rolled along the Spar Deck. The flooding, which began early on the 10th of November, progressed during the worsening weather and sea conditions and increased in volume as the vessel lost effective freeboard, finally resulting in such a loss of buoyancy and stability that the vessel plunged in the heavy seas.

4. The following factors contributed to the loss of FITZGERALD:

a. The winter load line assigned to FITZGERALD under the changes to the Load Line Regulations in 1969, 1971 and 1973 allowed 3 feet, 3¼ inches less minimum freeboard than had been allowed when the vessel was built in 1958. This overall reduction in required freeboard also reflected a reduction in Winter Penalty for Great Lakes vessels. Not only did the reduction in minimum required freeboard significantly reduce the vessel's buoyancy, but it resulted in a significantly increased frequency and force of boarding seas in the storm FITZGERALD encountered on 10 November. This, in turn, resulted in an increased quantity of water flooding through loosely dogged hatches and through openings from topside damage.

b. The system of hatch coamings, gaskets, covers and clamps installed on FITZGERALD required continuing maintenance and repair, both from routine wear because of the frequent removal and replacement of the covers and from damage which regularly occurred during cargo transfer. That the required maintenance was not regularly performed is indicated by the fact that the crew of the vessel had no positive guidelines, in the form of Company requirements or otherwise, concerning such maintenance. That the required repairs were not regularly performed as damage occurred is indicated by the fact that significant repairs had been required during the previous winter lay-up period and by the fact that more repairs of the same nature were expected, since a general item to repair hatch covers and coamings had been included in the work list for the winter lay-up which FITZGERALD was approaching when it was lost. It is concluded that the system of cargo hatch coamings, gaskets, covers and clamps which was installed on FITZGERALD and the manner in which this system was maintained did not provide an effective means of preventing the penetration of water into the ship in any sea condition, as required by Coast Guard Regulations.

c. Whether all the cargo hatch clamps were properly fastened cannot be determined. In the opinion of the Marine Board, if the clamps had been properly fastened, any damage, disruption or dislocation of the hatch covers would have resulted in damage to or distortion of the clamps. But, the underwater survey showed that only a few of the clamps were damaged. It is concluded that these clamps were the only ones, of those seen, which were properly fastened to the covers and that there were too few of these and too many unfastened or loosely fastened clamps to provide an effective closure of the hatches.

d. The cargo hold was not fitted with a system of sounding tubes or other devices to detect the presence of flooding water. It is not known whether any efforts were made to determine if water was entering the cargo hold. If the hold had been checked at a time when the level of the water was below the cargo surface, the extent of flooding could not have been determined. It is inconceivable that flooding water in the cargo hold could have reached a height to be seen, without a seasoned Master taking more positive steps for vessel and crew safety than were reported. Therefore, it is concluded that the flooding of the cargo hold was not detected.

e. The cargo hold was not fitted with transverse watertight bulkheads. As a result, the flooding water which entered could migrate throughout the hold, extending the effect of the flooding and aggravating any trim which existed.

5. At sometime prior to 1530 on 10 November, FITZGERALD experienced damage of sufficient magnitude to cause the Master to report topside damage and a list. Significantly, the Master of FITZGERALD reported the damage rather than the incident which caused it. It is the opinion of the Marine Board that the incident, while possibly of a serious nature, was not of such extent as to have caused, by itself, the loss of the vessel and further, that the full extent of the incident was not perceived by vessel personnel. The Master noted the list and topside damage and incorrectly concluded that the topside damage was the only source of flooding. He began what he believed were adequate, corrective measures—pumping spaces which would receive flooding from damaged vents—and thus felt the problems were under control.

The topside damage could have been caused by the vessel striking a floating object which was then brought aboard in the heavy seas. This also could have resulted in undetected damage opening the hull plating above or below the waterline and additional unreported damage to topside fittings, including hatch covers and clamps. Intake of water into the tunnel or into one or more ballast tanks through the damaged vents and opened hull would have produced the reported list and increased the rate of cargo hold flooding. The most likely area of damage would have been in the forward part of the ship. The vessel had entered a snowstorm approximately one-half hour before the topside damage was reported. In addition, FITZGERALD's radars were reported inoperative shortly after the damage was reported, and may have been malfunctioning for some period before the report. Both the reduced visibility from the snow storm and the radar malfunction would, in the opinion of the Marine Board, have reduced the likelihood that the crew of the vessel could have detected the object in sufficient time to take effective action to avoid it.

The topside damage could have been caused by some unidentified object on board breaking away in the heavy seas. Flooding through such damage could have caused a list. While there were objects on deck which might have come adrift and knocked off a vent cap or damaged a hatch coaming, the only items on deck which had enough mass to do sufficient damage to the hull to cause a sustained list were a hatch cover, the hatch cover crane, or the spare propeller blade. If such extensive damage had occurred, a seasoned Master would have reported it. Such a report was not received.

The topside damage and list could have been caused by a light grounding or near grounding on the shoals north of Caribou Island. Although their testimony is not fully consistent, both the Master and the Watch Officer on ANDERSON indicated that FITZGERALD passed within a few miles of Caribou Island and that they had a conversation concerning the closeness of

FITZGERALD to the shoals north of the island. It is considered possible that a light grounding or near grounding on these shoals could have occurred. The vessel could have been damaged from the grounding, from the effect of the violent seas which would be expected near the shoals, or from the shuddering that the vessel would have experienced as it passed near the shoals. The damage could have been on deck, below the water line, or both, leading to the reported topside damage and list. The Marine Board is unable to reconstruct the trackline of FITZGERALD south of Michipicoten Island, however, FITZGERALD was observed to pass two to three miles off Michipicoten Island West End Light from which position a single course change to 141°T would have taken the vessel directly to Whitefish Point on a track well clear of the shoal areas off the northern tip of Caribou. Had there been a delay in making the course change after passing Michipicoten, FITZGERALD would have passed closer to the shoals. But, the distance between Michipicoten and the shoals is such that it appears that a delay in making the course change of upwards of an hour would have been required to cause FITZGERALD to have actually reached the shoals.

The list could have been caused by a localized hull structural failure, resulting in the flooding of a ballast tank or tanks. There is no correlation between such an occurrence and the reported loss of vents and fence rail. The survey of those parts of the wreckage which could be seen showed no evidence of brittle fracture.

The Marine Board concludes that the exact cause of the damage reported cannot be determined, but that the most likely cause was the striking of a floating object.

6. In the opinion of the Marine Board, the flooding from the damage reported, and from other damage which was not detected, most likely occurred in the forward part of the vessel, resulting in trim down by the bow. By the time the damage was reported by FITZGERALD, the flooding of the cargo hold had reached such an extent that the cargo was saturated and loose water existed in the hold. Because of the trim by the bow, this water migrated forward through the non-watertight screen bulkheads which separated the cargo holds, further aggravating the trim and increasing the rate of flooding.

7. Because there were neither witnesses nor survivors and because of the complexity of the hull wreckage, the actual, final sequence of events culminating in the sinking of the FITZGERALD cannot be determined. Whatever the sequence, however, it is evident that the end was so rapid and catastrophic that

there was no time to warn the crew, to attempt to launch lifeboats or life rafts, to don life jackets, or even to make a distress call.

Throughout November 10th the vessel was subjected to deteriorating weather and an increasing quantity of water on deck. With each wave that came aboard, water found its way into the cargo hold through the hatches. As the vessel lost freeboard because of this flooding and as the sea conditions worsened, the frequency and force of the boarding seas increased, and so did the flooding. The Master of the vessel reported that he was in one of the worst seas that he had ever seen. It is probable that, at the time he reported this, FITZGERALD had lost so much freeboard from the flooding of the cargo hold that the effect of the sea was much greater than he would ordinarily have experienced. Finally, as the storm reached its peak intensity, so much freeboard was lost that the bow pitched down and dove into a wall of water and the vessel was unable to recover. Within a matter of seconds, the cargo rushed forward, the bow plowed into the bottom of the lake, and the midships structure disintegrated, allowing the submerged stern section, now emptied of cargo, to roll over and override the other structure, finally coming to rest upside-down atop the disintegrated middle portion of the ship.

Alternatively, it is possible that FITZGERALD sank as a result of a structural failure on the surface, resulting from the increased loading of the flooding water. However, this is considered less likely because such a failure would have severed the vessel into two sections on the surface, and one or the other, if not both sections would have floated for a short while. With the weather conditions that existed at the time FITZGERALD was lost and, in particular, with the winds in excess of 50 knots, if either or both of the pieces had floated for any time, significant drifting would have occurred. But, the survey of the wreckage showed that the two main pieces were within a ship length, thus little or no drifting took place.

8. There is no evidence that the crew of FITZGERALD made any attempt to use any lifesaving equipment, or that lifesaving equipment or its performance contributed in any way to this casualty. The condition of the lifeboats recovered indicates that the boats were torn away from their chocks, grips and falls. The condition of the life rafts recovered indicates that they were released from their float-free racks and inflated as they were designed to. One raft was damaged, partly when it floated onto the rocky shoreline and partly by a search party which punched holes in it to allow water to drain out during the recovery operation.

Testimony of witnesses indicates that a successful launching of a lifeboat would have been extremely difficult in the weather and sea conditions which prevailed at the time FITZGERALD was lost. This testimony also indicates that Great Lakes mariners have little confidence that lifeboats could be launched successfully in other than moderate wind and sea conditions, and given the choice, they would use the inflatable rafts as the primary means of abandoning a sinking ore carrier. Their confidence in the capability of the rafts was tempered by stated beliefs that a raft could not be boarded safely once it was launched and waterborne and that they would inflate it on deck and wait for it to float free from the sinking vessel. This illustrates that although Great Lakes mariners understand the difficulties inherent in disembarking from a stricken vessel their level of understanding of the use and capability of inflatable life rafts is inadequate. In the opinion of the Marine Board, the appraisal by crewmen that they have small chance of survival on abandoning a stricken vessel in a rough seaway could influence them to stay with the stricken vessel rather than attempt abandonment.

The present requirement for posting a placard containing life raft launching instructions is not considered sufficient to train crewmembers in the proper use of this primary lifesaving equipment. The placard is, however, considered a valuable aid in assisting and reinforcing other crew training.

Lifeboat drills were held on FITZGERALD during the 1975 season, but were not held on a weekly basis as required by regulations. The level of training of the crew in the use of lifeboats and life rafts is indeterminate.

There is no evidence to indicate that any of the crewmembers of FITZGER-ALD escaped from the vessel at the time of its loss. However, if they had, their chances of survival would have been significantly enhanced if they had been provided with equipment to protect them against exposure.

9. The twenty-nine crewmen on board FITZGERALD are missing and presumed dead.

10. It was fortunate that the Steamer ARTHUR M. ANDERSON was in the area of and in radiotelephone communication with FITZGERALD on the afternoon and evening of 10 November. Without the presence of this vessel, the loss of FITZGERALD would not have been known for a considerable period of time, possibly not until the following day, and, at the latest, when the vessel failed to arrive at the unloading dock.

11. The testimony of witnesses indicates a conflict as to the time that the Coast Guard was first notified of the problems with FITZGERALD. The Marine

Board concludes that the first notification that the Coast Guard received of the problem with FITZGERALD was at approximately 2025 Eastern Standard Time on 10 November in a radiotelephone call from CAPT Cooper, Master of ANDERSON. At the time of this call, the actual loss of FITZGERALD was neither comprehended by CAPT Cooper nor conveyed to the Coast Guard. The Coast Guard radio watchstander who received the call, attempted to communicate with FITZGERALD, without success, and advised the Rescue Coordination Center. The second call from CAPT Cooper to the Coast Guard, at approximately 2100, 10 November, did express a grave concern that FITZGERALD was lost, and rescue efforts were initiated. It is concluded that the time period which elapsed in evaluating and reporting the loss of FITZGERALD did not contribute to the casualty or high loss of life, because FITZGERALD sank suddenly, with all hands trapped on board.

12. In the opinion of the Marine Board, in a tragedy of this magnitude, occurring, as this one did, in extreme weather conditions, vessels in the area and SAR aircraft must be relied upon as the first source of assistance.

The response by the merchant vessels in the area to the Coast Guard's request for assistance was in keeping with the finest traditions of mariners. The response of the vessels ARTHUR M. ANDERSON and WILLIAM CLAY FORD is considered exemplary and worthy of special note. These vessels proceeded to the scene on the night of 10 November and searched under conditions of extreme weather and sea on 10 and 11 November. The response of the Canadian vessel HILDA MARJANNE, which got underway but was forced back by weather, is also worthy of note.

The response by Coast Guard SAR aircraft from Air Station Traverse City was timely. The first aircraft was not launched until 51 minutes after it was ordered because it was necessary to load flares for the night search. The launching of three aircraft within one hour and thirty-five minutes is within the response requirements called for by the Ninth Coast Guard District SAR Plan. The request for and dispatch of additional SAR aircraft from Coast Guard Air Station Elizabeth City, NC, from the U. S. Navy, from the Michigan Air National Guard, and from Canadian SAR forces was also timely.

The only Coast Guard surface unit in an SAR standby status which was close enough to respond within a reasonable time and was large enough to cope with the weather and sea conditions which prevailed at the time was the Buoy Tender WOODRUSH at its home port in Duluth, MN. WOODRUSH, on a six-hour standby status, was underway within two and one-half hours. The Marine Board concludes that the response by the WOODRUSH was timely. The wind and sea conditions precluded the use of the Harbor Tug NAUGATUCK stationed at Sault Ste. Marie, which had operating limitations imposed on its use outside harbor waters. The small craft designed for coastal operations which were available in Lake Superior were unsuitable for search 15 miles offshore in the high sea state then existing. It is concluded that there is a need for additional surface forces with SAR capability to improve the overall search and rescue posture in Lake Superior.

13. Because ANDERSON was following FITZGERALD, providing navigational assistance and observing FITZGERALD to be on a trackline heading for the entrance to Whitefish Bay and because the wreckage was found on a trackline headed for the entrance to Whitefish Bay, it is concluded that the outages of Whitefish Point light and radio beacon did not contribute to the casualty.

14. The progress of the severe storm which crossed Lake Superior on 9 and 10 November was adequately tracked by the National Weather Service and the weather reports and weather forecasts adequately reflected its path and severity. Weather forecasts were upgraded in a timely manner and a special warning was issued. Estimates of wind velocity by persons on vessels in the storm were higher than those forecast and also higher than those reported by shoreside stations, however, the overall severity of the storm was generally as forecast and reported. It is concluded that mariners on Lake Superior on 10 November were adequately warned of the severe weather and that the Master of FITZGERALD was aware of the severity and location of the storm.

15. Testimony of licensed Great Lakes mariners indicates the cargo hold of a Great Lakes ore carrier cannot be dewatered if it is loaded with a cargo of taconite pellets. The Marine Board is unable to determine the validity of this as a general proposition or whether it affected the loss of FITZGERALD.

16. The Loading Manual which was developed for FITZGERALD did not comply with the requirements of the Load Line Regulations. Since the only loading information available to the Marine Board is the total cargo carried on down-bound voyages, whether FITZGERALD was ever subjected to unacceptable stresses cannot be determined.

17. The underwater survey of the wreckage and the detailed study of the photographs taken show no apparent relationship between the casualty and the discrepancies found and reported at the Spar Deck Inspection conducted on 31 October 1975.

18. The hydrographic survey performed by CSS BAYFIELD basically confirmed the data indicated on chart L.S.9 and Canadian chart 2310. In addition, this survey showed that the northern end of the shoals north of Caribou Island extends approximately one mile further east than indicated on Canadian chart 2310.

19. The nature of Great Lakes shipping, with short voyages, much of the time in very protected waters, frequently with the same routine from trip to trip, leads to complacency and an overly optimistic attitude concerning the extreme weather hazards which can and do exist. The Marine Board feels that this attitude reflects itself at times in deferral of maintenance and repairs, in failure to prepare properly for heavy weather, and in the conviction that since refuges are near, safety is possible by "running for it." While it is true that sailing conditions are good during the summer season, changes can occur abruptly, with severe storms and extreme weather and sea conditions arising rapidly. This tragic accident points out the need for all persons involved in Great Lakes shipping to foster increased awareness of the hazards which exist.

20. There is no evidence of actionable misconduct, inattention to duty, negligence, or willful violation of law or regulation; on the part of licensed or certificated persons, nor evidence that failure of inspected material or equipment, nor evidence that any personnel of the Coast Guard, or any other government agency or any other person contributed to the cause of this casualty.

RECOMMENDATIONS

It is recommended:

1. That Part 45 of Title 46 of the United States Code of Federal Regulations (Great Lakes Load Lines) be amended immediately to rescind the reduction in minimum freeboard brought about by the 1969, 1971 and 1973 changes to the Load Line Regulations.

2. That any subsequent amendments to the Great Lakes Load Line Regulations as they apply to ore carriers, such as FITZGERALD, reflect full consideration of the necessity for a means of detecting and removing flooding water from the cargo hold and for watertight sub-division of the cargo hold spaces. Such an appraisal should take due cognizance of:

   a. The severe weather and sea conditions encountered by these vessels and the resulting high degree of deck wetness, and,

   b. The inherent difficulty in meeting and maintaining a weathertight standard with the system of hatches, coamings, covers, gaskets and clamps used on FITZGERALD and many other Great Lakes vessels.

3. That the owners and operators of Great Lakes ore carrying vessels undertake a positive and continuing program of repair and maintenance to insure that all closures for openings above the freeboard deck are weathertight, that is, capable of preventing the penetration of water into the ship in any sea condition. This program should include frequent adjustment of hatch clamping devices and vent closures and prompt repair of all hatches, coamings, covers and clamping devices found damaged or deteriorated.

4. That Part 45 of Title 46 of the United States Code of Federal Regulations be amended to require closing and securing of hatches when underway in open waters and closing of vent caps when underway in a loaded condition. A visual inspection of the closure of hatch covers and vent caps should be conducted and logged by a licensed officer prior to sailing in a loaded condition.

5. That the Coast Guard undertake a program to evaluate hatch closures presently used on Great Lakes ore carriers with a view toward requiring a more effective means of closure of such deck fittings.

6. That the owners and operators of Great Lakes vessels, in cooperation with the maritime unions and training schools, undertake a program to improve the level of crew training in the use of lifesaving equipment installed on board the vessels and in other emergency procedures. This program should specifically include training in the use of inflatable life rafts and afford crews of vessels the opportunity to see a raft inflated.

7. That Part 97 of Title 46 of the United States Code of Federal Regulations be amended to require crew training in launching, inflation and operation of inflatable life rafts.

8. That the Coast Guard institute a continuing program of inspections and drills for Great Lakes vessels prior to each severe weather season. The severe weather season should correspond to the Winter Load Line season, i.e., 1 November through 31 March. Under this program, just before the severe weather season began, there would be an inspection to verify that the crew had been trained in the use of the lifesaving equipment and drills would be conducted with the crew then on board the vessel. There would be a physical inspection of the Spar Deck and all critical structural and

non-structural members exposed to damage from cargo loading and off-loading equipment including, but not limited to, hatch coamings, hatch covers, vent covers, tank tops, side slopes, hatch-end girders, arches, spar deck stringers, and spar deck plating. Additionally, all emergency drills would be witnessed, and alarms, watertight closures, navigation equipment and required logs would be inspected.

9. That the Coast Guard take positive steps to insure that the Masters of Great Lakes vessels are provided with information, as is required by the regulations, concerning loading and ballasting of Great Lakes vessels, and that the information provided include not only normal loaded and ballasted conditions, but also details on the sequences of loading, unloading, ballasting, deballasting and the intermediate stages thereof as well as information on the effect upon the vessel of accidental flooding from damage or other sources.

10. That the Coast Guard complete, as soon as possible, the studies, currently underway, which concern primary lifesaving equipment, its launching, and disembarkation from stricken vessels. And, that measures be implemented promptly to improve the entire abandon ship system, including equipping and training personnel, automatic launching of equipment and alerting rescue forces.

11. That the Coast Guard schedule maintenance status for buoy tenders and icebreakers located in the Great Lakes so as to maximize surface search and rescue capability during the severe weather season, consistent with their primary missions.

12. That Subpart 94.60 of Title 46 of the United States Code of Federal Regulations, which requires emergency position indicating radio beacons (EPIRB), be amended to include requirements for such beacons on vessels operating on the Great Lakes during the severe weather season.

13. That the Coast Guard promulgate regulations which require vessels operating on the Great Lakes during the severe weather season to have, for each person on board, a suit designed to protect the wearer from exposure and hypothermia.

14. That navigation charts showing the area immediately north of Caribou Island be modified to show the extent of the shoals north of the island and

that this modification be given the widest possible dissemination, including Notices to Mariners.

15. That the Coast Guard foster and support programs dedicated to increasing awareness, on the part of all concerned with vessel operations, inspection and maintenance, of the hazards faced by vessels in Great Lakes service, particularly during the severe weather season. The programs should make maximum use of company safety programs, safety bulletins, publications and trade journals.

16 That no further action be taken and that this case be closed.

W. W. BARROW, *Rear Admiral, USCG Chairman*
A. S. ZABINSKI, *Captain, USCG Member*
J. A. WILSON, *Captain, USCG Member*
C. S. LOOSMORE, *Commander,*
USCG Member and Recorder

LAKE CARRIERS' ASSOCIATION

LETTER OF DISSENT

MR. WEBSTER B. TODD, JR.

CHAIRMAN

NATIONAL TRANSPORTATION SAFETY BOARD

800 INDEPENDENCE AVENUE, S. W.

WASHINGTON, D. C. 20594

SUBJECT: COAST GUARD INVESTIGATION REPORT DATED JULY 26, 1977

ON THE FITZGERALD SINKING

Dear Mr. Chairman:

The lake shipping industry, proud of its safety record through the years, completely rejects the Coast Guard theoretical cause of the FITZGERALD sinking. We are setting forth the basis for our position and urge that our statement be considered in your deliberations in the case.

Lake Carriers' Association consists of 15 domestic bulk shipping companies on the lakes. 135 vessels are involved with a registered gross of 1,395,065 tons.

Owners and operators have a paramount interest in navigation safety. In addition to their prime asset, an experienced crew, there is a significant investment in the vessel and value of any cargo on board. Where changes in design or regulations are found necessary from operating experience or casualties, there is no question as to a corrective course of action. When changes running into millions of dollars are recommended based only on a **possible** cause of an accident, industry most vigorously objects. And further, when the possibility is poorly supported by known factors, industry is even more upset.

In its conclusions, the Coast Guard Marine Board stated: ". . . the proximate cause of the loss of the S/S EDMUND FITZGERALD cannot be determined."

In his action on the Board's findings, conclusions and recommendations, the Commandant stated: "With regard to opinions as to the causes of damage and the final sequence of events, an analysis has been made which demonstrates the possibility of capsizing and/or foundering. The analysis of various stages of flooding indicates that bending moment magnitudes and distribution would not support a conclusion of general structural failure as a primary cause of the casualty."

"The Commandant concurs with the Board that the most probable cause of the sinking was the loss of buoyancy resulting from massive flooding of the cargo hold. This flooding most likely took place through ineffective hatch closures. As the boarding seas rolled over the spar deck, the flooding was probably concentrated forward. The vessel dove into a wall of water and never recovered, with the breaking up of the ship occurring as it plunged or as the ship struck the bottom. The sinking was so rapid and unexpected that no one was able to successfully abandon ship."

It should be emphasized that the proximate cause of the sinking could not be determined, so any theoretical rationale advanced could only be a **possible** cause. Thereafter the recommendations of the Board with general approval of the Commandant proceed on structural and hatch closure details with specificity as if the actual cause of the sinking had been determined.

The Coast Guard has pointed its finger at ineffective hatch closures as the most likely cause of the sinking. Let's examine that thesis, then look at another much more likely cause.

The present hatch covers are an advanced design and are considered by the entire lake shipping industry to be a most significant improvement over the telescoping leaf covers previously used for many years. The one-piece covers have proven completely satisfactory in all-weather operations without a single vessel loss in almost 40 years of use. Closure clamps have been greatly improved over the years to the present cast steel clamps that have also been found to be completely satisfactory in service.

Raised coamings that support the hatch covers on non-self-unloading vessels sustain minor damage from time to time by shore based unloading equipment. It is necessary to have periodic repairs and straightening done on such vessels. The Board noted that some work was scheduled for the FITZGERALD at her next shipyard availability. But the Board failed to note that this is an annual winter layup work item for most straight deck vessels, such as the FITZGERALD, depending on the unloading docks traded at. The FITZGERALD was in a trade that involved much less damage than many other similar vessels. There was nothing unusual about this repair item on the next shipyard work list. It is important to note that the spar deck inspection of the FITZGERALD, conducted ten days before the sinking by the Coast Guard OCMI at Toledo and the American Bureau of Shipping, the classification society relied upon by the Coast Guard, revealed no significant damage of the hatch coamings or closure fittings.

We call attention to almost forty years' experience with the current type of hatch covers and closure clamps that have been improved during the period. If ineffective closings exist, as alleged by the Coast Guard, surely during the forty years operating experience there would have been watery cargo to unload, be it ore, coal, grain or stone. This not only would have been readily apparent, but also a costly problem that vessel and cargo owners would not tolerate. If significant water did enter the cargo holds in this manner during a downbound voyage there would be a corresponding change in draft. Draft readings are recorded by the vessel before leaving the port, by the Corps of Engineers at the Soo Locks and by the vessel upon arrival at the unloading port. Periodically the Coast Guard checks the drafts. There are few unexplained changes that have occurred enroute, and none of these were accompanied by water accumulation in the cargo holds . . . in almost forty years of experience.

The Board has pointed to improper hatch closure procedures being observed on other vessels to support the contention that those on the FITZGERALD probably were not closed properly. We submit that there is no validity to such an imputation theory. What might have been observed on one or more vessels in other than heavy weather conditions should under no circumstances be assumed to have been the case on the FITZGERALD in the weather she was experiencing. Consequently, we question the Coast Guard's conclusions on hatch closure procedures.

The Master of the ANDERSON reported that his vessel and the FITZGERALD had proceeded more or less together across Lake Superior at their normal speeds. Based on weather forecasts and deteriorating northeasterly weather, they both worked up to the lee of the Canadian shore as they proceeded eastward. At 0953 the ANDERSON reported that the vessels were not taking any green water aboard, only spray. At 1152 the ANDERSON again reported that conditions were normal. In eastern Lake Superior on the afternoon of November 10, as the vessels changed course to pass between Michipicoten and Caribou Islands, the wind started hauling around to the south and eventually to the northwest.

At 1520 the Second Mate logged ANDERSON abeam Michipicoten Island West End Light at a distance of 7.7 miles. The seas were beginning to build rapidly from the northwest and the Master changed course to 125 degrees. This new course was "shaped up" to clear Six Fathom Shoal north of Caribou Island and to reach a point 8 miles off the island. The FITZGERALD was 17 miles ahead and to the right of dead ahead. The FITZGERALD was then observed to open further to the right of ANDERSON's heading. This would have put the FITZGERALD in the vicinity of the Six Fathom Shoals area. The Master of the ANDERSON testified at the Coast Guard inquiry that he had told the Mate on watch that the FITZGERALD was closer to this shoal than he wanted the ANDERSON to be. No plot of the FITZGERALD was maintained.

When the FITZGERALD departed Superior on November 10 her draft was 27 feet, 2 inches forward and 27 feet, 6 inches aft. The Master of the ANDERSON reported 10–15 foot waves experienced above Caribou Island and as high as 25 feet below Caribou as the seas built up from the northwest winds coming across the lake. Steady winds as high as 43 knots were recorded by the ANDERSON at 1520; winds at 58 knots were logged at 1652.

Between 1530 and 1535, or 10 to 15 minutes after the FITZGERALD was observed by the ANDERSON to be in the Six Fathom area, the FITZGER-ALD advised the ANDERSON of a list, some fence rail damage and the loss of two ballast tank vents. The FITZGERALD advised she was slowing down to permit the ANDERSON to catch up and keep track of her. She also reported that both of her pumps were going. Presumably this meant two 7,000 GPM ballast pumps. It was not until 1610 or 1615 that the FITZGERALD advised her radars were not working and asked the ANDERSON to provide navigational assistance. Note that this does not establish just when the radars became inoperative.

It should be emphasized that minutes after passing Six Fathom Shoal FITZGERALD reported a list, two ballast tank vents had carried away and two ballast pumps were in use. Capacity of the two pumps was 14,000 gallons per minute. Each vent opening in the deck would be eight inches in diameter, so the amount of water entering two eight-inch vents could readily have been handled by the ballast pumps. With the two pumps operating there should have been no list from this source of water, particularly in as short of time as 10 to 15 minutes. Captain Cooper of the ANDERSON testified that "he took that list which seemed to be real fast". Within the time frame involved, such a list can only be readily explained by holing of the vessel's ballast tanks caused by striking Six Fathom Shoals.

It should be noted that there was no report of hatch damage or hatches opening up. Water on the main deck would have resulted in a compressive action, pushing the hatch covers more tightly on their gaskets, rather than lifting them. There was no indication water was entering the holds from topside other than the small amount coming through the two openings. It should be kept in mind that the hatch covers are on coamings raised two feet above the main deck.

Had the water causing the list been entering the cargo hold from topside the amount of water passing aft to the cargo hold suction would have been insufficient to support even one ballast pump. It is also questionable whether water in the cargo hold would have resulted in a list since it would not have been restricted to one side of the vessel. Moreover, if flooding commenced in the forward part of the vessel and forward trim were affected, as theorized by the Coast Guard, the suction point, which is located in the after cargo hold, would have been elevated and pumping would not have been possible. Yet the vessel had two pumps going and the Master reported the FITZGERALD was holding her own at that time, which indicated that water was being pumped and **could not have come through the cargo holds**!! The damage then had to be on the bottom and, since there was no indication of any structural failure, must have been caused by an external force such as shoaling.

Considering that the vessels had only been underway for a day, that no damage or abnormally severe weather was experienced up to early afternoon on November 10, that no mention was made of hatch cover damage or loss, it becomes all too apparent that the quantity of water needed to sink the FITZGERALD could not have seeped through the hatch covers.

After the initial damage caused by shoaling, the vessel labored in heavy quartering seas for over three hours as it proceeded towards Whitefish Point. Thus, excessive working from rolling and pitching was inevitable, accompanied by progressive extension of the initial damage. As the vessel filled up gradually from the bottom to the point where its buoyancy was marginal, a large wave or series of heavy waves could have raised the stern, starting the bow's dive underwater, never to recover. Since the pilothouse was on the bow it would have gone under immediately, leaving no opportunity to alert the crew or radio for help.

The Marine Board indicated that taconite pellets can absorb up to 7 percent moisture. Without explanation this information is "illusive". Under optimum conditions, pellets can contain up to 7 percent moisture, the average amount is less. Not stated is the fact that they contain 3 to 5 percent in the stockpile and when loaded in the cargo holds. Under exposure to moisture they can perhaps absorb 1 or 2 percent **more over a period of time.** There have been statements by the Coast Guard that the pellet cargo could soak up 2,000 tons of water and leave no telltale moisture in the bottom of the hold.

Hatch covers could have been blown off by the compressed air in the cargo compartments as water entered from the sides or bottom. This is a well-known phenomenon based on experience in vessel sinkings. Or hatch covers could have been sprung from the weight of pellets as the vessel dove to the bottom. These same actions would have sprung or broken hatch clamps. Contrary to the Board's findings, the underwater pictures do not support a conclusion that the hatch clamps were not closed properly.

The Coast Guard indicated that a study would be undertaken to determine whether present system for hatch closures on lake vessels can be improved. The industry is always interested in improved equipment or procedures, so such a study is supported.

If the ineffective hatch closure theory is not plausible, then what is likely to have happened? The Coast Guard quickly dismissed the possibility of shoaling near Caribou Island. The reason given was that an accurate track in that area could not be determined from the ANDERSON officers' testimony. Indeed, there was a lack of preciseness that would have been invaluable in proving or disproving the shoaling theory. The ANDERSON's Master, having no inkling of serious trouble on the FITZGERALD, did not record the position of either vessel. Even though not recorded at the time, this experienced Master nonetheless determined from his observations that the FITZGERALD had passed through the Six Fathom (36 feet) Shoal area near Caribou Island. After the fact, when the FITZGERALD was known to be lost, he did not broadcast the information by radio, but made a "confidential" report to his home office by telephone at the first opportunity. His report was taped by the home office.

The Master of the ANDERSON did not volunteer that information when he first appeared as a witness in the Inquiry but the tape was subsequently offered to the Board by his company because of its pertinency to the hearing.

The navigation position data near Caribou Island furnished by the Master of the ANDERSON is materially strengthened by direct radar observations, in contrast to the confusing reconstructed track line produced by the Marine Board. On Page 2149 of the Board Report, Captain Cooper stated he simultaneously had **both** the FITZGERALD and Caribou on his radar, and he was positive that the FITZGERALD went over the shoals. Captain Cooper meticulously avoided the shallower waters because of the heavy seas normal there in such storm conditions.

The significant point is the simultaneous radar observation of Caribou and the vessel. When one object is fixed (Caribou), the distance can be rather accurately determined without any concern for relative motion, bearings, track lines, position, speed or heading. The radar is equipped with concentric ring scales enabling the experienced observer to estimate distances between objects on its screen.

The result of the hydrographic survey of the Caribou Island shoal waters conducted by Canadian Hydrographic Service, at the request of the Coast Guard Marine Board looking into the FITZGERALD sinking, is described on Pages 86 and 87 of the Report. It should be particularly noted that the survey identifies a shoal less than six fathoms deep more than one mile farther east than any in the Six Fathom Shoal cluster depicted on the latest navigation charts. This verified shoal was in the track of the FITZGERALD, as observed by the ANDERSON, thus making shoaling even more certain as the start of the fateful events leading to the sinking. This fact could be considered along with the taped report of the ANDERSON's Master.

Loadline changes . . . In view of the foregoing, and since the Marine Board found there was no structural failure, nor has any experience or data been cited showing that 1969, 1971 or 1973 changes in the Loadline Regulations were improper or unwise, this recommendation should be dismissed.

To qualify for a reduction in freeboard the Coast Guard has imposed a group of conditions that enhance ships' safety. Only those ships which incorporated certain structural features were eligible to take advantage of the specified draft increases. For example, in 1969, for a 600′ ship to gain 5.5 inches of draft it would have to be constructed in compliance with recently upgraded ABS rules; have steel, one-piece, watertight hatch covers—instead of boards and tarpaulins; have steel deckhouses; be proven structurally suitable for the resulting loaded draft in all operating conditions; and have under deck passages, or tunnels, permitting personnel to move fore and aft in safety.

There has been an implication that a ship receives a loadline assignment precisely calculated in accord with the structural stresses imposed by the deadweight corresponding to the loadline draft. Ignored is the fact that the scantlings used must satisfy a number of criteria, including the imperical— and generally conservative rules of a classification society. The truth is that, in the first instance, a vessel's freeboard is set by its length, depth, deck height or shear pattern, extent and stanchness of superstructures and deckhouses, and the efficacy of a number of fittings such as watertight closures, freeing ports and means of protecting the crew. Then, it must be proven that the structural strength is commensurate with the loads corresponding to that freeboard draft.

In every instance, when a ship seemingly becomes eligible for a freeboard decrease by reason of a subsequent amendment to the loadline regulations, it is necessary to prove to the Coast Guard and the classification society that the vessel's structure measures up to the deeper loading. At this time, furthermore, many details of structure and equipment come under the scrutiny of these regulatory agencies with the result that they are generally—and expensively—upgraded. Thus it may be seen that decreased freeboard or increased draft is not a present lightly bestowed by the Coast Guard, rather, **quid pro quo** in the form of safety enhancement is demanded for these allegedly perilous inches.

Watertight compartmentation . . . Some background may be helpful to counter the thinking that lake vessels have no watertight compartments and are merely one large "bathtub".

Great Lakes vessels are designed by competent naval architects based on criteria developed and published by one of the worldwide classification societies (American Bureau of Shipping and Lloyds Registry on the Great Lakes) and the regulations of the United States or Canadian Coast Guard. Additionally, a proposed design must be submitted and approved by both a classification society and the governmental regulatory authority. The basic strength standard and the loadline assigned a vessel is in accordance with the international regulation under joint agreement of the United States and Canadian governments.

Great Lakes vessels are designed with segregated ballast tanks. This means that the ship has tanks designed exclusively for water ballast and it is not necessary to utilize the cargo hold for water ballast when in the light condition. These tanks provide a double shell over the entire bottom of the cargo hold and vertically up the sides to about the loaded water line on most ships. Tunnels under the weather deck have watertight doors and afford watertight integrity several feet above the main deck. However, the envelope extends to the weather deck on some designs. The typical Great Lakes bulk vessel has six to nine ballast tanks on each side. Each tank is divided port and starboard by a watertight center vertical keelson and fore and aft by a watertight bulkhead. Additionally, the ship is divided into complete watertight compartments by the collision bulkhead forward and the engine room bulkhead aft. Afterpeak tanks are watertight and extend vertically to one deck below the weather deck.

These watertight subdivisions and ballast tanks afford a substantial margin of safety in case the shell of the vessel is penetrated allowing water to flood one or more of the compartments. Damage control can be exercised through the use of a combination of ballast pumps, compressed air applied to the tanks and use of the collision tarps.

A claim has been made that while lake vessels may lack watertight subdivisions between cargo holds, ocean going vessels are required to have water-tight bulkheads between cargo spaces. Actually there is no basic requirement for a seagoing **cargo** ship to have any watertight subdivision beyond the collision bulkhead, machinery space bulkhead(s) and the afterpeak bulkhead. Further subdivision to meet floodability criteria is required only when free-board less than "Steamer" or Type "B" freeboard is desired.

Since 1970 vessels built under Title XI Mortgage Insurance Procedures are required to have "one compartment" watertight stability. Whether or not required, our members are moving towards improved watertight compart-mentation in new construction. Accomplished in that manner, the cost is not prohibitive, as compared to retrofitting.

In a further effort, and in the light of the foregoing, Maritime Adminis-tration has recently invited bids on a contract to consider the practicality of further watertight compartmentation on lake vessels.

Lake shipping safety in general . . . A few additional comments will up-date the status and progress of our safety efforts. At the House Merchant Marine and Fisheries Committee Coast Guard oversight hearings at the Soo on July 16, 1976, I listed a number of steps under consideration by govern-ment and industry that would, in my opinion, be a quantum step forward safety-wise.

Hull monitoring . . . First is the development of a hull monitoring sys-tem with an appropriate pilothouse readout to interpret hull actions in all-weather situations and to alert the master that trouble is developing. No mat-ter what survival systems are available for the vessel personnel, if they don't know they are in trouble, such as was apparently the case on the FITZGER-ALD, safety will not prevail. A contract is in process by MARAD to pull avail-able technology together to develop and test such a monitoring system on a lake vessel. Much of the preliminary stress measurement procedures have already been accomplished on lake vessels.

Develop an all-weather capsule . . . In my opinion, lifeboats, as we have known them through the years, are obsolescent today. This is not only because of current technology, but also reduced professionalism in today's seamen.

We have recommended a change in Coast Guard regulations to permit development and use of survival equipment other than the traditional life rafts and lifeboats. The changes are still under consideration. There is not much incentive for such investment until the future is clarified.

Since recommending development of a "survival capsule" for shipboard use, interest has been expressed by several firms in this country. And in Norway, government, shipping and classification society authorities have developed a 36-man capsule that can be ejected from a ship's deck. This is especially advantageous where fire or other hazardous cargoes are involved. Our cargoes on the lakes don't fall into this category, so we are more interested in a capsule that can be boarded in all-weather and can float free if the vessel sinks.

Survival suits . . . On August 11, 1977, after considerable study, the Coast Guard approved two survival suits for shipboard use. This eliminated the liability problem in using lifesaving equipment that does not have Coast Guard approval.

Improved weather forecasting . . . A number of changes are underway that should result in improved marine weather forecasting for the lakes. Weather buoys, the assignment of marine forecasters, more vessels reporting weather data, looking at the lakes as a weather system for marine purposes and better communications are under consideration or in process. This, together with improved meteorological training of deck officers, will further enhance safety of lake shipping.

Position keeping on the lakes . . . Since it is now almost certain that the FITZGERALD grounded on a shoal above Caribou Island, and there is no evidence of structural failure, we must conclude there was a navigation problem, not a design weakness nor a hatch closure deficiency.

What was the navigation problem and how can we minimize it for other vessels?

We know that the FITZGERALD advised the ANDERSON at 1610 to 1615 that his radars were not working and asked for navigation assistance. But we don't really know just when the radars went out or how. Did both go at the same time from a large wave action? Where was the vessel in relation to the Six Fathom Shoals area above Caribou?

The east side of Caribou Island is relatively low so wave action would have distorted radar signals giving an impression of being farther from the island than actually was the case. The radio beacon at Whitefish Point was not operating. Bearings from this beacon would have indicated the vessel's position east or west from the shoal area. This signal would have been especially critical under the circumstances involved.

Two changes are underway that will improve navigation in the future, one will be especially helpful. As part of the national navigation plan, Loran-C coverage for the lakes is to be provided by the Coast Guard by 1980. This remarkably accurate position finding system is not affected by visibility, sea return or other weather conditions. It will be the principal means of navigation, complementing radar, and will obsolete radio beacons on the lakes. Consequently, completion of the Loran-C coverage should be expedited.

The other change is a requirement for fathometers on lake vessels. The bottom characteristic of the lakes and the limited bottom information shown on charts will limit the usefulness of this equipment, but it may be of some help in special situations.

And finally, the uncharted shoal **less** than six fathoms deep over one mile east of Six Fathom Shoal north of Caribou Island will be shown on future navigation charts of eastern Lake Superior.

Mr. Chairman, the lake shipping industry and its professional naval architect advisors can find NOTHING in the available factors to support the Coast Guard's thesis that the sinking resulted from poor hatch closure procedures. We can't identify one such factor, whereas, such factors do support shoaling as the cause of the sinking.

If we can provide any other information or assistance, please call on us.

Respectfully submitted,

LAKE CARRIERS' ASSOCIATION
Paul E. Trimble
Vice Admiral USCG (Ret.)
President

NATIONAL TRANSPORTATION SAFETY BOARD

WASHINGTON, D.C. 20594

MARINE ACCIDENT REPORT

ADOPTED: MAY 4, 1978

SS EDMUND FITZGERALD SINKING IN LAKE SUPERIOR

NOVEMBER 10, 1975

CONTENTS

INTRODUCTION

This casualty was investigated by a U.S. Coast Guard Marine Board of Investigation which convened at Cleveland, Ohio, on November 18, 1975. A representative of the National Transportation Safety Board observed part of the proceedings. The Safety Board has considered all facts pertinent to the Safety Board's statutory responsibility to determine the cause or probable cause of the casualty and to make recommendations.

The Safety Board's recommendations are made independently of any recommendations proposed by the Coast Guard. To assure public knowledge of all Safety Board recommendations, all such recommendations are published in the Federal Register. If the Coast Guard does not accept some of these Safety Board recommendations, the Coast Guard is required to set forth in detail the reasons for such refusal. This is one of the means by which the Safety Board exercises its responsibility of assessing the safety, operating, and regulatory practices of the U.S. Coast Guard.

SYNOPSIS

About 1915 EST on November 10, 1975, the Great Lakes bulk cargo vessel SS EDMUND FITZGERALD, fully loaded with a cargo of taconite pellets, sank in eastern Lake Superior in position 46°59.9' N, 85°06.6' W, approximately 17 miles from the entrance to Whitefish Bay, MI. The ship was en route from Superior, WI, to Detroit, MI, and had been proceeding at a reduced speed in a severe storm. All the vessel's 29 officers and crewmembers are missing and presumed dead. No distress call was heard by vessels or shore stations.

The Safety Board considered many factors during the investigation including stability, hull strength, operating practices, adequacy of weathertight closures, hatch cover strength, possible grounding, vessel design, loading practices, and weather forecasting.

The National Transportation Safety Board determines that the probable cause of this accident was the sudden massive flooding of the cargo hold due to the collapse of one or more hatch covers. Before the hatch covers collapsed, flooding into the ballast tanks and tunnel through topside damage and flooding into the cargo hold through nonweathertight hatch covers caused a reduction of freeboard and a list. The hydrostatic and hydrodynamic forces imposed on the hatch covers by heavy boarding seas at this reduced freeboard and with the list caused the hatch covers to collapse.

Contributing to the accident was the lack of transverse watertight bulkheads in the cargo hold and the reduction of freeboard authorized by the 1969, 1971, and 1973 amendments to the Great Lakes Load Line Regulations.

INVESTIGATION
The Accident

About 0830 [all times are Eastern Standard based on the 24-hour clock] on November 9, 1975, the SS EDMUND FITZGERALD began loading 26,116 long tons of taconite pellets at Burlington Northern Railroad Dock No. 1 in Superior, WI. This pier, known as a "chute pier," is equipped with built-in storage bins, known as "pockets," which are usually filled before a vessel arrives. Chutes are lowered from each "pocket" to direct the cargo into the hatches of the vessel. Most of the "pockets" are filled with 300 tons of taconite pellets; however, a few pockets are filled with 100 tons or 200 tons. These smaller amounts of cargo are used during the final phase of loading to trim the ship for departure.

Loading was completed about 1415 on November 9. The chief mate informed dock personnel that the vessel's final drafts were 27 feet 2 inches forward and 27 feet 6 inches aft. Drafts were taken after receipt of the taconite pellets and 50,013 gallons of No. 6 fuel oil, delivered by a barge which came alongside while the cargo was being loaded.

Neither shipboard nor dock personnel experienced difficulties while loading the cargo nor was any difficulty or damage reported by the crew of the FITZGERALD. Shoreside personnel saw the ship's crew replacing the hatch covers after loading.

Upon departure at 1415, the FITZGERALD proceeded at full speed of 99 rpm, approximately 16.3 mph. About 1630, the SS ARTHUR M. ANDERSON departed Two Harbors, Minnesota, with a similar cargo en route to Gary, Indiana. Separated by 10 to 20 miles, the two vessels proceeded on similar courses across Lake Superior.

Because of predicted deteriorating weather, the receipt of storm warnings at 0200 on November 10, and discussions by radiotelephone, the FITZGERALD and ANDERSON departed the recommended shipping lanes along the southern shore of Lake Superior, and proceeded northeastward south of Isle Royal, then eastward along the northern shore, and then southeastward along the eastern shore. This departure from the recommended track allowed the two vessels to take advantage of the lee provided by the Canadian shore. This is a generally accepted practice among Great Lakes mariners to avoid adverse sea conditions during fall and winter storms when the wind direction makes this lee available. During the first 10 to 11 hours of the voyage, the ANDERSON was ahead of the FITZGERALD; however, about 0300 on November 10, the faster FITZGERALD pulled slightly ahead.

The FITZGERALD made routine weather reports at 0100 and 0700 on November 10. In the normal morning report to the company office, the FITZGERALD said her estimated time of arrival at Sault Ste. Marie was indefinite because of bad weather.

As the FITZGERALD and the ANDERSON approached the eastern shore, the FITZGERALD proceeded farther east than the ANDERSON before changing to a southeasterly course toward Michipicoten Island. Since the FITZGERALD traveled a greater distance at a higher speed, the distance between the two vessels remained almost constant. About 1252, the ANDERSON was abeam Otter Island at a range of 10.8 miles, and the FITZGERALD was 8 miles ahead and slightly east of the ANDERSON's track. (See figure 1.) At that point, the FITZGERALD was about 17 miles north-northwest of Michipicoten Island.

At 1350, the ANDERSON changed course to 230° T to allow more sea room west of Michipicoten Island because the wind was predicted to haul to the northwest. At this time, the FITZGERALD was 2½ to 3 miles southwest of Michipicoten Island, and she advised the ANDERSON that she would "continue on" although she was "rolling some." The FITZGERALD continued southeastward toward Whitefish Point on a course of 141° T while the ANDERSON proceeded southwestward to about 11 miles west of Michipicoten Island and changed course to 130° T at 1445. At this time, the FITZGERALD was observed to be about 16 miles ahead, a position 9 miles south of Michipicoten Island. At 1520, the ANDERSON changed course to 125° T at a position 7.7 miles southwest of Michipicoten Island. The FITZGERALD was 16 miles ahead and slightly to the right of the ANDERSON's trackline.

About 1530, the FITZGERALD, then in a position northeast of Caribou Island, called the ANDERSON and reported, "I have a fence rail down, have lost a couple of vents, and have a list." The FITZGERALD further advised that she would "check-down" to allow the ANDERSON to close the distance between the vessels. The ANDERSON asked the FITZGERALD if the pumps were going and the reply was, "Yes, both of them."

About 1610, the FITZGERALD advised the ANDERSON that both her radars were inoperative and asked that the ANDERSON keep track of the FITZGERALD and provide navigational assistance. At 1634, the ANDERSON changed course to 141° T in a position 7.5 miles, 035° T from the north end of Caribou Island and observed the FITZGERALD 14 to 15 miles ahead and slightly to the right of the ANDERSON's heading flasher. At 1728, the ANDERSON fixed her position 10.5 miles east of Caribou Light, determined that the FITZGERALD was 15 miles ahead and slightly left (east) of the

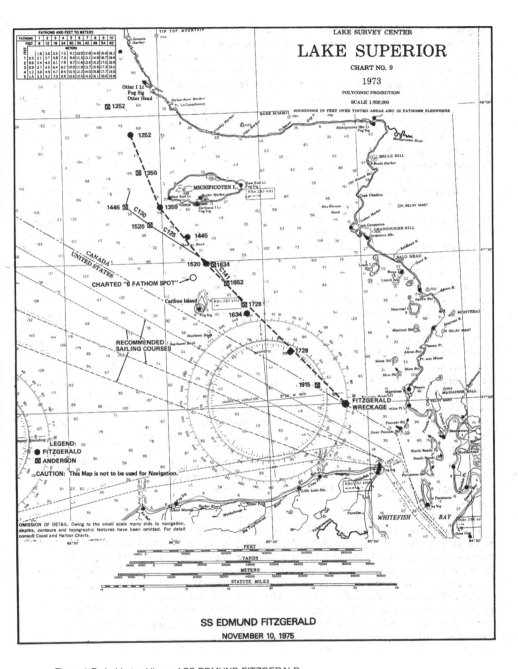

Figure 1. Probable tracklines of SS EDMUND FITZGERALD
and SS ARTHUR M. ANDERSON on November 10, 1975.

ANDERSON's heading flasher, and advised the FITZGERALD that White-fish Point was 35 miles from the FITZGERALD on a bearing of 144° T. The FITZGERALD replied that she "wanted to be 2½ miles off Whitefish Point," and appeared to be steering for that position.

About 1639, the Coast Guard station at Grand Marais, MI, advised the FITZGERALD, in response to her inquiry, that the radio beacon at Whitefish Point was not operating.

Between 1700 and 1730, a Great Lakes registered pilot on board the north-bound Swedish vessel AVAFORS, in a position near Whitefish Point, answered a call from the FITZGERALD and said that Whitefish Point Light was operat-ing but that the radio beacon was still off. During a radiotelephone conversation between the two vessels, the master of the FITZGERALD apparently spoke to personnel aboard the FITZGERALD while the radiotelephone remained on the transmit mode. The master was overheard saying, "Don't allow nobody on deck," followed by some conversation concerning a vent, which was not understood aboard the AVAFORS. The master advised the AVAFORS that the FITZGERALD had a "bad list," had lost both radars, and was taking heavy seas over the deck in one of the worst seas he had ever encountered.

About 1820, the ANDERSON advised the FITZGERALD that the FITZGERALD was working to the left of the ANDERSON's heading of 142° T and determined by radiotelephone that the FITZGERALD was steering 141° T.

At 1900, the ANDERSON advised the FITZGERALD that she was 10 miles ahead and 1 to 1½ miles to the left (east) of the ANDERSON's heading flasher. At 1910, the ANDERSON advised the FITZGERALD of northbound traffic 9 miles ahead of her. In response to a question about her problems, the FITZGERALD replied, "We are holding our own."

This was the last radiotelephone conversation with the FITZGERALD. When the ANDERSON's radarscope was checked about 1920, there was no radar contact with her. Visibility increased about this time and although lights on shore more than 20 miles away and lights of a northbound vessel 19 miles away could be seen, the FITZGERALD, which should have been approxi-mately 10 miles away, was not visible.

Between 1920 and 2030, the ANDERSON tried calling the FITZGERALD on VHF-FM radiotelephone, but got no response. At 2032, the ANDERSON notified the Coast Guard that the FITZGERALD may have suffered a casualty.

Wreckage identified as that of the FITZGERALD was located in posi-tion 46°59.9' N, 85°06.6' W in 530 feet of water in eastern Lake Superior just north of the International Boundary in Canadian waters. This position correlates with the last position of the FITZGERALD as reported by the ANDERSON.

Crew Information

The crew of the FITZGERALD consisted of the following 29 persons: a master, 3 licensed deck officers, a chief engineer, 4 licensed engineering officers, and 20 unlicensed personnel. No survivors were found and no bodies were recovered.

The master and chief mate were experienced Great Lakes mariners, having been licensed since 1938 and 1941, respectively. Both men held valid licenses as Master and First Class Pilot for Great Lake vessels of any gross tonnage. The other mates held valid licenses as First Class Pilot for Great Lakes vessels of any gross tonnage which were first issued in 1969 and 1973, respectively. The engineering officers were similarly experienced.

The master had been employed by the vessel's operator since 1938, had been employed as master since 1951, and had served as master of the FITZGERALD since April 1972.

The chief mate had been employed by the vessel's operator since 1947 in various capacities, including relief master in 1966 and 1971, and had served aboard the FITZGERALD as chief mate since April 1975.

Vessel Information

The FITZGERALD was one of a fleet of 14 to 18 vessels operated by the Columbia Transportation Division between 1972 and 1977. The Coast Guard casualty records for the company fleet did not reveal any heavy weather damage during this period.

The FITZGERALD was a conventional "straightdecker" Great Lakes bulk cargo vessel. (See figure 2.) It was 729 feet long, 75 feet in breadth, 39 feet in depth, 13,632 gross tons, and 8,686 net tons. It was propelled by a 7,500-hp, steam turbine and was built as Hull 301 at Great Lakes Engineering Works, River Rouge, Michigan, in 1958. The vessel was owned by Northeastern Mutual Life Insurance Company and operated by the Columbia Transportation Division of the Oglebay Norton Company.

The vessel had a 860,950-cubic-foot cargo hold divided by two nonwatertight transverse "screen" bulkheads. Outboard and below the cargo hold were eight ballast tanks divided at the centerline into port and starboard tanks. (See

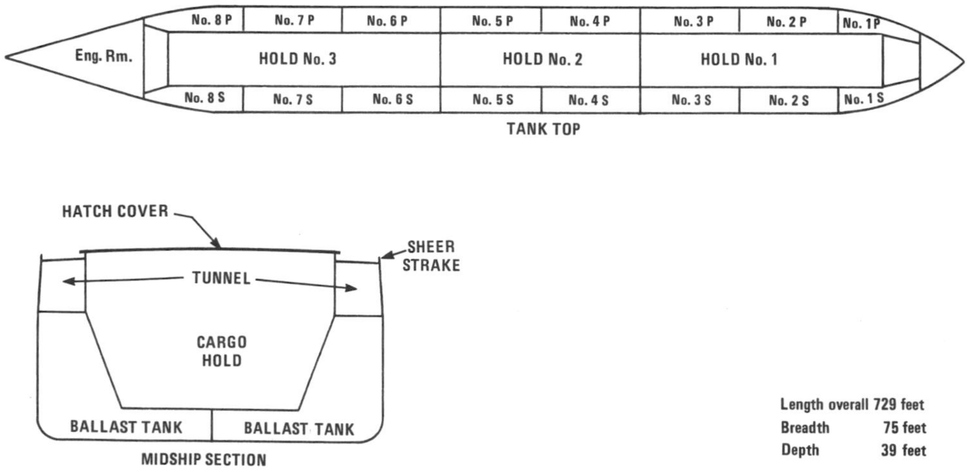

Figure 2. Arrangement of SS EDMUND FITZGERALD.

figure 2.) The forward deckhouse contained the pilot house and accommodations for the deck crew. The engine room was located aft, above which were the rest of the accommodations and the crew's messing facilities. Below the weather deck and above the ballast tanks were two tunnels, one port and one starboard, used for access between the accommodation areas during adverse weather. The sheer strake extended $15^3/_8$ inches above the weather deck at side and was connected to the stringer plate by a riveted gunwale bar.

There were 21 cargo hatch openings. Each opening measured 11 feet longitudinally and 48 feet transversely and had a 24-inch coaming above the weather deck. Each opening was made weathertight by a single-piece steel hatch cover. The hatch covers were made of $5/_{16}$-inch stiffened plate with a $9/_{16}$-inch rubber gasket around the underside of the plate's perimeter. Each hatch cover was secured by 68 manually operated "Kestner" clamps arranged on 2-foot centers. Each clamp had an adjustment bolt which determined the force applied by the individual clamp and therefore controlled the deflection of the hatch cover, the compression of the rubber gasket, and the weathertightness of the hatch opening. There were no written procedures concerning maintenance or adjustment of the hatch clamps or gaskets. An electrically operated hatch cover crane which ran on rails outboard of the cargo hatch openings was used for lifting the hatch covers.

Access to the cargo hold was provided through two 30-inch hatches through the weather deck located at the "screen" bulkheads fitted on 24-inch coamings, through doors from the tunnels, and through doors at the main deck level (i.e., the deck level below the weather deck) at the forward and after ends of the cargo hold.

Two 8-inch-diameter vent pipes which extended 18 inches above the weather deck were fitted for each ballast tank. The port and starboard access tunnels had similar vents extending 30 inches above the weather deck located forward and aft. In addition, each ballast tank was fitted with a remote water level indicator device, called a "King Gage," located in the lower engineroom near the ballast pumps. The only means of detecting water in the cargo hold or access tunnel was by visual inspection. Federal regulations do not require that Great Lakes vessels be equipped with instruments to indicate trim or list.

The bilge and ballast system consisted of a piping system connected through manifolds and valving to four 7,000 gallon-per-minute main pumps and two 2,000 gallon-per-minute auxiliary pumps. The ballast system could be used to de-water the cargo hold through two suctions located at the aftermost end of the No. 3 cargo hold, port and starboard. The tunnels could be drained by manually operated drains connected to the ballast tanks.

The following radiotelephone equipment was located in the pilothouse and chartroom: Two VHF-FM, 12-channel, 25-watt radiotelephones operated from vessel's power; one VHF-FM 12-channel, 25-watt radiotelephone operated from rechargeable batteries located in the pilothouse; one AM, 8-channel, 100-watt radiotelephone operated from vessel's power; one AM, emergency, 50-watt radiotelephone including channel 51 (2182 kHz), operated from rechargeable batteries. The FITZGERALD also had a radio direction finder and two surface scan radar sets. No fathometer was required and none was installed.

After her delivery in 1958, the FITZGERALD operated essentially unchanged until 1969 when a diesel-powered bow thruster was installed. During the winter of 1971–1972, the main propulsion plant was converted from coal to oil and the coal bunkers were converted to fuel oil tanks. An automatic boiler combustion and feed-water control system was installed as part of this conversion.

Between 1958 and 1973, the FITZGERALD was permitted three reductions in the minimum freeboard required by 46 CFR Part 45. (Freeboard on the FITZGERALD was the distance from the maximum draft permitted to the weather deck at side.) A comparison of the requirements for Great Lakes cargo vessels and those for vessels operating on the oceans shows that for vessels of similar dimensions, the freeboard required for a Great Lakes Load Line and that required for ocean service would be approximately the same. However, the longitudinal strength required for a Great Lakes vessel is approximately one-half that required for a vessel in ocean service. The following table shows the freeboards assigned to the FITZGERALD:

MINIMUM REQUIRED FREEBOARD

Date	Midsummer	Summer	Intermediate	Winter
Originally assigned when vessel was built	11 feet-10¾ inches	12 feet-6¾ inches	13 feet-6¾ inches	14 feet-9¼ inches
3 July 69	11 feet-4½ inches	12 feet-½ inch	13 feet-¾ inch	14 feet-3½ inches
17 Sept 71	11 feet-4½ inches	12 feet-½ inch	13 feet-¾ inch	13 feet-2 inches
13 Sept 73	10 feet-5½ inches	11 feet-2 inches	11 feet-2 inches	11 feet-6 inches

46 CFR 45.5 states that midsummer freeboard applies May 1 through September 15; summer freeboard applies April 16 through April 30 and September 16 through September 30; intermediate freeboard applies October 1 through October 31 and April 1 through April 15; and winter freeboard applies November 1 through March 31.

As part of the requirements for obtaining the freeboards assigned on September 13, 1973, all vents were to be at least 30 inches above the weather deck.

However, under 46 CFR 45.133(b), the FITZGERALD was permitted to have ballast tank vents extending to only 18 inches above the weather deck because the 30-inch height interfered with handling cargo on the ship.

No major structural problems were detected during the operating years of the FITZGERALD. Some cracking was detected in the keelson connection to the shell plating; however, during the winter layup of 1968–1969, this condition was corrected by redesign and repair. Only minor cracks were observed thereafter. Some minor fractures were detected in the hatch coamings and the gunwale bar which were caused by original construction faults and original design detail defects. These minor fractures were repaired and the design details were corrected during the winter layup of 1973–1974 and no subsequent fractures were found.

During its operating years, the FITZGERALD sustained damage from one grounding, one collision, and several instances of striking lock walls. In these instances, all the damaged structure was removed and replaced as original. The FITZGERALD was last drydocked in Cleveland, Ohio, in April 1974, when the accessible areas of the interior and exterior structure and hull plating were examined and all damage was satisfactorily repaired.

During the winter layup of 1974–1975 and while the Coast Guard was conducting the inspection for certification, the American Bureau of Shipping (ABS) conducted an annual survey of the hull, machinery, and boilers; completed part of the continuous machinery survey; and conducted an annual load line inspection. These surveys were completed on April 9, 1975, with no outstanding requirements that affected the structural integrity of the hull.

The FITZGERALD was last inspected by the Coast Guard and the ABS on October 31, 1975. Four minor structural defects in way of the hatches were noted and the Coast Guard ordered these defects to be repaired before the 1976 shipping season. The structural defects consisted of: A 1-inch notch in the plate in way of hatch No. 13; a 1-inch gouge in the plate in way of hatch no. 15; a 10-inch crack in No. 16 hatch end girder; and a 1-inch crack at the intersection of No. 21 hatch coaming and hatch end girder. All four defects probably resulted from damage from offloading equipment and did not affect the strength of the hull girder.

Cargo Information

The FITZGERALD was carrying about 26,116 long tons of National Taconite Pellets. Taconite pellets are manufactured by a process known as "oxide pelletizing." This process begins with the mining of iron ore (magnetite), concentrated with the addition of bentonite, processed into balls of $^3/_8$-inch to $^5/_8$-inch diameter, and fired at temperatures of 2,200° F to 2,400° F, which changes its composition to relatively nonmagnetic hemotite. This process produces almost spherical pellets containing 67 percent iron, which are easily handled by belts and bulk cargo handling equipment. Taconite pellets weigh from 127 to 140 pounds per cubic foot, will absorb approximately 8 to 9 pounds (6 to 7 percent by weight) water per cubic foot, can contain up to 27.5 pounds of water in the interstitial void spaces in each cubic foot of pellets, and exhibit an angle of repose (the angle between the horizontal and the slope of a freestanding pile of the material) of approximately 260 either wet or dry.

Great Lakes bulk carriers are loaded to have as little trim, heel, and midship deflection as possible. Cargo is distributed so that the vessel does not hog; however, 1 inch of sag is considered acceptable. During loading, the crew monitors the forward, aft, and midship drafts, and small amounts of cargo are added at selected locations to achieve the desired drafts when the loading is almost completed.

On the upbound voyage, en route to loading ports in the upper lakes, Great Lakes bulk carriers use water ballast to obtain the desired draft and trim to insure sufficient vertical clearance upon arrival at the loading berth. During loading operations, ballast water is pumped out at the same time cargo is loaded to maintain correct vertical clearances.

Meteorological Information

On November 8, 1975, a storm was generated over the Oklahoma Panhandle. By 0700 on November 9, the storm was centered over south-central Kansas and the National Weather Service (NWS) predicted that the storm would travel in a northeasterly direction and pass just south of Lake Superior by 1900 on November 10.

At 1300 on November 9, the storm was centered over the northeast corner of Kansas and the NWS predicted that the storm would shift to a more northerly direction, pass over Lake Superior east of Michipicoten Island, and by 1900 on November 10 be over James Bay, Canada.

At 1900 on November 9, the NWS issued gale warnings (expected winds from 34 to 47 knots) for all of Lake Superior. Winds in the eastern half of the lake were predicted to be "east to northeast, increasing to 25 to 37 knots during the night, and northeasterly by Monday afternoon (November 10), waves 5 to 10 feet." At 2239, on November 9, the forecast was revised to "easterly winds 32 to 42 knots, becoming southeasterly Monday morning, and west to southwest 35 to 45 knots Monday afternoon, rain and thunderstorms, waves 5 to 10 feet increasing to 8 to 15 feet Monday."

At 0100 on November 10, the storm was located over central Wisconsin, had a minimum barometic pressure of 29.24 inches of mercury and was moving at an average speed of 29 knots. At 0100 on November 10, the FITZGERALD was about 20 miles south of Isle Royal and reported winds from 030° T at 52 knots and waves of 10 feet.

At 0200 on November 10, NWS issued a storm warning (expected winds over 48 knots) predicting "northeast winds 35 to 50 knots, becoming northwesterly 28 to 38 knots, waves 8 to 15 feet."

At 0700 on November 10, the FITZGERALD was about 45 miles north of Copper Harbor, Michigan, and reported winds from 050° T at 35 knots and waves of 10 feet.

At 1034 on November 10, the NWS predicted "north to northwest winds

32 to 48 knots this afternoon becoming northwesterly 25 to 48 knots tonight and westerly 20 to 30 knots Tuesday, waves 8 to 16 feet decreasing Tuesday."

At 1300 on November 10, the storm center had crossed Lake Superior to the west of Michipicoten Island and was over White River, Ontario. At 1300 on November 10, the ANDERSON was 20 miles northwest of Michipicoten Island and reported winds from 150° T at 20 knots, waves of 12 feet; the M/V SIMCOE was 15 miles to the southwest of the ANDERSON and reported winds from 270° T at 44 knots and waves of 7 feet. At the same time, Stannard Rock Weather Station reported winds from the west-northwest at 50 knots, gusting to 59 knots, and the Whitefish Point Station reported winds from the south-southwest at 19 knots, gusting to 34 knots.

At 1639, on November 10, the NWS predicted for Eastern Lake Superior: "Northwest winds 38 to 52 knots with gusts to 60 knots early tonight and northwesterly winds 25 to 35 knots diminishing Tuesday, waves 8 to 16 feet tonight, decreasing Tuesday."

At 1900, on November 10, as the storm center passed over the southern tip of James Bay, Canada, the ANDERSON reported winds from 300° T at 50 knots, waves of 16 feet, and Stannard Rock reported wind west-northwest (292.5° T) at 40 knots, gusting to 65 knots. The highest winds recorded by Stannard Rock were west-northwest at 56 knots gusting to 66 knots at 1700 on November 10.

The log of the ANDERSON shows the following on November 10:

1. At 1350, just north of Michipicoten Island, the winds were northwest by west at 5 knots.

2. At 1445, west of Michipicoten Island, the winds were northwest at 42 knots.

3. At 1520, just south of Michipicoten Island, the winds were northwest at 43 knots.

4. At 1652, north east of Caribou Island, the winds were northwest at 52 knots.

The master of the ANDERSON testified that 10 or 12 miles north of Caribou Island, the seas were running 12 to 18 feet, and south of Caribou Island, the seas were running 18 to 25 feet. He further testified that he observed winds gusts of 70 or 75 knots.

A NWS meteorologist testified that before the FITZGERALD sank, the average sustained wind speed was 45 knots from the northwest for a period of

6 to 7 hours and that these conditions would produce waves with a significant height of 15 feet. He also testified that there are usually 4 or 5 intense storms on the Great Lakes during the fall to spring shipping seasons. A storm of the intensity of the one recorded on November 10 would not occur every year; however, more intense storms have been recorded on the Great Lakes.

Wreckage

Because of the weather conditions following the sinking of the FITZGERALD and because the wreckage was lying on the bottom of Lake Superior in 530 feet of water, a comprehensive examination of the damage to the FITZGER-ALD was not undertaken until May 1976. At that time, a task force was formed, including representatives from the Coast Guard Marine Board of Investigation, the National Transportation Safety Board, the U.S. Navy Supervisor of Salvage, the Naval Undersea Center, and Seaward, Inc. of Falls Church, Virginia, an engineering consultant firm under contract to the U.S. Navy Supervisor of Salvage to make a visual survey of the wreckage using the USN CURV III System under contract to the USCG. The CURV III is an unmanned, deep-diving vehicle controlled from the surface and capable of television and still photography. This vehicle made 12 dives with a total of 56 hours 5 minutes bottom time and recorded 43,255 feet of videotape and 985 still color photographs.

The results of the CURV III visual survey and three earlier side-scan sonar surveys were assembled and reviewed by Seaward, Inc., which prepared a sketch of the wreckage (see figure 3), and artists' conceptions of the wreckage from several viewpoints. (See figures 4 to 8.)

The wreckage lies approximately 17 miles northwest of Whitefish Point, Michigan. The wreckage consists of an upright bow section, an inverted stern section, and debris from a missing 200-foot midship portion. The bow section is 276 feet long, inclined 15° to port from the upright, extends from the stem to a location between hatches Nos. 8 and 9, and is buried in mud up to the 28-foot draft mark.

There was extensive damage to the forward deckhouse and there were several holes in the bow shell plating. The rest of the shell plating extending back to the rupture was intact. The No. 1 hatch cover was entirely inside the No. 1 hatch and showed indications of buckling from external loading. Sections of the coaming in way of the No. 1 hatch were fractured and buckled inward. The No. 2 hatch cover was missing and the coaming on the No. 2 hatch was fractured and buckled. Hatches Nos. 3 and 4 were covered with mud; however, one corner of hatch cover No. 3 could be seen in place. Hatch cover No. 5 was missing. A series of 16 consecutive hatch cover clamps were observed on the No. 5 hatch coaming. Of this series, the first and eighth were distorted or broken. All of the 14 other clamps were undamaged and in the open position. The No. 6 hatch was open and a hatch cover was standing on end vertically in the hatch. The hatch covers were missing from hatches Nos. 7 and 8 and both coamings were fractured and severely distorted. The bow section abruptly ended just aft of hatch No. 8 and the deck plating was ripped up from the separation to the forward end of hatch No. 7.

The stern section was upside down and inclined 10° from the vertical away from the bow section. All bottom plating was intact from the stern to a location between hatches Nos. 17 and 18 where the vessel had separated. The rudder and propeller were undamaged with the rudder positioned no more than 10 degrees from centerline.

SS EDMUND FITZGERALD
NOVEMBER 10, 1975

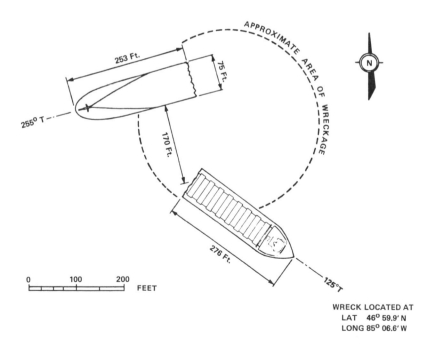

Figure 3. Sketch of relative positions of bow and stern section.

SS EDMUND FITZGERALD
NOVEMBER 10, 1975

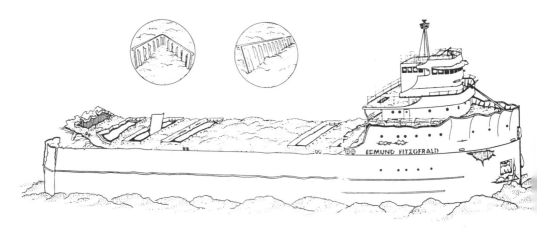

Figure 4. Sketch of bow section from starboard.

SS EDMUND FITZGERALD
NOVEMBER 10, 1975

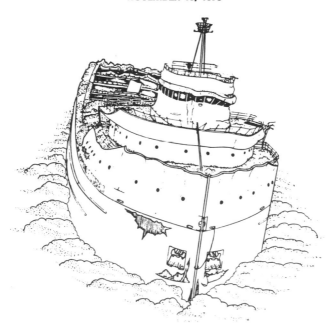

Figure 5. Sketch of bow section from ahead.

SS EDMUND FITZGERALD
NOVEMBER 10, 1975

Figure 6. Sketch of bow section from astern.

SS EDMUND FITZGERALD
NOVEMBER 10, 1975

Figure 7. Sketch of stern section from ahead.

SS EDMUND FITZGERALD
NOVEMBER 10, 1975

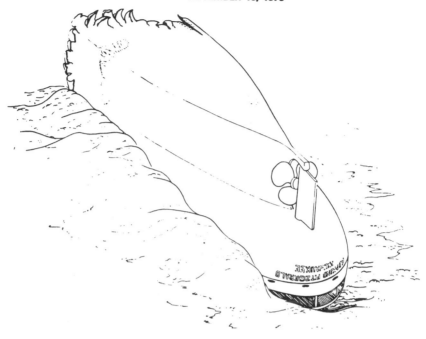

Figure 8. Sketch of stern section from astern.

There was mud-covered wreckage extending out from the ruptured end of the stern section, but no identification of what part of the ship it came from can be determined. Three hatch coamings and a hatch cover were lying next to the stern section. One of the hatch coamings bore the numeral 11.

A few of the deck vents on the starboard side of the bow section could be seen above the mud. One vent near hatch No. 5 was torn away from the deck, leaving an opening in the deck at the base of the vent pipe. The vents on the port side of the bow section were covered with mud. Neither the spare propeller blade nor the hatch cover crane was visible and they have not been located.

Survival Aspects

The Coast Guard Certificate of Inspection issued on April 9, 1975, authorized the FITZGERALD to carry 49 persons, although it had only 29 crewmen aboard on November 10, 1975. The required lifesaving equipment, as stated on the certificate was: 1 lifeboat on port side for 50 persons; 1 lifeboat on starboard side for 50 persons; 2 inflatable liferafts for 25 persons each; 24 life rings; and 83 life preservers.

The two lifeboats and one 25-person liferaft were located aft and one 25-person liferaft was located forward. The inflatable rafts were installed in racks designed to allow the rafts to float free and automatically inflate.

Fire and boat drills conducted in good weather while the FITZGERALD was moored indicated that a conventional lifeboat could not be launched in less than 10 minutes. Testimony indicated that as much as 30 minutes would be required to launch a lifeboat in a seaway and that a lifeboat probably could not be launched successfully and boarded in the seaway experienced by the FITZGERALD at the time of her loss. Most witnesses felt that a Great Lakes vessel could be abandoned more successfully with an inflatable liferaft rather than with a lifeboat.

Coast Guard regulations require fire and boat drills to be conducted at least weekly. The logbooks of the FITZGERALD were lost with the vessel; however, records available from the offices of Columbia Transportation Division indicate that 14 fire and boat drills were conducted between April 12 and October 31, 1975.

Based on the 49 persons permitted by the Certificate of Inspection, U.S. Coast Guard regulations require: 1 life preserver for each of the 49 persons, 25 as a required 50 percent excess, 2 in each lifeboat, 3 for the wheelhouse watch, and 2 in the engine room.

After an intensive search by U.S. Coast Guard and Canadian Coast Guard surface and air units, Michigan Air National Guard aircraft, and U.S. and Canadian merchant vessels between November 10 and 13, 1975, no survivors were found and no bodies were recovered. Ontario Canadian Provincial Police conducted numerous shoreline searches. The total lifesaving equipment recovered was: 1 lifeboat, one-half of another lifeboat, 2 inflatable liferafts, and 21 lifejackets or lifejacket pieces.

On November 10, the only Coast Guard surface search and rescue units available for open water deployment were the Buoy Tender WOODRUSH, located 300 miles from the accident at its home port in Duluth, Minnesota, and the Harbor Tug NAUGATUCK located at Sault Ste. Marie, MI. However, the NAUGATUCK is restricted from operating in open water when winds exceed 60 knots and, therefore, was directed not to proceed beyond the entrance to Whitefish Bay. All other Coast Guard surface units were either too far away or in a repair status.

Waterway Information

Only three navigational charts covering the area between Michipicoten Island and Whitefish Bay are available. These charts are:

a. Lake Survey Chart No. 9, "Lake Superior," which shows all of Lake Superior at a scale of 1:600,000 published by the U.S. National Oceanic and Atmospheric Administration (NOAA).

b. Canadian Chart 2310, "Lake Superior, Caribou Island to Michipicoten Island," which shows the area from slightly north of Michipicoten Island to slightly south of Caribou Island at a scale of 1:97,280 is published by the Canadian Hydrographic Service.

c. Lake Survey Chart No. 92, "Lake Superior, St. Mary's River to Au Sable Point," which shows the southeastern portion of Lake Superior from Sault Ste. Marie to just south of Caribou Island and west to Au Sable Point Light at a scale of 1:120,000 also is published by NOAA.

Great Lakes mariners normally use NOAA Lake Survey Chart No. 9 for navigation on Lake Superior. Larger scale charts are available for smaller areas, including harbors, where more detail is required. Lake Survey Chart No. 9 contains the following note: "Owing to the small scale, many aids to navigation, depths, contours, and topographical features have been omitted. For details, consult Coast and Harbor charts."

Lake Survey Chart No. 9 shows bottom contours of less than 3 fathoms and less than 5 fathoms around Caribou Island by blue shading in two tones. Two locations of charted depths of 6 fathoms are shown northeast and northwest of the shaded areas. The extent of shoaling with depths in excess of 5 fathoms but less than 10 fathoms is not shown and the mariner is not made aware of the extent of the shoal area north of Caribou Island known as North Bank, as identified on Canadian Chart 2310.

After this accident, the Coast Guard requested the Canadian Hydrographic Service to conduct a hydrographic survey of the area north of Caribou Island to confirm the charted soundings and to update the charted data. Current charts are based on a survey conducted by the Canadian Hydrographic Service in 1916 and 1919.

The Canadian Hydrographic Service conducted a survey from May 19 to July 8, 1976, and from August 7 to September 30, 1976. The survey included the waters between Michipicoten Island and Caribou Island bounded by latitudes 47°10' N and 47°45' N and longitudes 85°33' W and 86°11' W. Soundings were obtained by echo soundings and geographic positions were determined by use of a special three-station mini fix system.

The results of the survey were reduced to a datum of 182.99 meters (599.85 feet) above the International Great Lakes Datum. This base datum is within 0.53 foot of the datum used on current charts.

The hydrographic survey conducted by the Canadian Hydrographic Service of the area north of Caribou Island produced bottom contours very close to those shown on Canadian Chart 2310. In some locations on North Bank, some soundings were less than charted depths; however, in all instances these locations are within the 10-fathom curve as shown on Chart 2310. No soundings less than 10 fathoms were indicated either north or east of the charted 10-fathom curve.

Columbia Transportation Division, the operator of the FITZGERALD, conducted an independent hydrographic survey of the shoal area north of Caribou Island. Water depths were determined by sonic devices, lead line, and direct measurement by divers. The results of this survey show water depths that vary slightly from the Canadian survey. These differences can be attributed to the rocks and boulders on the bottom and the various tracklines on which soundings were recorded.

A former chief mate of the FITZGERALD testified that between September 13 and October 3, 1975, the FITZGERALD discharged at Toledo, Ohio. Because of the FITZGERALD's deep draft, she was not able to pull up to the dock and had to lay off some 12 feet each time. The ship seemed to plow its way toward the dock every trip, he said. Similar "groundings" of other Great Lakes bulk cargo vessels during discharge at various ports were observed by Coast Guard Marine Inspectors during the winter of 1976 and the spring of 1977 and by Safety Board personnel during the summer of 1977.

Tests and Research

The Safety Board analyzed the structure of the FITZGERALD's hatch covers to determine the forces necessary to cause their failure. The analysis assessed several possible failure modes and several possible draft conditions caused by flooding of either the cargo hold, the tunnel, or the ballast tanks. The results of the analysis indicated that boarding seas could have induced sufficient stresses to cause the catastrophic failure of one or more of the hatch covers when the FITZGERALD's freeboard was reduced by the flooding. The resulting catastrophic structural failure would have allowed rapid massive flooding of the cargo hold.

Other Information

Operating Instructions

Many Great Lakes bulk cargo vessel operators advised the Safety Board that they give their masters operating instructions concerning navigation in adverse weather and ice. These instructions are general and are usually verbal although some companies provide their masters with written policy. All the companies contacted stated that the final operational decisions concerning vessel navigation are made by the master whether to sail, delay sailing, divert to avoid adverse weather and sea conditions, anchor, or seek shelter. Each master is expected to use his experience to evaluate the most current and accurate weather information in deciding the best course of action for the safety of his ship.

Great Lakes vessels covered by the 1973 Great Lakes Load Line Regulations (46 CFR 45.105) are required to have on board, in a form approved by the Commandant, USCG, sufficient information to enable the master to load and ballast the vessel so that unacceptable stresses in the vessel's structure are avoided. Testimony taken at the Coast Guard Marine Board of Investigation and subsequent inspections by the U.S. Coast Guard indicate:

1. The loading information provided Great Lakes vessels is not always used by the master.

2. The FITZGERALD's loading information provided no information on intermediate stresses during the loading sequence nor any information on any aspect of unloading.

3. The FITZGERALD's loading information was prepared for a two-belt loading system such as that used at Silver Bay, MN, the FITZGERALD's normal point of loading. It did not contain information directly applicable to a chute dock, such as the one at which the FITZGERALD loaded on November 9, 1975.

4. The FITZGERALD's loading information did not contain information on ballasting or deballasting in conjunction with loading and unloading.

Navigation Information

Navigation on Lake Superior normally is accomplished, as was the case aboard the ANDERSON, using Lake Survey Chart No. 9, described in waterway information.

An accurate record of the navigational tracklines of the FITZGERALD and the ANDERSON was not available. Information from which investigators determined a probable trackline for the FITZGERALD consisted of logs and charts from the ANDERSON, considerable testimony from the master and the mates of the ANDERSON, and weather messages filed by both the ANDERSON and the FITZGERALD. The ANDERSON was navigated by radar ranges and bearings and determined the positions of the FITZGERALD by radar observations. The crew of the ANDERSON did not plot the FITZGERALD's actual geographic position.

The radar presentation aboard the ANDERSON consisted of a relative bearing display on a plan position indicator (PPI) scope. The vessel's head was always toward the top of the scope and bearings were clockwise relative to the centerline of the ship. Range was determined from directly reading a dial indicating the distance from the center of the scope (the vessel's position) to a movable electronic indicator on the scope or by estimating a target's distance from fixed, electronically displayed range rings on the scope. On the 24-mile range display, these fixed range rings were shown at intervals of 4 miles.

Accurate bearings relative to ship's head could be read directly from the bearing ring surrounding the PPI scope. To obtain an accurate true bearing, the relative bearing had to be added to the ship's true heading at the time the bearing was taken. There is no testimony to indicate that the crew of the ANDERSON did this to obtain true bearings of the FITZGERALD or other targets they observed.

Testimony indicated that the ANDERSON's navigation was based primarily on bow and beam bearings, although range was sometimes determined. Further, the testimony did not always clearly state that both radar ranges and radar bearings were always obtained. The testimony indicated that at times the term "radar bearing" was used to indicate either range or bearing or both values. Beam bearings are relative to the ship's centerline and may be in error, depending upon the instantaneous heading of the vessel when the beam bearing is taken.

The ANDERSON plotted an intended course and did not start a new trackline plot in those positions where a fix did not fall on the intended trackline. At times, the ANDERSON determined her position and did not log or plot the data, steered courses other than those charted or logged, and changed course without simultaneously fixing her position. These procedures made reconstruction of a track difficult. Also, an analysis of the testimony and other data relating to the navigation of the ANDERSON and the FITZGERALD indicated that some of the information regarding the navigational plots was not consistent. In attempting to reconstruct the navigational tracks of the two vessels, greater credibility was given to positions based on radar information and routine log entries of navigational information from the ANDERSON than to visual estimates of the FITZGERALD's position given a month after the accident. (See figure 1.)

Testimony indicated that when the FITZGERALD and the ANDERSON were north of Michipicoten Island, they were on converging courses heading toward a point 2½ to 3 miles west or southwest of West End Light. Information from other Great Lakes mariners indicated that 141° T is a usual course from West End Light to Whitefish Bay and this trackline is well clear of any shoal areas.

ANALYSIS
The Sinking

An analysis of the wreckage itself did not give any conclusive evidence as to the cause of the sinking of the FITZGERALD. However, an analysis of the final events in conjunction with the wreckage indicated that the FITZGERALD experienced massive flooding of the cargo hold just before she sank.

When the master of the FITZGERALD first reported topside damage to the vessel at 1530 on November 10, he stated he had a fence rail down, had lost two vents, and had "both" pumps going. Flooding was occurring in one or more ballast tanks, the tunnel or a combination of ballast tanks and the tunnel. At the same time, because of the severe sea conditions, water was entering the vessel's cargo hold through nonweathertight hatch covers. Between 1530 and the sinking, the FITZGERALD's deck was awash with green water. Since the sheer strake extended 15⅜ inches above the weather deck for the entire length of the vessel at side, water would have been trapped on deck. The combined effect of the water in the ballast tanks, the tunnel, the cargo hold, and on deck would have decreased the vessel's freeboard, permitted more water to enter the cargo hold, and increased any trim or list initiated by the ballast tank or tunnel flooding.

The Safety Board determined through its structural analysis of the hatch covers that the sea state, combined with the loss of freeboard and the trim caused by flooding, could have imposed sufficient hydrostatic loads to cause a hatch cover failure and collapse under static loading.

The Safety Board calculations assumed a wave height of 25 feet. This was based on the ANDERSON's observations of significant wave heights from 18 to 25 feet. A significant wave height of 25 feet means that the average height of the one-third highest waves is 25 feet. The Safety Board also calculated that, by 1915 on November 10, sufficient water had entered the hull of the FITZGERALD to reduce its freeboard to near zero at hatch No. 1. With zero freeboard, a wave of 25 feet in height would yield a static head of 12.5 feet. This static head was sufficient to cause hatch cover failure. 46 CFR 45.145 required that hatch covers be designed assuming a minimum 4-foot head of water.

The quartering seas would cause a "piling" effect in the area behind the forward deckhouse and thus increase the static head. Any stresses caused by the dynamic forces of the boarding seas would have added to the static stresses and would have accelerated the hatch cover failure.

The hatch cover failure would have been severe enough to allow rapid massive flooding of the cargo hold. Since there were no watertight bulkheads within the cargo hold, the flooding water would have progressed throughout the hold within minutes, causing the vessel to sink bow first to the bottom of the lake. Upon impact with the bottom, the midship portion disintegrated and the stern section rolled over, coming to rest upside down.

The cargo hold was not fitted with a system of sounding tubes or other devices to detect the presence of flooding water. The only suctions for the bilge pumping system in the cargo hold were located aft in cargo hold No. 3 port and starboard. Testimony indicated that it is almost impossible to pump water from the cargo hold when there is bulk cargo aboard. The cargo tends to clog the strainer and prevent the flow of water into the bilge well where the pump takes suction. This inability to dewater the cargo hold indicates that the ballast pumps were taking suction on the ballast tanks where the system was normally effective for dewatering. There was no bilge suction for either tunnel; therefore, flooding was probably occurring in the ballast tanks or the tunnel which drains into the ballast tanks, or both.

Because of the large capacity of the FITZGERALD ballast pumps (four of 7,000-gpm capacity and two of 2,000-gpm capacity), the flooding must have been occurring through openings other than just the damaged ballast tank vents, or the tunnel must have been flooding at a rate greater than could be drained into the ballast tanks. Any flooding through the vent openings or tunnel drains into the ballast tanks would have been removed within a matter of minutes by the ballast pumps and the vessel's list should have been eliminated.

The FITZGERALD did not explain what caused the damage to the fence rail and the vents. However, whatever caused this damage probably also caused some localized structural damage to the vessel's hull plating. This damage to the hull plating would have permitted flooding into the tunnel and into the ballast tanks faster than the pumps could remove the water and thereby eliminate the list. The topside damage could have been caused by the vessel striking a floating object which was brought aboard by heavy seas or by some object on board, such as the hatch cover crane or spare propeller blade, breaking away in the heavy seas.

After the FITZGERALD's master reported damage at 1530, the sea conditions became worse. Ten or 12 miles north of Caribou Island, the seas were 12 to 18 feet high, and below Caribou Island, the seas were 18 to 25 feet. Any structural damage to the shell plating would have propagated under the higher stress levels caused by these sea conditions and would have increased the rate of water flooding into the ballast tanks, or the tunnel, or both.

Visual inspections by Coast Guard Marine Inspections during the winter of 1976 and the spring of 1977 and by Safety Board personnel during the summer of 1977 indicate that hatch covers on Great Lakes vessels are not maintained weathertight.

A detailed analysis of the amount of water that could have entered the cargo holds through openings between the hatch covers and the hatch coamings of the FITZGERALD on November 10, 1975, was made by both the Coast Guard and the Safety Board. Both analyses show that the current hatch design used on Great Lakes vessels, such as the FITZGERALD, would have permitted significant amounts of water to enter the FITZGERALD's cargo hold under the sea conditions encountered on November 10, 1975.

The effect of this flooding on both trim and list could have been determined by the use of trim and list indicating instruments. The instruments also could have provided an indication of the rate of change of trim and list by comparing a series of readings at various times. The change of trim and list would have indicated if progress was being made by pumping or if conditions were getting worse.

Between 1700 and 1730, the master of the FITZGERALD told the AVA-FORS that "I have a 'bad list,' I have lost both radars, and am taking heavy seas over the deck in one of the worst seas I have ever been in." In order for the FITZGERALD to have developed a "bad list" 2 hours after the list was first reported, the flooding rate into the ballast tanks must have exceeded the vessel's pumping capacity or flooding through the openings between the hatch covers and the hatch coamings must have contributed significantly to the list. Because of the severe sea condition, the master probably did not realize the extent of flooding in the cargo hold, and he had no means of detecting the flooding until the water level exceeded the height of the cargo. At 1910, the FITZGERALD reported that "We are holding our own;" however, shortly thereafter the FITZGERALD sank.

Because there were neither witnesses nor survivors, and because the scattered wreckage on the lake bottom does not indicate a definite mode of hull failure, the actual sequence of events culminating in the sinking of the FITZGERALD cannot be completely substantiated. Two possibilities are discussed below.

First, the increased weight of the flooding water could have caused a massive structural failure while the FITZGERALD was still on the surface, which caused the vessel to break into two sections. However, an analysis of various flooding conditions indicated that the stress levels from longitudinal bending moments were well below that which would cause a structural failure on the surface. The proximity of the bow and stern sections on the bottom of Lake Superior indicated that the vessel sank in one piece and broke apart either when it hit bottom or as it descended.

Therefore, the FITZGERALD did not sustain a massive structural failure of the hull while on the surface.

Second, the reduced freeboard and loss of transverse stability from flooding could have caused the FITZGERALD to capsize. If three or less adjacent ballast tanks on the same side of the vessel were completely flooded, the FITZGERALD would not have capsized. The vessel also would not have capsized if water had entered only the cargo hold through openings between the hatch covers and the hatch coamings. In each case, the roll angle would not have been sufficient to produce a cargo shift. However, under the combined effects of flooding two ballast tanks, the tunnel, and the cargo hold, the FITZGERALD would have capsized within minutes. If the vessel had capsized, however, all the hatch covers would probably have been torn away by the force of the shifting taconite pellets. The underwater survey of the wreckage showed that hatch covers Nos. 3 and 4 were still in place. The final position of the wreckage indicated that if the FITZGERALD had capsized, it must have suffered a structural failure before hitting the lake bottom. The bow section would have had to right itself and the stern portion would have had to capsize before coming to rest on the bottom. It is, therefore, concluded that the FITZGERALD did not capsize on the surface.

Possible Grounding

Safety Board investigators considered the possibility that flooding resulted from a grounding which ruptured the hull plating in the area of some ballast tanks, but rejected this possibility for the following reasons:

- A reconstruction of the FITZGERALD's most probable trackline shows her path to be about 3 miles from the nearest position where grounding could have occurred.

- No gouges, scraps, fractures, indentations, or other indications of grounding were visible on the exposed bottom plating on the after section of the wreckage. These observations were made during a close examination of the exposed bottom plating by underwater television from the CURV III. Damage to the bottom plating of a vessel from grounding on boulders in the rocky shoal north of Caribou Island during the severe sea conditions would probably have extended into the bottom plating of the stern section.

- The FITZGERALD's full speed was reported to be 16.3 mph. At this speed, it was impossible for the FITZGERALD to pass through her 1520 position, as determined by the ANDERSON from radar observations, and reach the nearest position at which grounding could occur by 1530. Although the list was not reported until 1530, the Safety Board concludes that topside damage occurred before 1520 and that the list was caused by flooding through the topside damage for a period of time. Even if massive damage could have been sustained at 1530 and instantaneous flooding could have occurred, it is unlikely that the FITZGERALD would have instantly reported the damage. If an immediate report had been made it probably would have mentioned damage more serious than just a list, the loss of a rail, and damage to the vents.

Probable Trackline

In reconstructing the ANDERSON's probable trackline, the Safety Board relied primarily upon the ship's log entries concerning fixes taken at 1520 and 1652, the courses steered, and the reported speed of 14.5 mph. Subsequent testimony indicated a course change at 1652, which was not logged and a fix taken at 1701, which also was not logged. These times do not correlate with the other navigational data. Instead, calculations indicate that course was probably changed at 1634 and the fix probably was obtained at 1734. With these time corrections, the ANDERSON's track correlates with the fixes, times, courses, and speeds given in the testimony of the ANDERSON's master and mate.

The reconstruction of the positions of the ANDERSON and the FITZGERALD from Otter Head to the position of the FITZGERALD's wreckage shows that the most probable trackline of the FITZGERALD runs from a position 2½ to 3 miles southwest of West End Light on Michipicoten Island on a course of 141° T toward Whitefish Bay. The position southwest of West End Light was confirmed by radar observations aboard the ANDERSON. A preponderance of the evidence confirms that the FITZGERALD's positions were close along this trackline at intervals from 1350 throughout the afternoon. The wreckage of the FITZGERALD was found 1½ miles east of this trackline.

About 1520, the FITZGERALD was about 16 miles ahead and slightly to the right of dead ahead of the ANDERSON, a position about 7 miles north by east from Caribou Island. This position correlated well with the FITZGERALD's most probable course and speed. The master of the ANDERSON testified that between 1530 and 1540, the FITZGERALD was about 17 miles ahead and 1 or 1½ points (about 11 to 170) to the right of the ANDERSON's heading flasher. During his testimony, before the Marine Board, the master indicated a position on a chart about 4 to 5 miles northeast of Caribou Island. Although these two descriptions are not compatible, in both cases the FITZGERALD would have been east of the 10-fathom curve. The relative motion of the FITZGERALD, on course 141° T as observed from the ANDERSON on course 125° T, caused the FITZGERALD's bearing to increase to the right.

To reconstruct the FITZGERALD's probable trackline between 1252 and 1915 the Safety Board used information from the ANDERSON's logs and from radar data testified to by the ANDERSON's master and mate. An analysis of the FITZGERALD's course and speed from 1252 to a position southwest of West End Light indicates that the earliest time she could have changed course to 141° T was 1359, using her previous speed of 16.3 mph. The segment of the track between 1359 and 1520 shows the FITZGERALD made 13.1 mph on a track of 144° T. The segment of the track between 1520 and 1915 shows the FITZGERALD made 11.8 mph on a track of 139° T. These calculated speeds indicate the FITZGERALD reduced speed before 1530 when she reported topside damage and a list and said she would reduce speed.

Based on radar data observed by the ANDERSON, the FITZGERALD's position at 1350 (1359), 1445, 1520, 1652 (1634), 1701 (1728), and 1915 correlate with the 141° T course reported by the FITZGERALD and the Safety Board's calculated speeds. (See figure 1.)

The trackline of the FITZGERALD lies 2.75 miles east of Chummy Bank and 2.5 miles east of the 10-fathom curve outlining the shoal area north of Caribou Island known as North Bank. Some testimony placed the FITZGER-ALD closer to North Bank; however, the course of 141° T from West End Light to Whitefish Bay is well known to Great Lakes navigators and this was the intended track of both the ANDERSON and the FITZGERALD. The ANDERSON was navigated to return to this trackline at 1634 for the final leg of her voyage. At this time the FITZGERALD was observed to be almost dead ahead of the ANDERSON when her heading was 142° T.

Although the FITZGERALD could have departed from the usual trackline of 141° T from West End Light to Whitefish Bay to pass over the shoal area north of Caribou Island and then return to the 141° T trackline at a position observed by the ANDERSON at 1634, this departure is unlikely. The distance from the 1520 position of the FITZGERALD to the closest point where grounding could occur was 3.3 miles. To reach this point at 1530, a course change of 64° and an increase of speed to 19.8 mph would have been required. The FITZGERALD's full speed was 16.3 mph.

During a taped conversation with his office, which was made a part of the record, the ANDERSON's master stated that the FITZGERALD "passed right over that 6-fathom spot." (See figure 1.) The Canadian Hydrographic Service survey shows the water depth at this charted "6-fathom spot" is 52 meters (28.4 fathoms). If the FITZGERALD, whose draft was more than 27 feet, had passed through this position on a course of 141° T the vessel would have had to pass within ¾ of a mile of the north tip of Caribou Island and through an area where the depth is less than 21 feet. Furthermore, the position of the charted "6-fathom spot" is more than 5 miles west of the FITZGERALD's 1520 position testified to by the ANDERSON's mate and her 1540 position testified to by the ANDERSON's master. The Safety Board concludes that the statement on the tape referring to the FITZGERALD passing over the charted "6-fathom spot" is not supported by the evidence.

Other Safety-Related Findings

Although not directly contributing to the sinking of the FITZGERALD, several items were uncovered during the investigation of this accident that affect the safety of Great Lakes bulk cargo vessels and are discussed below:

Fathometers

The shoal waters near Michipicoten Island and Caribou Island, as well as other locations in Lake Superior, are not isolated spots. The bottom contour around these shoal areas is usually gradual enough that the change of water depth will provide adequate warning that a vessel is approaching a shoal area if the water depth is measured with a fathometer.

A fathometer can be used to determine a trackline made good in most areas by comparing a series of observed depths to the charted depths. This easy determination of a vessel's position and progress would be a significant aid to a mariner if other navigational instruments fail, as was the case of the FITZGERALD. A fathometer is most useful when vessels are navigating in restricted waterways, such as the waters of the Great Lakes, where all navigational information is important.

Charts

The small scale of Lake Survey Chart No. 9, which the FITZGERALD probably used, limited the amount of detail that could be shown on chart. The shoal area north of Caribou Island is not shown on the chart within a bottom contour line greater than 5 fathoms; and a charted depth of 6 fathoms, shown approximately 5 miles north-by-west from Caribou Island, appears to be an isolated shallow spot. The Canadian Hydrographic Service survey did not show any sounding as low as 6 fathoms in this position, and no isolated shoal spots were detected.

Canadian Hydrographic Service Chart 2310 shows this shoal area known as North Bank in considerably more detail than does Lake Survey Chart No. 9 and the bottom contour lines were confirmed by the 1976 Canadian Hydrographic Service survey of the area. No isolated spots of shoal water were located, and all soundings of less than 10 fathoms fell within the 10-fathom curve shown on Canadian Chart 2310.

Testimony that the FITZGERALD passed over a "6-fathom spot" highlights the need for additional information to be shown on Lake Survey Chart No. 9 about North Bank where the water depth is between 5 and 10 fathoms. Although the probable trackline of the FITZGERALD was east of this shoal area, greater detail of this area would be useful to mariners.

Groundings at Cargo Facilities

Although groundings did not contribute to the loss of the FITZGERALD, testimony and visual observations by U.S. Coast Guard Marine Inspectors and Safety Board personnel indicate that the increased drafts permitted under the 1973 Great Lakes Load Line Regulations have increased the number and severity of "groundings" at loading and discharge berths because of insufficient water depth alongside.

Since Great Lakes vessels are normally drydocked only every 5 years, the extent of damage from these "groundings" will probably not be apparent for some years. They may result in reduced plate thickness or minor structural failures. Damage by "groundings" may lead to major structural failure under the stresses imposed by a seaway.

Weather Forecasting

At 1639, on November 10, the NWS predicted for eastern Lake Superior northwest winds 38 to 52 knots with gusts to 60 knots, and waves 8 to 16 feet. The observed winds by the ANDERSON and by the Stannard Rock Weather

Station during the afternoon of November 10 were in the range of 40 to 58 knots from the west-northwest, gusting to 65 knots. These observations confirm the NWS predications. However, the wave height prediction was not accurate. The ANDERSON observed waves 18 to 25 feet during the afternoon of November 10. This is 12 to 75 percent greater than the predicted maximum wave height. A NWS meteorologist testified that under the observed wind conditions, current techniques would have predicted 15-foot waves. This indicates that the NWS does not have adequate wave height prediction techniques for the Great Lakes.

Loading Information

Testimony indicated that adequate loading information is not being provided to Great Lakes bulk carriers as required by 46 CFR 45.105. Great Lakes bulk carriers may be overstressing their hull structure during loading and unloading. Although this overstressing may not cause a massive structural failure during loading and unloading, the overstressing may cause a minor structural failure or low cycle fatigue in structural members, which could lead to a massive structural failure in a seaway.

Vessel Design

Normally, the maximum wave heights and wave lengths encountered on the Great Lakes are considerably less than the wave heights and wave lengths encountered in the open ocean. For this reason, Great Lakes bulk cargo vessels are designed to a longitudinal structural strength standard approximately one-half that required for vessels on an ocean voyage. The limiting sea state used in structural design also determines the requirements for freeboard and hatch cover design, even though this limiting sea state may be exceeded on the Great Lakes.

The above reflects a difference in design philosophy between that applicable to Great Lakes vessels and that applicable to ocean ships. Ocean ships are designed for the maximum expected sea conditions because they may be in the middle of the ocean when they encounter a severe storm, with no place to seek shelter. Great Lakes vessels, however, have relatively short voyages and can either delay sailing or seek shelter en route when severe storm conditions are expected or encountered. Therefore, masters must be informed of the maximum sea conditions for which Great Lakes bulk cargo vessels are designed and must be prohibited from operating under weather conditions which exceed the vessel design limits.

Emergency Position Indicating Radio Beacons

Great Lakes vessels are not required to have emergency position indicating radio beacons (EPIRB's) and none was provided aboard the FITZGERALD. The EPIRB is a battery-operated radio transmitter designed to transmit an emergency signal when it is manually turned on. The EPIRB is installed in such a manner that it will float free if the vessel sinks. When the EPIRB floats free, its transmitter is automatically placed in operation and the emergency signal will be transmitted.

The emergency signal can be received by shore stations, aircraft, and other vessels, and the location of the transmitter can be determined by means of radio direction finders and triangulation. The location of a distress or potential distress allows search and rescue efforts to be concentrated in a small area and increases the probability of finding survivors.

Although the ANDERSON lost visual and radar contact with the FITZGERALD about 1915, the ANDERSON was not convinced that the FITZGERALD had sunk for more than an hour. When the ANDERSON became convinced the FITZGERALD was lost she advised the U. S. Coast Guard by VHF-FM radiotelephone of her concern. The reason for this delay was that there was no distress call from the FITZGERALD. If the FITZGER-ALD had been fitted with an EPIRB, a distress signal would have been transmitted immediately when the FITZGERALD sank. This EPIRB would have alerted rescue units sooner and reduced the search area.

As in many catastrophic marine accidents, the FITZGERALD did not have time to broadcast a distress call over its own radio equipment. Had the ANDERSON not been in contact with the FITZGERALD by radio and radar, the loss of the FITZGERALD and a good estimate of her position would not have been known for many hours and the search area for possible survivors would have been greatly expanded.

Search and Rescue

Although not contributing to the loss of life in the sinking of the FITZGER-ALD, the Coast Guard's surface search and rescue capability was extremely limited on November 10. The only Coast Guard surface unit that was large enough to cope with the weather and sea conditions, that was not under repair, and that was close enough to respond within a reasonable time was the WOOD-RUSH, 300 miles away. The small craft designed for coastal operations, which were available in Lake Superior, were unsuitable for searching 15 miles offshore under the prevailing sea conditions. Additional surface search and rescue units on the Great Lakes that are capable of operation in severe weather conditions are needed.

CONCLUSIONS
Findings

1. The FITZGERALD's hatch covers were not weathertight and allowed water to enter the cargo hold over an extended period. This water was not detected because it migrated down through the cargo. There was no method provided for sounding the cargo other than visual observations, nor was there any method for dewatering the cargo hold with the vessel trimmed by the bow.

2. Amendments to the Great Lakes Load Line Regulations in 1969, 1971, and 1973 allow Great Lakes bulk carriers to load deeper. This deeper loading increased deck wetness which caused an increase in the flooding rate through nonweathertight hatches or other nonweathertight openings.

3. The topside vents and fence rail were damaged before 1520 either by a heavy object coming adrift on deck or by a floating object coming aboard with the seas. The FITZGERALD's hull plating probably was damaged also; the damage propagated and caused flooding of the ballast tanks and tunnel.

4. Flooding of ballast tanks and the tunnel caused trim and a list. Detection of ballast tank flooding prompted the ballast pumps to be started. However, the flooding rate through the hull damage, which was propagating, increased and exceeded the capacity of the pumping system.

5. The hull stress levels, even with a substantial amount of flooding, were low enough that the hull girder did not fail before the sinking.

6. The forces on the hatch covers caused by boarding seas were sufficient to cause damage and collapse. These forces increased as flooding caused a list and reduced the vessel's freeboard.

7. Flooding of the cargo hold caused by one or more collapsed hatch covers was massive and progressed throughout the hold. Flooding was so rapid that the vessel sank before the crew could transmit a distress call.

8. The vessel either plunged or partially capsized and plunged under the surface. The hull failed either as the vessel sank or when the bow struck the bottom.

9. The availability of a fathometer aboard the FITZGERALD would have provided additional navigational data and would have required less dependence on the ANDERSON for navigational assistance.

10. The most probable trackline of the FITZGERALD, from west of Michipicoten Island to the position of her wreckage, lies east of the shoal areas north and east of Caribou Island; therefore, damage from grounding would have been unlikely.

11. The shoal area north of Caribou Island is not shown in sufficient detail on Lake Survey Chart No. 9 to indicate the extent of this hazard to navigation. A contour presentation of this hazard would allow mariners to better assess this area and would help to eliminate the erroneous conclusion that there are isolated spots of shallow water, where in fact there is a large area of shoal water less than 10 fathoms deep.

12. Insufficient water depth has been observed at some loading and discharge piers. "Groundings" of vessels at these locations induce hull stresses of unknown magnitudes and create the potential of undetected hull damage and wear.

13. Although the National Weather Service accurately predicted the direction and velocity of the wind expected over the eastern end of Lake Superior on November 10, 1975, the predicted wave heights were significantly less than those observed.

14. Loading information on the FITZGERALD and other Great Lakes bulk cargo vessels was not adequate.

15. Great Lakes bulk cargo vessels normally can avoid severe storms. The limiting sea state for Great Lakes bulk cargo vessels should be determined, and the operation of vessels in sea states above this limiting value should be restricted.

16. The presence of an EPIRB aboard the FITZGERALD would have provided immediate automatic transmission of an emergency signal which would have allowed search units to locate the position of the accident. The accurate location of this position would have reduced the extent of the search area.

17. Installation of trim and list indicating instruments on the FITZGERALD would have provided the master an early indication of flooding that would have an adverse effect on the vessel. These instruments would have given an indication of whether the master's corrective action was adequate.

18. The surface search and rescue capability of the Coast Guard on November 10 was inadequate.

Probable Cause

The National Transportation Safety Board determines that the probable cause of this accident was the sudden massive flooding of the cargo hold due to the collapse of one or more hatch covers. Before the hatch covers collapsed, flooding into the ballast tanks and tunnel through topside damage and flooding into the cargo hold through nonweathertight hatch covers caused a reduction of freeboard and a list. The hydrostatic and hydrodynamic forces imposed on the hatch covers by heavy boarding seas at this reduced freeboard and with the list caused the hatch covers to collapse.

Contributing to the accident was the lack of transverse watertight bulkheads in the cargo hold and the reduction of freeboard authorized by the 1969, 1971, and 1973 amendments to the Great Lakes Load Line Regulations.

RECOMMENDATIONS

As a result of its analysis of this accident, the National Transportation Safety Board made the following recommendations:

To the U.S. Coast Guard:

- "Insure that all hatch covers, hatch coamings, and vents are in good repair and are capable of being made weather-tight during the annual inspections of all Great Lakes bulk cargo vessels before the spring shipping season and at inspections before the winter load line season. (Class II, Priority Action) (M-78-10) (Issued March 23, 1978)

- "Use the ship-rider program by Coast Guard Marine Inspectors and hatch cover inspections at cargo loading facilities to prevent sailing of any vessel found lacking in weathertight integrity. (Class II, Priority Action) (M-78-11) (Issued March 23, 1978)

- "Report the number of hatch cover inspections made of Great Lakes bulk cargo vessels and of sailings prevented or restricted due to nonweathertight closures over the next 2 years so that an accurate accounting can be made of the problem in reassessing minimum freeboard requirements. (Class II, Priority Action) (M-78-12) (Issued March 23, 1978)

- "Investigate, together with the American Bureau of Shipping, the effects that the deeper drafts permitted under the 1969, 1971, and 1973 amendments to the Great Lakes Load Line Regulations, have had on the structural strength of Great Lakes bulk cargo vessels. Note any damage or bottom plating wear over the next 2 years caused by the groundings of these vessels during loading, unloading, or navigation in restricted-depth waterways. Evaluate the effect this damage and wear might have on the structural strength of these vessels in a seaway, and jointly report the finding. (Class II, Priority Action) (M-78-13) (Issued March 23, 1978)

- "Determine if reduction in the minimum freeboard requirements for Great Lakes vessels permitted by the 1969, 1971, and 1973 amendments to 46 CFR Part 45 increases the potential for vessel flooding because the designs of weathertight closures are not adequate, and report the findings. (Class II, Priority Action) (M-78-16)

- "Initiate a design study to improve the current weathertight hatch cover and clamp designs used on Great Lakes bulk cargo vessels with a view toward requiring a more effective means of closure of such fittings. (Class II, Priority Action) (M-78-17)

- "Insure that the masters of Great Lakes bulk cargo vessels have the loading information required by 46 CFR 45.105, including the proper sequences for simultaneous loading and deballasting or unloading and ballasting. (Class II, Priority Action) (M-78-18)

- "Require that the masters of all Great Lakes cargo vessels that are not required by 46 CFR 45.105 to have loading information be provided with such information, including the proper sequence for simultaneous loading and deballasting or unloading and ballasting. (Class II, Priority Action) (M-78-19)

- "Require that a Great Lakes cargo vessel meet a minimum level of subdivision and damage stability to prevent the foundering of the vessel because of flooding through one hatch or flooding because of damage in a limited area of the vessel. (Class II, Priority Action) (M-78-20)

- "Require a means of detecting water in the cargo holds of a Great Lakes vessel so that her master will have an early indication of flooding and can take any necessary corrective action. (Class II, Priority Action) (M-78-21)

- "Amend 46 CFR 56.50-50 to require an effective bilge pumping system on Great Lakes bulk cargo vessels so that if the vessel has trim by the bow and is listing, water can be removed from any portion of the cargo hold. (Class II, Priority Action) (M-78-22)

- "Require instruments in the wheelhouse to detect changes in both trim and heel on Great Lakes bulk cargo vessels so that changes in trim and heel caused by the presence of water or changes in cargo configuration can be detected. (Class II, Priority Action) (M-78-23)

- "Require that the information supplied to the master of Great Lakes cargo vessels on loading and stability also include information on the vessel's ability to survive flooding (e.g., trim and heel results after assumed damage) so that the master can take appropriate corrective action or formulate timely plans to effect crew evacuation. (Class II, Priority Action) (M-78-24)

- "Require that Great Lakes vessels have emergency position indicating radio beacons (EPIRB's) so that vessels lost or in serious danger can be located rapidly and accurately. (Class II, Priority Action) (M-78-25)

- "Determine, in conjunction with the American Bureau of Shipping, the limiting sea state applicable to the design of Great Lakes bulk cargo vessels including freeboard and longitudinal strength, and report the findings. (Class II, Priority Action) (M-78-26)

- "Prohibit the navigation of Great Lakes vessels in wind and wave conditions which exceed the limiting sea state used for vessel design. (Class II, Priority Action) (M-78-27)

- "Determine, in conjunction with the American Bureau of Shipping, the design criteria used to determine the structural adequacy of hatch covers and report the findings. Evaluate the design criteria and impose more stringent standards if indicated. (Class II, Priority Action) (M-78-28)

- "Require that all Great Lakes bulk cargo vessels have a fathometer. (Class II, Priority Action) (M-78-29)

- "Increase the surface search and rescue capability on the Great Lakes during severe weather periods. (Class II, Priority Action) (M-78-30)"

To the American Bureau of Shipping:

- "Insure that the closures on the freeboard deck of all Great Lakes bulk cargo vessels are capable of being made weathertight in accordance with the annual survey requirements of 46 CFR 42.09-40. (Class II, Priority Action) (M-78-14) (Issued March 23, 1978)

- "Investigate, together with the U.S. Coast Guard, the effects that the deeper drafts permitted under the 1969, 1971, and 1973 amendments to the Great

Lakes Load Line Regulations have had on the structural strength of Great Lakes bulk cargo vessels. Note any damage or bottom plating wear over the next 2 years caused by the 'groundings' of these vessels during loading, unloading, or navigation in restricted-depth waterways. Evaluate the effect this damage or wear might have on the structural strength of these vessels in a seaway, and jointly report the findings. (Class II, Priority Action) (M-78-15) (Issued March 23, 1978)

- "Determine, in conjunction with the U.S. Coast Guard, the limiting sea state applicable to the design of Great Lakes bulk cargo vessels including freeboard and longitudinal strength. (Class II, Priority Action) (M-78-31)

- "Determine, in conjunction with the U.S. Coast Guard, the design criteria used to determine the structural adequacy of hatch covers. (Class II, Priority Action) (M-78-32)"

To the National Oceanic and Atmospheric Administration:

- "Revise Lake Survey Chart No. 9 showing the areas between Michipicoten Island and Caribou Island in Lake Superior to reflect the findings of the survey performed by the Canadian Hydrographic Service. (Class II, Priority Action) (M-78-33)

- "Evaluate the current methods of forecasting wave heights on the Great Lakes to determine if these methods accurately predict actual wave heights. (Class II, Priority Action) (M-78-34)"

BY THE NATIONAL TRANSPORTATION SAFETY BOARD
/s/ JAMES B. KING
Chairman
/s/ FRANCIS H. McADAMS
Member
/s/ ELWOOD T. DRIVER
Member
/s/ PHILIP A. HOGUE
Member

KING, Chairman, filed a concurring statement.
  (See concurring statement below.)
HOGUE, Member, dissented. (See dissenting statement below.)

Concurring Opinion of James B. King, Chairman:

I agree fully with the report adopted by the majority, but because of the importance of the accident and the controversy it has engendered, I believe it worthwhile to address in some detail the contentions which the dissent raises. The dissent offers eight contentions to support its version of the probable cause, and this opinion will discuss each in turn.

The first contention, upon which the dissent principally rests, is that Captain Cooper of the ANDERSON stated after the accident that he believed that the FITZGERALD had grounded north of Caribou Island. This statement: (1) was contradicted by Captain Cooper himself under circumstances more likely to elicit a correct recollection and (2) is inconsistent with the independent navigational evidence. The statement upon which the dissent relies was not made under oath, was made without benefit of charts, with no other witnesses present, and without cross-examination. When Captain Cooper had an opportunity to testify before the Marine Board and to refer to navigational charts, he contradicted his statement concerning a grounding, and charted a trackline for the FITZGERALD which corresponds to the trackline presented in the report.

At the Marine Board Captain Cooper and Chief Mate Clark both testified that the FITZGERALD was not near the shoal area. Captain Cooper testified that at 1540 the FITZGERALD was in the position the ANDERSON reached when she changed course to 141° T. This position is well clear of the shoal. Chief Mate Clark testified that when the ANDERSON changed course to 141° T the FITZGERALD was right on their heading flasher and "Maybe he didn't go in there (close to Caribou Island)."

Moreover, the "grounding" statement is inconsistent with the independent navigational evidence. First, the "6-fathom spot" to which Captain Cooper referred to is noted in Lake Survey Chart No. 9 but was later determined by hydrographic survey not to exist. Second, the FITZGERALD could not have passed over the "6-fathom spot" on a course of 141° T without coming and remaining hard aground just north of Caribou Island in less than 4 fathoms of water. Moreover, it would have been physically impossible for the FITZGERALD to travel from her 1520 position obtained by the ANDERSON to a position in which grounding would have been possible by 1530. Such a journey would have required that the FITZGERALD proceed through mountainous seas at a speed greater than her top speed, nor is there any evidence of grounding in the approximately 270 ft. of exposed bottom plating on the FITZGERALD stern.

The dissent's second contention is the Captain McSorley's report of a list and vents and fence rail down occurred when the FITZGERALD was in the shoal area, and indicates that the FITZGERALD had grounded. As mentioned above, the probable trackline shows that the FITZGERALD was not near a shoal area. In any event, a grounding could not have caused loss of the two vents. The two vents are massive, and a heavy impact above the deck level would have been required. The reported list, which the dissent takes to indicate grounding at that moment, could not have developed instantaneously. Whatever event caused the list had to have occurred sometime before 1520.

The dissent's third contention, closely parallel to that just discussed, is that loss of the fence rail must have been caused by hogging. As discussed above, impact by a heavy object would have been required to knock down the vents. The object which knocked down the vents could also easily have knocked down the fence rails. Thus, although hogging could have caused loss of the fence rail, it could not have caused loss of the vents. On the other hand, impact by a heavy object could have caused the loss of both.

As a fourth contention, the dissent cites the testimony of Mr. Steam and Captain Webster. These two opinions, of course, are speculations of persons who were not near the FITZGERALD at the time of the casualty. As mentioned previously, these opinions are inconsistent with the navigational evidence.

The fifth contention is that because Captain McSorley was a competent master he would have insured that all hatch covers were secured. Captain McSorley's competence was unquestioned, but investigations have disclosed that a number of competent Great Lakes bulk cargo vessels do not maintain weathertight hatches. During the lay-up period of 1976–1977 the Coast Guard conducted an extensive program of hatch cover inspections to insure that the clamps were properly adjusted and that the hatches were weathertight. The hatch clamps were frequently adjusted while the Coast Guard inspector was still aboard to show that the hatch covers would pass a hose test for weathertightness. Many times the hatch clamps were tightened to the point of failure without achieving the weathertightness of the closure. Furthermore, even after this extensive program, Safety Board investigators found loose clamps and nonweathertight hatch covers on Great Lakes bulk cargo vessels during the fall of 1977.

Moreover, dogging the hatches closed does not insure weathertightness. The clamps must also be properly adjusted. Although Captain McSorley may have insured that the FITZGERALD hatch were dogged closed, the clamps were not properly adjusted. Evidence of improper clamp adjustment is seen in the video tapes of the wreckage at hatch No. 5 where the hatch cover is missing and of a series of 18 consecutive hatch clamps only 2 are damaged and the remaining 16 are undamaged and are in the open position. Had these clamps been properly adjusted, they would all have been damaged or the hatch would have remained in place.

Calculations indicate that each of the 68 clamps on FITZGERALD's hatch covers must apply about 2,400 pounds at force to insure a tight seal from the gasket. Furthermore, Great Lake masters believe the weight of the hatch cover alone, about 14,000 pounds, would make the hatch cover weathertight. Calculations indicate more than 178,000 pounds is required.

A sixth contention, also concerning hatch covers, is that there is not testimony to insure that the FITZGERALD ever arrived in port without dry cargo. Although there is no testimony concerning wet cargo, 26,116 tons of taconite could absorb 4 to 6.7 percent water by weight (1044 to 1750 tons) without any free water being seen in the cargo hold. On occasions Great Lakes bulk cargo vessels have arrived in port with 2 to 4 inches of water in the cargo hold.

The dissent also argues that the tracklines of the ANDERSON and the FITZGERALD and their relative positions could not be reconstructed as stated in the Coast Guard Report. After extensive analysis of the testimony, the tracklines in the report of the vessel were reconstructed using logged times and positions. Although the data used were not of the "navigation textbook quality" the testimony does match the reconstructed tracklines if some times are adjusted. By calculating courses and speeds from positions "logged as normal course of business" the errors of time are evident.

The differences in relative bearing as observed by the ANDERSON's master and mate can be explained by the fact that the two bearings were taken 20 minutes apart. Furthermore, the motion of the FITZGERALD relative to the ANDERSON, on courses 141° T and 125° T, respectively, would have caused the bearings to drift right.

The dissent's final contention is that the FITZGERALD was steering various courses between Michipicoten Island and Caribou Island between 1359 and 1520. The standard usually accepted trackline for this route is 141° T. Great Lakes vessels depart from the recommended tracklines to take advantage of the lee provided by shore as did the ANDERSON and the FITZGERALD. The ANDERSON changed her course to 230° T while north of Michipicoten Island to allow for a predicted wind shift to the northwest and to allow herself more searoom from a lee shore. At the time of this wind shift the FITZGERALD was south of Michipicoten Island and had no reason to alter course from the accepted track of 141° T. Any course change the FITZGERALD would have made to reduce the rolling of the vessel would have been to the east. A course change to a course more southerly than 141° T would have produced more pronounced rolling and would have been unacceptable to the master.

I have reviewed the dissent carefully and given careful consideration to Member Hogue's opinions, but I am unable to find the evidence in the testimony or reports which would permit me to join him.

s/ JAMES B. KING
Chairman May 4, 1978

Dissenting Opinion of Philip A. Hogue, Member:

The most probable cause of the sinking of the SS EDMUND FITZGERALD in Lake Superior on 10 November 1975, was a shoaling which first generated a list, the loss of two air vents, and a fence wire. Secondarily, within a period of 3 to 4 hours, an undetected, progressive, massive flooding of the cargo hold resulted in a total loss of buoyancy from which, diving into a wall of water, the FITZGERALD never recovered.

In its conclusions, the Coast Guard, on p. 94 of its report, states, "At sometime prior to 1530 on 10 November, FITZGERALD experienced damage of sufficient magnitude to cause the Master to report topside damage and a list. Significantly, the Master of FITZGERALD reported the damage rather than the incident which caused it. (Underscoring supplied.) It is the opinion of the Marine Board that the incident, while possibly of a serious nature, was not of such extent as to have caused, by itself, the loss of the vessel and further, that the full extent of the incident was not perceived by vessel personnel." I totally concur with that Marine Board opinion.

The record indicates that the FITZGERALD was in all respects seaworthy prior to the commencement of her final voyage. Testimony as to the prudence and competence of her Master, Captain McSorley, is abundant. Paraphrasing the words of various witnesses, he was the best captain of the best ship in the fleet operated by the Oglebay-Norton Company. In recognition of this reputation, crew members specifically sought employment on the SS EDMUND FITZGERALD. Further, available evidence indicates that Captain McSorley would not commence a voyage into predicted bad weather without first insuring that all the hatch covers were effectively secure.

Like the Marine Board of the Coast Guard or the majority of the Members of the National Transportation Safety Board, I could speculate or surmise in the first instance that flooding into the cargo hold took place through ineffective hatch covers or in the second instance that flooding took place due to the failure of hatch cover Number One due to massive seas. I reject these arguments because neither of them is fully cognizant of the ramifications of the first reported list, the loss of two vents and fence railing at approximately the precise time the FITZGERALD was reportedly in or over shoal waters.

Between the first reported damage and the time of the sinking, approximately 3 to 4 hours later, seas of 25 to 30 feet and winds gusting to 80 knots were variously observed. Without exception, expert testimony has affirmed the fact that seas in shoal waters are inherently more violent and wild than in open water. It follows, therefore, that subsequent to her initial sustained damage, the FITZGERALD suffered progressive damage from laboring, rolling, and pitching for the next 3 to 4 hours as it proceeded toward Whitefish Point Light.

At or about 1730, Captain Woodard aboard the Swedish vessel AVAFORS received a report from Captain McSorley stating the FITZGERALD had a "bad list," had lost both radars and was taking heavy seas over the deck in one of the worst seas he had ever been in. In approximately 2 hours from the initial report of a list, the FITZGERALD had acquired a "bad list" and sustained the loss of both radars.

Approximately 1 hour 40 minutes later at or about 1910, the FITZGERALD reported it was holding its own. This was the last transmission ever heard from the FITZGERALD. Aside from the expert testimony elicited at the Coast Guard Marine Board hearing, it is self-evident that Captain McSorley had a damaged ship, and that he did not know how damaged she was. It is true that initial damage to the FITZGERALD could have been sustained by other means, but it would be a most unlikely coincidence that damage was sustained at the same approximate time that she was reported by Captain Cooper of the SS ANDERSON to be in close or over shoal waters.

Despite the difficulty experienced, in retrospect, by Captain Cooper days later before the Coast Guard Marine Board, in pinpointing the position of the FITZGERALD over various and sundry shoals, the fact remains that in his most fresh, spontaneous and free report of the accident to his company less than 24 hours after the accident, Captain Cooper variously stated, "I AM POSITIVE HE WENT OVER THAT SIX (6) FATHOM BANK!" and "I KNOW DAMN WELL HE WAS IN ON THAT THIRTY–SIX (36) FOOT SPOT, AND IF HE WAS IN THERE, HE MUST HAVE TAKEN SOME HELL OF A SEAS." "I SWEAR HE WENT IN THERE. IN FACT, WE WERE TALKING ABOUT IT. WE WERE CONCERNED THAT HE WAS IN TOO CLOSE, THAT HE WAS GOING TO HIT THAT SHOAL OFF CARIBOU, I MEAN, GOD, HE WAS ABOUT THREE MILES OFF THE LAND BEACON."

In other testimony before the Coast Guard Marine Board, Captain Cooper testified that he told the Mate on watch on the ANDERSON that the FITZGERALD was closer to the six (6) fathom shoal north of Caribou Island than he wanted the ANDERSON to be.

No one knows of a certainty how long the FITZGERALD had a list or had other topside damage prior to the conversation between Captain Cooper and Captain McSorley at or about 1530.

Neither does anyone know for sure exactly which vents were initially lost.

It is reasonable to assume, from all that is known of Captain McSorley, that his first report of damage was based on damage sustained immediately prior to 1530 and that it was no small consideration that caused Captain McSorley to ask the ANDERSON to stay with him, saying, "I will check down so that you can close the distance between us."

Quoting from the Coast Guard Marine Board on pp. 90 and 91, the following information is deemed highly relevant:

"The only information available on the position and trackline of Fitzgerald is in the weather reports sent by FITZGERALD and in testimony of the Master and Watch Officers of the SS ARTHUR M. ANDERSON, which was following FITZGERALD, in voice radio communication with it, and observing it visually and on radar. The weather reports from FITZGERALD scheduled at 1300 and 1900, 10 November, were not received.

"The position of FITZGERALD relative to that of ANDERSON cannot be reconstructed. Information available is based on the recollections of the Master and Watch Officers on ANDERSON, since the relative position of FITZGERALD was observed intermittently on the radar, but not recorded. Testimony on these observations is inconsistent. For example, the Officer on watch on ANDERSON recalled that FITZGERALD was 'a shade to the right of dead ahead,' as FITZGERALD passed northeast of Caribou Island, while the Master thought it was a point and a half to the right at that time.

"The Master and the Watch Officers on ANDERSON testified at length as to the position and trackline of ANDERSON in the afternoon and evening of 10 November. An analysis of this testimony shows that the vessel was navigated by radar ranges and bearings, that, at times, positions were determined but not logged, that course changes were made without simultaneous determination of position, that positions were determined as much as twenty minutes from the time that course changes were made, and that the courses steered varied from course logged because of the expected drift. The Marine Board attempted to reconstruct the trackline of ANDERSON and found that in order for the vessel to have steered the courses and have been at the positions at the times testified to, the speed of the vessel would have varied from a low of 5 mph to a high of 66 mph. But the Master testified, and the engineering log confirmed, that throughout the period, ANDERSON maintained a steady speed, turning for 14.6 mph.

Accordingly, it is concluded that the times and positions reported by officers of ANDERSON were not sufficiently accurate to allow the trackline of either FITZGERALD or ANDERSON to be reconstructed."

In order for me to concur with the Safety Board's majority, I have to assume that the true positions and tracklines of the FITZGERALD were those that would have been pursued in normal weather and that she remained well clear of shallow water and shoals.

I strongly doubt that was the case because Captain Cooper and Captain Pulcer, the former Master of the FITZGERALD, both testified that despite the general use of traffic lanes on Lake Superior, heavy weather contributed to the selection of ship courses. Indeed, on the day of the sinking, Captain Cooper of the ANDERSON originally intended to clear Michipicoten about 2 to 2½ miles off. Nonetheless, due to weather, he finally cleared Michipicoten West End Light by 7.7 miles. Thereafter, he steered a number of courses ranging from 125 degrees to 141 degrees. All factors considered, it is my assumption that the FITZGERALD was variously steering various courses and for approximately the same reasons. In fact, if the FITZGERALD had also been 7.7 miles off Michipicoten, instead of 2.2 miles as estimated or recollected, and steering 141 degrees, she certainly would have been in the shoal waters Captain Cooper reported to his company.

Considering the fact that no testimony has ever been produced to show that the FITZGERALD had ever arrived in port without dry cargo and the overall success of the hatch covers generally in use on the Great Lakes for many years, I have great difficulty accepting the argument that one or more of the hatches on the FITZGERALD on the day of the accident were either nonwatertight or that they failed prior to the first report of damage. If, in fact, hatch failure or loss of weathertight integrity occurred prior to the FITZGERALD's sinking, I can only surmise that such failure or failures occurred subsequent to the first list reported on or about 1530 and prior to the sinking on or about 1910.

I place great credence in Captain Cooper's testimony that the FITZGERALD was in proximity or over shoal waters; first, because his judgment is the most expert to be found at the scene and as much as anything else, the FITZGERALD reported her first casualties at that almost exact time. I could have doubts of one fact or another, but putting two and two together plus the subsequent events, I am strongly convinced that the FITZGERALD received her first damage as I have indicated and that from that time until the sinking, the FITZGERALD's condition deteriorated beyond the Captain's knowledge and beyond recovery.

Naval Architect Richard A. Steam, on p. 1227 of the Marine Board of Investigation stated, "If there was a list, it must have been—if it was any substantial amount of list, it must have been from a fracture in the hull caused by grounding or other means."

Captain Cooper on pp. 565 and 566 of the Marine Board of Investigation Report stated, "I believe that she was cracked somewhere. She was taking water fast enough because what he told me was that, 'I have a list and I am taking water' and I said, 'Have you got your pumps on?' and he said, 'Both of them.'"

On p. 2140, Captain Cooper stated, "I have never known a ship to lose a fence rail in a seaway."

On pp. 2152 and 2153, Captain Cooper stated again, "The only solution I can have to a fence rail breaking is—you can't break one by sagging a ship, but you would have to bend the ship, hog it up in the middle, to put such a tension on the fence rail that you would break it." "That is five-eighths wire rope with three strands running in through there. You might break one, but you can't conceivably think of breaking three."

On p. 2490, Captain Delmore Webster states, "I think he set over on one of those shoals and that was the moment that his fence rail broke."

All of the foregoing expert testimony strongly supports the conclusion that the initial list and loss of fence railing were induced by shoaling.

On p. 1962, Captain Woodard, the pilot on the Swedish vessel AVAFORS stated, "It was one of the biggest and wildest seas I have ever been in, I mean fast." On p. 1963, he said, "The sea was straight up and down and a lot of them were coming at you. It was not like big rollers."

Without exception, vessels in the vicinity of the FITZGERALD's sinking absolutely refused to consider turning around in such severe wind and sea conditions.

After studying all available information, it is my firm conclusion that the FITZGERALD shoaled and sustained her initial damage shortly before 1530 and that thereafter, the various workings of the vessel and loss of watertight integrity led to her sudden and totally unexpected sinking.

/s/ PHILIP ALLISON HOGUE
Member May 9, 1978

The Witnesses

DONALD A. AMYS, a general foreman for Burlington Northern for six years, supervised the loading of the *Fitzgerald.*

ROY T. ANDERSON, holder of a first-class pilot's license since December 1970, was second mate of the *Arthur M. Anderson.*

LEDOLF BAER, an authority on wave forecasting, served as director of the Oceanographic Services office headquartered in Rockville, Maryland.

PHILIP M. BRANCH, a Coast Guardsman employed by Group Sault Ste. Marie, was on duty monitoring weather and distress signals on the night of November 10, 1975.

LLOYD BRESLAU, assistant director for Physical Science and Technology at the Coast Guard Research and Development Center in Groton, Connecticut, ran the side-scan sonar during the search for the wreckage of the *Edmund Fitzgerald.*

MORGAN E. CLARK, first mate of the *Arthur M. Anderson,* holder of a first-class pilot's license since 1951, had been sailing on the Great Lakes for twenty-nine years.

WILLIAM CLEARY had worked as a naval architect for the Coast Guard since 1961.

JESSE B. "BERNIE" COOPER began sailing on the Great Lakes in 1937, starting as a deckhand and progressing until he commanded his own vessels. He had been the master of the *Arthur M. Anderson* for three years prior to the loss of the *Edmund Fitzgerald.*

CHARLES CORBETT, chief of Marine Environmental Protection for the Coast Guard office in Cleveland, assisted in the search for, and analysis of, the oil spill left by the *Edmund Fitzgerald.*

CLARENCE E. DENNIS, an employee at Burlington Northern for thirty-four years, had spent fifteen years as a boat loader in Superior, Wisconsin, at the time of the *Fitzgerald*'s final loading.

RICHARD A. FELDTZ, a hull superintendent for the Columbia Transportation Division of Oglebay Norton, last inspected the *Edmund Fitzgerald* on October 31, 1975.

HORTON E. GAFFORD was commanding officer of the Marine Inspection Office in Toledo, Ohio, at the time of the *Fitzgerald* sinking.

THOMAS E. GARCIA was a former deckwatch on the *Edmund Fitzgerald.*

JAMES J. GORDON, a marine hull inspector with the Coast Guard, was stationed at the Marine Safety Office in Toledo, Ohio.

HARRY C. HILGEMANN, sailing since 1965, was a wheelsman on the *Arthur M. Anderson*.

DONALD HILSEN worked briefly as a watchman on the *Edmund Fitzgerald*. He described his duties as "general maintenance of the ship, keeping it clean, handling the winches and taking groceries aboard [and] standing a ladder watch."

EDGAR M. JACOBSEN, marine superintendent for Oglebay Norton, held a master's license since 1943.

ALBERT JACOVETTI, a twelve-year commander of Great Lakes freighters, was pilot of the *Nanfri* on November 10, 1975.

WILFORD JEANQUART was a surveyor for the American Bureau of Shipping in Toledo, Ohio.

WILLIAM E. KENNEDY, a twenty-three-year veteran at the National Weather Service Forecast Office in Cleveland, collected weather data from the weather boats on the Great Lakes.

ROBERT KURZLEB, an oceanographic engineer, was employed by Seaward, Inc., in Falls Church, Virginia, at the time of the *Fitzgerald* sinking.

GERALD LANGE was a former first mate on the *Edmund Fitzgerald*.

JOHN H. LARSON, a seaman on the Great Lakes for twenty-two years, worked as a watchman on the *Edmund Fitzgerald* for five seasons, most recently in 1973.

CHARLES H. LINDBERG, a nineteen-year sailor on the Great Lakes, served on the *Fitzgerald* during two shipping seasons: as a deck-watch and wheelsman in 1964 and as a watchman and wheelsman in 1974.

DANIEL C. MANIA, stationed at the Marine Inspection Office in St. Ignace, Michigan, inspected the *Fitzgerald*'s recovered lifeboats.

ROBERT W. MASON, Chief Merchant Marine Technical Branch, was stationed at the Ninth District Coast Guard office in Cleveland, Ohio.

ROBERT L. MAY, a twenty-year veteran of Great Lakes shipping, was a wheelsman on the *Arthur M. Anderson*.

CHARLES A. MILLRADT, commander of the Coast Guard Group, Sault Ste. Marie, Michigan, had been a commissioned officer in the Coast Guard for just over twenty years at the time of the *Fitzgerald* accident. He was part of the search and rescue team looking for survivors.

CHARLES R. MUMFORD, an RCC controller at the Ninth Coast Guard District office in Cleveland, assisted in the *Fitzgerald* search effort.

ROBERT O'BRIEN was master of the *Benfri.*

RICHARD ORGEL served as third mate on the *Fitzgerald* for a month in 1972. He held a master's license for fifteen years.

WILLIAM R. PAUL was a Coast Guard inspector stationed in Toledo, Ohio.

PETER PULCER commanded the *Edmund Fitzgerald* from 1966 to 1971.

ANDREW RAJNER, a first mate employee on Oglebay Norton vessels, served as third mate on the *Fitzgerald* in 1965 and acted as temporary first mate on the *Fitzgerald* from September 12 to October 3, 1975.

JAMES A. RIVARD JR., chief of the Search and Rescue Branch of the Ninth Coast Guard District in Cleveland, directed the overall search efforts when the *Edmund Fitzgerald* was reported missing.

SIDNEY L. SPINNER, a fleet engineer, worked for the Columbia Transportation Division of Oglebay Norton.

RICHARD A. STEARN, a naval architect, founded the firm of naval engineers R. A. Stearn, Inc., in 1946.

CHARLES W. STUDSTILL, a hull inspector, retired from the Coast Guard in 1974. He inspected the *Fitzgerald* in dry dock at the American Shipyard in Lorain, Ohio, on April 20, 1974.

JAMES W. VILLAR served as manager of Research and Development of the Cleveland Cliffs Iron Company beginning in 1968.

RAYMOND R. WALDMAN worked as the meteorologist in charge of the National Weather Forecast Service in Chicago.

CHESTER WALTER, a Coast Guard hull inspector stationed in Toledo, Ohio, inspected the *Edmund Fitzgerald* on March 19, 1975.

DELMORE R. WEBSTER, temporary master of the *J. Burton Ayers,* was a former *Fitzgerald* crew member.

GARY WIGEN, usually stationed at the Coast Guard station in Grand Marais, Michigan, was working a radio watch in Sault Ste. Marie when he received a call from the *Edmund Fitzgerald* on November 10, 1975.

CEDRIC WOODARD, skipper of the *Avafors* and holder of a master's license since 1942, sailed for the last time on November 10, 1975.

Glossary

ACCESS TUNNELS—long tunnels running beneath the spar deck on either side of the cargo hold, allowing crewmen to move between the front and back of a ship during inclement weather

AFT (OR AFTER DECK)—back, or stern, section of the ship

BALLAST—added weight, usually lake water, to lower the ship in the water and add stability

BALLAST PUMPS—pumps that remove water from a boat's ballast tanks

BALLAST TANKS—large, watertight storage tanks below the cargo hold, on the starboard and port sides of the ship, in which ballast is stored

BALLAST TANK VENT—pipe running from a ballast tank to the spar deck, allowing air to be removed from the ballast tank

BEAM—the width of a boat at its broadest point

BOW—front or forward section of a ship

BOW THRUSTER—small propeller, located on the ship's bow, used to help in maneuvering

BULKHEAD—partition used to divide sections of a ship's hold

CAPTAIN (OR MASTER)—commander, or chief officer, of a ship

CAPSIZE—roll onto a side or turn over

CHIEF ENGINEER—crewman in charge of a ship's engine

DAVITS—small cranes on board a ship, especially a pair used for suspending and lowering a lifeboat

DE-BALLASTING—the process of pumping or expelling water from a ship's ballast tanks

DRAFT—depth of a ship's hull beneath the waterline

FATHOM—a measure of depth equal to six feet

FETCH—the distance traveled by wind or waves across open water

FIRST MATE—the second in command of a ship

FLOTSAM—floating debris of wreckage

FOLLOWING SEAS—waves moving in the direction of the wind, following a vessel moving in the same direction

FORE (OR FOREDECKS)—forward, or bow section of a ship

FOUNDER—to fill with water and sink

FREEBOARD—distance between the waterline and the spar deck

GREEN WATER—solid water, rather than spray, washing over the decks of a ship

GROUNDING—striking bottom, or running completely aground

HATCH COAMINGS—raised rims around the hatch openings upon which the hatch covers are fixed

HATCH COVERS—large, flat sheets of steel that cover the hatch coamings and prevent water from entering the cargo hold

HATCHES—openings in the ship's spar deck, through which cargo is loaded

HOGGING—the bending down of the fore and back of a ship with no support for the middle

HOLD—the large area of a ship in which cargo is stored

HULL—main body of a ship, upon which the decks and superstructures are built

KEEL—backbone of the ship, running the entire length of a ship, upon which the framework of the ship is built

KEELSON—reinforced "ribs" of a ship attached to the keel

KNOT—a measurement of speed, in nautical terms per hour, 1.15 statute miles per hour

LIST—a ship's leaning or tipping to one side

PILOTHOUSE (OR WHEELHOUSE)—enclosed deck in which the wheel and map room are located; the uppermost deck on a ship

POOP DECK (OR BOAT DECK)—highest point at the stern, on which lifeboats are stored

PORT—left side of a ship when you are facing the bow

SCREW—a ship's propeller

SHOAL—shallow area of water, usually marked by a sandbar, reef, or area of rising lake floor

SHOALING—striking, or bottoming out, against the bottom of a shallow area of water

SOO—common term for the locks at Sault Ste. Marie, Michigan

SPAR DECK (OR WEATHER DECK)—deck where the hatches are located

STARBOARD—right side of a ship when you are facing the bow

STERN—back or after section of a ship

STEWARD—ship's cook

SUPERSTRUCTURE—structures and cabins built above the hull of a ship

TACONITE—low-grade iron, usually processed and formed into small, marble-sized pellets

TEXAS—the deck, just beneath or behind the pilothouse, containing the captain's and mates' quarters

WHEELSMAN—crew member who steers the ship

WINDLASS—machine to lift anchors

WORKING—a ship's twisting, springing, and flexing in heavy seas

Michael Schumacher is the author of more than fifteen books, including *Mighty Fitz: The Sinking of the* Edmund Fitzgerald (Minnesota, 2012). He has written twenty-five documentaries on Great Lakes shipwrecks and lighthouses and is a frequent speaker at the annual Gales of November maritime conference. His previous books about the Great Lakes include *Wreck of the Carl D.: A True Story of Loss, Survival, and Rescue at Sea; November's Fury: The Deadly Great Lakes Hurricane of 1913* (Minnesota, 2013); and *Torn in Two: The Sinking of the* Daniel J. Morrell *and One Man's Survival on the Open Sea* (Minnesota, 2016). He lives in Wisconsin near the shores of Lake Michigan.